A Soldier in Search of Peace

A Soldier in Search of Peace

An Inside Look at Israel's Strategy

Major-General Avraham Tamir

Edited by Joan Comay

A Cornelia & Michael Bessie Book

HARPER & ROW, PUBLISHERS, New York
Cambridge, Philadelphia, San Francisco, Washington
London, Mexico City, São Paulo, Singapore, Sydney

Edited by Joan Comay. The editor would like to thank her husband
Michael for expert political advice, and Carol Dezent for invaluable help
in translating the original Hebrew manuscript.

FIRST U.S. EDITION

LIBRARY OF CONGRESS CATALOG CARD NUMBER: 87-46174
ISBN: 0-06-039088-3
88 89 90 91 92 HC 10 9 8 7 6 5 4 3 2 1

CONTENTS

CONTENTS

ILLUSTRATIONS

At a White House luncheon in honour of Prime Minister Shimon Peres

(Unless otherwise stated, all the photos are from the author's collection)

A Soldier in Search
of Peace

A PERSONAL PROLOGUE

One morning in December 1948, seven months after the State of Israel was born, I was shown into the office of David Ben-Gurion, Prime Minister and Minister of Defence.

I had just returned to the country after being released from a prisoner-of-war camp near Mafrak in Jordan. I had been taken captive in May 1948 when Jordanian troops wiped out Gush Etzion, an isolated group of four kibbutzim in the Hebron hills about twelve miles south-west of Jerusalem. Ben-Gurion knew, of course, what had happened there, but he now wanted a detailed, first-hand report from me, as I had been the Haganah commander in the battle. (The Haganah was the underground Jewish defence militia.) As he questioned me, he wrote notes in an exercise-book. The account took several hours.

I described to him the first attack on 4 May by a battalion of the Jordanian Arab Legion. (The Legion was a small, but efficient, regular army, trained and equipped by Britain; its commander was an Englishman, General Glubb Pasha, and most of its senior officers had been seconded from the British army.) We repulsed the attack but suffered heavy losses. I was severely wounded and laid up in the small kibbutz hospital.

On 12 May, the Legion launched a full-scale assault, supported by a horde of armed irregulars, mainly from the surrounding Arab villages. The battle lasted two days. We knew we faced hopeless odds as we could muster only 170 defenders, many of them women, armed with rifles, one mortar and four light machine-guns. The Legion shelled us heavily with its field artillery and threw twenty armoured cars into the attack. By the evening of the 14th, most of our defenders had been killed or wounded and our ammunition was exhausted. A radio message came through from Jerusalem ordering us to surrender, to save lives. After we had handed over our weapons, the irregulars came surging in, screaming with blood-lust. The Jordanian soldiers intervened and drove off the mob by firing into it, but not before we had incurred more casualties.

1

Next morning, the 15th, the wounded and other survivors were evacuated to Jordan. I was travelling in an ambulance when a Jordanian sergeant said to me boastfully, 'Your Ben-Gurion declared a state yesterday, but we will wipe it out in a week.' That was the first news I had that Israel had actually come into being. I burst into tears.

When our talk was over, Ben-Gurion asked me what I proposed to do. I told him that I hoped to start my university studies. We had by then practically won our War of Independence, having driven back the invading armies of Egypt, Jordan and Syria. He led me over to a map, pointing out the territory we now held, and said, 'You must go and see it all. That is the state we have to defend, and you must be one of the defenders. Off you go! Travel around, see it for yourself.'

I confess that my immediate response was, 'I haven't got a car.' He pressed a button and in came his military aide: 'Give Abrasha [my nickname] a jeep. He must see what has happened to the country while he was being held in Jordan. And then he will join the army.' I called my girlfriend, who was then serving in the fledgling air force, and for the next five days we drove through the length and breadth of Israel.

When I was sent from Jerusalem to Gush Etzion in March 1948, the country was still under the British Mandate and the Haganah, in which I served, was still an underground defence militia. I had now come back to a Jewish sovereign state and the Haganah had become the nucleus of the Israel Defence Forces (IDF).

On returning from the trip I enlisted, all thought of academic studies swept aside. I was then twenty-two years old. I would spend the next thirty-five years in uniform. I served in the infantry for ten years, commanding a battalion and then a brigade, and in 1958 I was posted to the General Staff. For many years after that I was occupied in planning for war: strategic analysis, military doctrine and the long-range development of our armed forces. Then, in 1973, the Yom Kippur War opened a new era of Israeli–Arab negotiations. From that time on, I was engaged mainly in planning for peace and was an active participant in the peace process.

To non-Israelis it may seem odd that a professional soldier should be a peacemonger. Yet six Israeli–Arab wars in little more than a generation have left my people with a deep longing for peace. We have few illusions about it. Even after the historic breakthrough with Egypt, we have remained hemmed in by Arab hostility in a chronically unstable region, and we must be prepared to defend ourselves at all times. For us, any move towards a settlement of the conflict carries with it both hope and risk. If we have to pull back from entrenched defence lines, we feel more vulnerable with each step backwards. For us, strategy for defence and strategy for peace are two sides of the same coin.

That is why we have been so insistent on writing the maximum of

2

safeguards into any Israeli–Arab agreement. It is sometimes said that we are obsessive about our safety and have developed an ingrained siege mentality. But other nations do not have to live in a small country without fixed frontiers or peaceful neighbours; nor do other nations have the same tragic story as the Jewish people, culminating in the horror of the Holocaust.

The painful paradox of our situation is that the road to peace has been through war. An Arab regime will only come to terms with the existence of Israel when it accepts that Israel is here to stay, and if it wants to get back territory held by Israel. President Sadat made the psychological leap from belligerency to coexistence. Yet there would have been no Israeli–Egyptian Peace Treaty if we had not gained possession of Sinai in a war forced upon us by Egypt in 1967.

Given our troubled history, it is remarkable that we have not become a militant people. Among the most ardent seekers of peace have been Israeli generals who have won fame in battle. Two men in particular come to mind: the late Moshe Dayan and Ezer Weizman.

During one of our discussions at Camp David, Weizman remarked that, 'Those who have made war best understand peace.' Menachem Begin gained a place in history as the Israeli leader who signed a peace treaty with the most important of the Arab states. Yet without Dayan and Weizman, there would have been no treaty for him to sign. In protracted and difficult negotiations, they strove in a pragmatic spirit to reconcile peace with security. I have worked closely for many years with these men and have tried as best as I can to follow their example.

PART ONE
ISRAEL'S PEACE
WITH EGYPT

1

THE STEP–BY–STEP APPROACH

In November 1977, Anwar Sadat, President of the Arab Republic of Egypt, arrived in Jerusalem and from the rostrum of the Knesset (Parliament) offered to make peace with Israel.

To us Israelis the event seemed unreal and dreamlike. One felt the wing-beats of history-in-the-making in the most historic of all cities. Surely Sadat was the most notable Arab visitor to Jerusalem since the Caliph Omar conquered the Holy Land in AD 636 and, out of respect, walked barefoot through the city gates.

Lest anything should happen to the Egyptian President, 10,000 Israeli soldiers, police and border police were involved in the security arrangements. There were moments when the whole country, glued to its television sets, held its collective breath – as when Sadat went to pray in the El Aksa mosque where, nearly thirty years earlier, King Abdullah of Jordan had been assassinated for the 'crime' of trying to reach a settlement with Israel.

The most striking and moving feature of the visit was the spontaneous surge of feeling that welled up from the people of Israel. In it was expressed the thirty years of living in a state of siege, the strain and anguish of six Israeli–Arab wars, and the deep longing for peace and normality.

The moment of euphoria would not last. As the speeches of Sadat and Prime Minister Menachem Begin in the Knesset indicated, there was a wide gulf between the parties over the basis for peace. Much of the Arab world had formed a Rejection Front that would go on wishing and aiming for Israel's destruction. Clearly, the obstacles to peace were still formidable. Yet something important and unexpected had happened: Israel's isolation from its Arab environment had been broken. There was open contact; there was the beginning of dialogue; there was fresh hope.

I had been through all those wars as a soldier. Only four years had passed since Saturday, 6 October 1973, which was Yom Kippur, the holiest day of the Jewish year. President Sadat, together with President

Assad of Syria, had chosen that day to launch the surprise assault that began another war. Now this same President Sadat stood before our Parliament and proclaimed, 'No more wars!' I asked myself, as did most of my fellow Israelis, whether he meant it, or whether this was a stratagem to make us give up the strategic territory we had gained in the Six Day War of 1967 and thus expose ourselves to fresh dangers.

The truth was that we had not recovered from the psychological shock of the Yom Kippur War and the intense wariness of Arab intentions left in its wake. Yet that war had produced one positive result: it had revived the dormant peace process. Before Sadat came to Jerusalem, two partial agreements had been concluded, one with Egypt and one with Syria. They were steps in the right direction – away from war and towards a political settlement of the Israeli–Arab conflict, however distant a goal that might appear.

At the end of the Yom Kippur War, the United Nations Security Council unanimously passed Resolution 338, sponsored by the United States and the Soviet Union. It reaffirmed Resolution 242 of 22 November 1967, which laid down the basis for a 'just and lasting peace' between the states concerned. Resolution 338 added a call for immediate negotiations 'under appropriate auspices'. The auspices agreed upon by the super-powers were a Geneva Conference with the participation of Israel and its four neighbouring Arab states, under the joint chairmanship of the United States and the Soviet Union. The invitations would be sent out by the UN Secretary-General, who would attend the opening meeting.

The formula was a device whereby the two superpowers paid lip-service to the United Nations but, in fact, intended to bypass it. The Conference met on 20 December 1973, heard speeches from the heads of the delegations, appointed a military committee and adjourned. It has never met again. As a framework for negotiations, the Geneva Confer-ence was unrealistic: the United States and the Soviet Union had conflicting policies and interests in the Middle East; every Arab spokesman was obliged to sound uncompromising in the hearing of his fellow-Arabs; and Syria did not attend at all and was represented by an empty chair.

After the Geneva meeting the United States launched its separate peacemaking effort, through the 'shuttle diplomacy' of the energetic Secretary of State, Dr Henry Kissinger. He and the Israeli Government shared the opinion that a direct leap from war to a comprehensive peace was not feasible. The only realistic approach was a step-by-step one, a series of partial agreements which would in time build up to a peace based on Resolution 242.

The first step was to stabilize the precarious military situation. Israel's forces had established a bridgehead across the Suez Canal, fanned out to the outskirts of the city of Suez, and cut off the Egyptian Third Army which was located east of the Canal. The two armies were thus intertwined. Exchanges of artillery fire continued, and there was a daily risk that hostilities would flare up again.

The official negotiations for a disengagement-of-forces agreement were conducted in a tent at Kilometre 101 on the Cairo–Suez highway. The two sides were represented by senior army officers, under the chairman-ship of General Siilasvuo of Finland, Interim Commander of the newly revived United Nations Emergency Force (UNEF). Arrangements were made regarding two topics: food supplies to the entrapped Egyptian Third Army and an exchange of prisoners of war. The real negotiations proceeded on the highest political level: Dr Kissinger sped back and forth between Cairo and Jerusalem; and Prime Minister Golda Meir, followed by Defence Minister Moshe Dayan, visited President Nixon in Washington.

An Israeli–Egyptian Disengagement-of-Forces Agreement was signed at Kilometre 101 on 18 January 1974. It required our troops to withdraw to a line ten to fourteen miles east of the Canal. A buffer zone between the armies was occupied by the UNEF, with a restricted zone for troops and armaments on either side. In consideration of the Israeli withdrawal, American military aid was increased.

The danger of war receded. Egypt started working to reopen the Canal to shipping and to restore the battered cities in the Canal zone. The influence of the United States, and of Dr Kissinger personally, was enhanced in the Middle East.

Disengagement with Syria on the Golan Heights was a much tougher proposition. It took nearly six months of exhausting negotiations, with Kissinger shuttling periodically between Damascus and Jerusalem, before a Disengagement-of-Forces Agreement was signed in Geneva on 5 June 1974, marking the formal end of the Yom Kippur War. Under the Agreement, Israel withdrew to the pre-war ceasefire line and, in addition, returned to Syria the garrison town of Kuneitra that had been in our possession since 1967. On the analogy of the Agreement with Egypt, an 'area of separation' with a restricted zone on either side was supervised by another UN peace force, the United Nations Disengagement Observer Force (UNDOF).

With the Disengagement-of-Forces Agreements established, the next political objective was to secure a more far-reaching interim agreement between Egypt and Israel. The negotiations dragged on from March to September 1975, and saw further rounds of Dr Kissinger's special brand of airborne diplomacy. We now had to face the crucial and complex question: in the absence of peace, how much more territory could be given up in Sinai without gravely undermining national security? On that question a crisis blew up between Jerusalem and Washington.

In June 1974, a new Israeli Government had taken office under Yitzhak Rabin, with Shimon Peres as Minister of Defence and Yigal Allon as Foreign Minister. It had to take account of the backwash of public disillusionment in Israel after the Yom Kippur War, and the country's deep distrust of Egyptian intentions. In this atmosphere, Israel was called upon to withdraw its troops a further substantial distance in Sinai; to surrender the vital Mitla and Gidi Passes that controlled three of the four main routes across Sinai; and to hand back to Egypt the offshore oil wells in Southern Sinai along the Gulf of Suez, including those Israel had developed. (This was the only source of energy under direct Israeli control. Its loss was rendered more serious by the Arab oil weapon exploited from 1973, and even more so at a later stage, when the Shah of Iran was swept out of power by the Khomeini revolution. Till then, Iran was Israel's main supplier of oil.)

The Israeli Government rejected these demands, and for the first time a crisis arose in Israeli–American relations that derived from stalled Israeli–Arab political negotiations. It would not be the last time. The course of the crisis aptly illustrated the use of 'the carrot and the stick' techniques employed by Washington to gain concessions from Jerusalem.

Kissinger arrived in Israel on 8 March 1975 and started shuttling between Jerusalem and Cairo. Two weeks later, he declared publicly that the talks had reached an impasse and he returned to the United States with his delegation. Through the media, Israel was made to appear to the American public as the party responsible for the breakdown in the talks, due to its intransigence on issues that would advance the course of peace. The Administration announced that its Middle East policy was being 'reappraised'; meanwhile, Israel's requests for military aid were frozen.

The Israeli Government reacted strongly and explained to the Knesset, the nation and the world why the concessions demanded of Israel would gravely undermine the country's security and could not be accepted. The mood in Israel was one of anger and defiance. An information campaign was launched in the United States to influence the Administration and public opinion. A conference of American Jewish leaders came out in support of Israel and – what mattered more to the President – a petition calling for renewed military and economic aid to Israel was signed by seventy-six members of the US Senate.

After further high-level contacts, the crisis was resolved. Israel's acceptance of the Interim Agreement, with the concessions that had been previously rejected, had become possible on the strength of certain bilateral American commitments. The United States undertook to ensure that Israel's oil imports would be maintained. There would be a long-range programme of American military and economic aid to strengthen Israel's defence capacity, including advanced types of weapons such as F-

15 and F-16 planes, M-60 tanks, hydrofoil naval boats and intelligence-gathering equipment. The United States would also inject a token early-warning American presence between the two armies on the ground.

The Interim Agreement was signed on 4 September 1975, nearly two years after the Yom Kippur War. By its terms, Israeli forces were to withdraw to a line thirty miles east of the Suez Canal and eight miles east of the Gulf of Suez. The demilitarized buffer zone occupied by the UNEF and the restricted zones on either side of it were accordingly relocated further to the east. Only police would be stationed in Southern Sinai. Cargoes to and from Israeli ports could pass through the Suez Canal, but only in non-Israeli vessels. A joint commission was set up to supervise the Agreement, under the aegis of General Siilasvuo.

A novel feature of the Agreement was the elaborate and sophisticated electronic early-warning system to prevent surprise attacks, which was set up in the vicinity of the Mitla Pass, within the UNEF buffer zone. Israel could retain its own station there, and Egypt could construct one if it chose. The United States set up three manned watch-stations and three unmanned sensor fields to be operated by 200 American civilian personnel, subject to the approval of Congress. In addition, US planes would carry out daily surveillance flights over the area and supply the data from them to Egypt, Israel and the UNEF.

In Israel, opponents of the Agreement charged that tangible and costly concessions were being made in exchange for paper promises by Egypt. The Rabin Government asserted in reply that there could be no movement towards peace without taking risks. The psychological importance of the Agreement was that it meant an irrevocable step by Sadat's Egypt away from war. Israel's gamble would pay off, with the signing of the Peace Treaty with Egypt four years later. Kissinger's ability to influence the parties to the negotiations on the two 1974 Disengage-ment-of-Forces Agreements and the 1975 Interim Agreement derived first and foremost from the fact that he was the person through whom the sides talked to each other. The Arab party did not wish to hold direct negotiations with Israel; they were willing to talk only through a mediator.

This enabled Kissinger to pass on to each party, on behalf of the other, whatever he thought would influence the negotiations in the direction he wanted. He would not disclose all the other side had said to him or all he had said to the other side. Maybe this indirect approach was unavoidable at that time, but it could never yield the mutual understanding and meeting of minds between parties that can only come about through face-to-face negotiations. In the later peace talks with Egypt, I dealt with the security arrangements in Sinai and gained much experience of the difference made by direct contact.

While Kissinger's shuttle diplomacy did yield important results, we had to remind ourselves that he was not (nor could any American mediator be) a neutral third party. He bore in mind throughout American strategic and economic interests in the Arab world – interests that did not always coincide with those of Israel.

In Jerusalem, Kissinger had his own way of creating an atmosphere of co-operation. Discussions were opened with an assessment by him of the strategic situation in the region. He indicated that the importance of a further Israeli–Egyptian agreement lay in keeping the Soviet danger to the free world at bay. He invoked the prospect of a broad strategic understanding between the United States and Israel for common purposes, accompanied by substantial American security and economic aid for Israel. I assume he created the same atmosphere amongst the Arabs by playing down the Israeli aspect and by stressing the importance of strategic co-operation between the United States and themselves. Kissinger also had a way of making threats, and I imagine he employed this method with both parties to gain compliance with his demands. He would say (or leak) on behalf of Egypt the attitude that, if an impasse was reached in the talks, the Egyptians would have no alternative but recourse again to war. (I am now sure such statements were not made to him in Cairo.) To the Egyptians he would say that if a deadlock were reached, the situation would relapse into war. In that case, they would be liable again to lose all of Sinai and incur once more the destruction of the towns along the Suez Canal. In addition, extremist factions inside and outside Egypt could foment a rebellion, which would quite likely lead to the downfall of the Egyptian Government and bring the country once more under Soviet control.

After the two Disengagement-of-Forces Agreements and the Interim Agreement with Egypt, the step-by-step approach to peacemaking in the Israeli–Arab conflict had exhausted itself. The reasons why there would be no further partial agreements are worth examining, since they throw light on the basic attitudes of the governments concerned.

Following the 1975 Agreement with Egypt, an anti-Egyptian Rejection Front emerged in the Arab world, led by Syria and the Palestine Liberation Organization (PLO). They maintained that separate agreements with Israel undermined the united Arab position, and that Israel had to withdraw completely from all the territories it had occupied in the Six Day War and return to the pre-1967 armistice lines. They demanded that the Geneva Conference be reconvened, with the participation of all the Arab states concerned as well as the PLO, constituting a single pan-Arab delegation. This would enable the Soviet Union, as co-chairman, to play an active role in Middle East negotiations as a counterweight to the United States, which was regarded as favouring Israel.

For its own reasons, the Soviet Union was determined to block separate American diplomatic initiatives and to thwart the rising United States influence that resulted. The Soviet Union, therefore, encouraged the Rejection Front, while itself refusing to recognize the 1975 Agreement.

Under these pressures Egypt would not consider another partial agreement, unless and until Israel concluded such agreements with Syria and Jordan.

Jordan had not taken part in the Yom Kippur War, except for sending an armoured brigade to Southern Syria which did not take part in the fighting. There was thus no need for a disengagement-of-forces agreement with Jordan. The situation that emerged from the Six Day War remained unchanged, with the border along the River Jordan. King Hussein lacked the capacity to make any agreement with Israel on his own, whether partial or final. After the bloody showdown in Jordan with the PLO in 1970–71 and its expulsion, Jordan had found itself virtually isolated in the Arab world and was slowly finding its way back into the fold. Other Arab governments regarded the PLO as the only legitimate spokesman for the Palestinian Arabs including those inhabiting the Israeli-occupied West Bank (Judea and Samaria)* and the Gaza Strip. These problems would face the King even if he could, by an agreement with Israel, regain all that Jordan had lost in the Six Day War, including East Jerusalem. But the King knew from his own secret contacts with Israeli representatives that there was no prospect of Israel making such an agreement. In brief, the King was in principle interested in coming to terms with Israel but in fact forced into immobility.

On the Golan Heights, neither Israel nor Syria was interested in further partial pacts after the 1974 Disengagement-of-Forces Agreement. Israel would not consider giving up more strategic territory on the Golan Heights and abandoning some of its settlements there unless it obtained peace with Syria in exchange. Here, too, there was a stalemate.

Lebanon had not taken part in the Yom Kippur War. Its border with Israel had remained unchanged from the beginning, and neither state had any territorial claims on the other. In any case, Lebanon was a weak and ethnically fragmented country. There was no factual basis for any Israeli–Lebanese interim agreement involving a partial withdrawal of Israel.

When the fighting stopped in the Yom Kippur War, I returned from the Suez Canal front to my post as head of the General Staff Planning Branch.

*The area west of the River Jordan which was occupied by Jordan from 1948 to 1967 is still generally known as 'the West Bank'. However, in Israel it is usually referred to by the ancient biblical names of 'Judea and Samaria'. To avoid confusion in the mind of the non-Israeli reader, the term used in this book is 'the West Bank'.

I had to reassemble my staff who, like myself, had gone off to emergency duties when the fighting started. We were much involved in the basic re-thinking of our defence strategy and the reorganization of our armed forces as a result of the war and the lessons it had taught. Our priority task, however, concerned the two 1974 Disengagement-of-Forces Agree-ments and the 1975 Interim Agreement with Egypt. I had to produce for the negotiations detailed proposals with maps regarding security arrange-ments in Sinai and on the Golan Heights. In each case, the aim was to create an effective system of safeguards against surprise attack while, at the same time, ensuring that the IDF retained a defensible line.

We carefully studied our previous experience with the armistice regime till 1967 and the ceasefire after that. In addition, Major Joel Singer, the Director of the International Law Section of the Military Advocate-General's Office, gathered together all the major post-war international agreements in the twentieth century that had a military component, including the Treaty of Versailles and the Korean and Vietnam treaties. We extracted from these documents any features of interest to us, such as demilitarized zones, limitation of forces, international supervision and early-warning systems.

At the same time, our architect Zalman Einav prepared the maps required. He was an acknowledged expert in this highly specialized field – extremely accurate and familiar with every contour on the ground. The problem with Einav was that he suffered emotionally when he had to depict our territorial concessions. At one stage he even protested to the Minister of Defence and the Prime Minister himself at our giving up areas that he thought vital to our security. I sometimes felt that his maps were drawn with a quill pen dipped in blood, not ink.

The security arrangements written into the 1974 and 1975 Agreements would provide valuable precedents several years later, when I was concerned with negotiating the Military Appendix to the Peace Treaty with Egypt.

Already in 1975, with the conclusion of the Interim Agreement, preparatory steps were taken to clarify our positions for future peace talks. As Minister of Defence, Shimon Peres formed a Joint Planning Branch of the Ministry of Defence and the General Staff, with myself as the head, directly responsible to him in matters of political strategy.

He charged me with preparing detailed proposals for a comprehensive peace settlement with Israel's four neighbouring Arab states – the so-called 'confrontation states'. In simple terms, I had to recommend how to exchange a security based on areas under Israel's control, which provided it with strategic depth, for a security based on a peace treaty or treaties which would bring the state of war to an end, provide security safeguards and normalize relations between Israel and its neighbours. For this purpose I set up within the Joint Planning Branch a special staff group, a kind of 'think-tank', that included representatives of the Foreign Ministry, the Intelligence Branch of the General Staff, the Mossad (External Intelligence) and academics from the strategic and political research institutes at the universities.

In 1976 I submitted to the Minister our policy recommendations (summarized in Chapter 8). But when the peace process actually started the next year, the Government which I had been serving was no longer in power.

2

THE STONY ROAD

Between the Sadat visit to Jerusalem and the signing of the Israeli–Egyptian Peace Treaty there were sixteen months of tough negotiations. We who took part in them had to travel a long and stony road, with the peace caravan halting at a number of way-stations: Cairo, Ismailia, Jerusalem, Leeds Castle in England, Camp David, Washington. For the most part, we emerged from these stations feeling like Omar Khayyam, who,

> Myself when young did eagerly frequent
> Doctor and Saint, and heard great argument
> About it and about, but evermore
> Came out by the same door wherein I went.

Nineteen seventy-seven was a watershed year in the political history of the State of Israel. From the beginning of independence Israeli politics had been dominated by the Labour movement, with successive governments headed by David Ben-Gurion, Moshe Sharett, Levi Eshkol, Golda Meir and Yitzhak Rabin. In the May 1977 elections, the right-wing Likud came to power. In the new coalition government under Menachem Begin, Moshe Dayan became Foreign Minister and Ezer Weizman Minister of Defence.

The peace programme of the Government was a projection of the views which the Likud had held in opposition. Its main points were:

- Return of the whole of Sinai to Egypt, on certain conditions.
- The peace border with Syria would not be the old international frontier but would remain on the Golan Heights.
- The peace border with Jordan would be the River Jordan; the West Bank and the Gaza Strip would be incorporated into Israel.

On the instructions of the new Minister of Defence, I set the Joint Planning Branch to draft proposals for security arrangements based on these peace policy objectives. On the peace front events unfolded rapidly. In September 1977, Dayan held secret talks in Morocco with Hassan

Tuhami, the Egyptian Deputy Premier, with King Hassan II as host. Through this roundabout channel, the message was conveyed from Begin to Sadat that Egypt could expect to regain all of Sinai in exchange for peace. On 19 November, Sadat journeyed to Jerusalem on the historic visit that made world news.

But the peace process initiated by the Sadat visit seemed to founder at the outset. Sadat published an interview lashing out at Israel, and at Begin personally, for not responding to his gesture by accepting the principles he had outlined for peace: complete withdrawal to the pre-1967 borders on all fronts and statehood for the Palestinian Arabs.

The United States now stepped on to the stage. President Jimmy Carter flew to Egypt and met Sadat at Aswan. He was followed by US Secretary of State Cyrus Vance and his top Middle East experts, who conducted talks in Cairo and then in Jerusalem. Elated by the belief that he had American support, Sadat overreached himself. He invited the other Arab states concerned to join Egypt, Israel, the United States and the United Nations at a great peace conference in Cairo. No Arab state accepted the invitation. After his rebuff, it was decided to play down the conference. It would only be a preparatory one with Egypt, Israel and the United States represented by senior officials, not political leaders. It met at Mena House, the renowned hotel at the Pyramids.

The Israeli delegation was headed by the Director-General of the Prime Minister's Office, Eliahu Ben-Elissar (later the first Israeli Ambassador to Cairo). Included in it were Meir Rosenne, Legal Adviser to the Foreign Ministry (later Israeli Ambassador to Washington), and myself as the representative of the Ministry of Defence.

The Egyptian delegation was led by their Ambassador to the United Nations, Abdul Meguid, with their Ministry of War represented by General Taha el-Magdoub and Brigadier Aweidi (with whom I had become well-acquainted during the negotiations in Geneva to finalize the military protocol of the 1975 Israeli–Egyptian Interim Agreement).

The Cairo Conference was a failure, and no progress was made on any of the issues in dispute. However, I used my time to have unofficial and useful talks with Magdoub and Aweidi, and I gained more understanding of the Egyptian positions on the essence of peace and on security arrangements. At the same time, Ezer Weizman, accompanied by two senior officers, met with the Egyptian Minister of War, General Abd-el Ghani Gamasi, at Jenklis near Alexandria. At this meeting, Weizman was able to form his own impressions of the Egyptian positions.

On the day the Mena House Conference opened, Premier Begin flew to Washington to discuss the Israeli Government's peace proposals with President Carter. On his way back, he stopped in London to brief Prime Minister Harold Wilson. At the same time, the 'Rejectionist' Arab states, led by Syria and Iraq, met at Tripoli in Libya. They denounced Sadat and called for a diplomatic and economic boycott of Egypt.

On 25 December, world attention focused on Ismailia on the Suez Canal, where Begin and Sadat met at a summit conference. They were accompanied by their respective Foreign Ministers, Moshe Dayan and Ibrahim Kamel, and their respective Ministers of Defence, Ezer Weizman and Abd-el Gamasi. Ben-Elissar and I travelled from Cairo to Ismailia in an official Egyptian car. The route we took brought back for me vivid memories of the Yom Kippur War, when I had been with the division that had established a bridgehead west of the Canal.

At the Conference, Begin presented Sadat with two documents containing a written set of peace plans. The first was a proposal for an Israeli–Egyptian peace treaty; the second was a proposal for Palestinian Arab self-rule in Judea, Samaria and the Gaza Strip, which would be implemented as part of the peace treaty.

The main elements of the peace treaty proposal were:

- Full normalization of all relations including diplomatic relations.
- Israeli withdrawal from all Sinai in two stages, within a period of two to five years after the signing of the treaty. The first stage would be an interim border stretching from El Arish on the Mediterranean coast to Ras Muhammad on the southern tip of the Sinai Peninsula. In the second stage, Israel would withdraw to the international border.
- The whole area of Sinai east of the Gidi and Mitla Passes would become a demilitarized zone under the supervision of a UN force.
- Egypt would continue to deploy only restricted forces in the zone between the Suez Canal and the Mitla and Gidi Passes, as stipulated in the Interim Agreement of September 1975.
- Israeli settlements would remain in the area controlled by the UN. They would be subject to Israeli administration and jurisdiction and would possess local powers of defence.
- Two of the three Israeli airfields in Sinai (Ophira, Etzion and Eytan) would serve civilians only and would be subject to Israeli management under UN supervision. The third airfield would remain in military use.
- The existing early-warning station in Sinai would remain under Israeli control.
- The Straits of Tiran and the Gulf of Akaba would be open to international navigation, as President Sadat had agreed in Jerusalem.
- These principles would remain in force until the year 2001, when they would be reassessed.

The main elements of Begin's proposal for self-rule in the West Bank and the Gaza Strip were:

- The military government in the West Bank would be dismantled and the Palestinian Arab inhabitants of these territories would be granted self-rule under an elected administrative council, located in Bethlehem.
- Israel would be responsible for security and public order in the territories.
- The Arab inhabitants would be given a choice between Israeli or Jordanian citizenship.
- A committee would be established including representatives of Israel, Jordan and the elected administrative council, which would examine existing legislation in the territories and would determine, by consent, which laws would remain in force, and what authority the administrative council would have to determine regulations.
- Israeli citizens would be entitled to buy land in the territories. Those Arab residents accepting Israeli citizenship would also be entitled to purchase land and settle anywhere in Israel.
- A committee comprising representatives of Israel, Jordan and the administrative council would determine regulations for the admission of Arab refugees to the territories in reasonable numbers.
- Freedom of movement and of economic activity in Israel, the West Bank and the Gaza Strip would be assured for all their inhabitants.
- Israel would maintain its claim to sovereignty over these territories while being fully aware that there were other claims to them. Israel, however, proposed that, in order to reach a peace settlement, the question of sovereignty should remain open.
- Regarding Jerusalem – Israel would present a separate proposal for the administration of the holy places of the three religions. This proposal would ensure freedom of access to the sites to members of each faith.

The above principles would be subject to reassessment after a period of five years.

There was initial optimism among the members of the Israeli delegation on the first day of the Ismailia Conference. We were soon disillusioned. Towards the end of the first day, Foreign Minister Kamel and Minister of State for Foriegn Affairs Butros Ghali rejected some of the key provisions of the Israeli peace plan. When Sinai was returned to Egypt, it would accept no continuing Israeli presence in it – neither military nor civilian settlements that were already there. The Palestinian Arabs in Israeli-occupied territory had to be given the right to self-determination and statehood, not just self-rule, as Israel proposed. Resolution 242 required Israel to return all territories taken by force and to withdraw on all fronts to the pre-1967 armistice lines. Egypt would not make a separate peace with Israel.

Clearly, the positions of the two parties were worlds apart. The Conference failed to produce agreement on a single specific question, or even on a set of general principles concerning the Palestinian problem. The only achievement was a decision to continue talks in two committees. The first would be a political committee with delegations from Israel, Egypt and the United States headed by their respective Foreign Ministers. The second would be a military committee comprising delegations from Israel and Egypt headed by their Ministers of Defence.

After the Ismailia Conference, I completed the material required for negotiations in the military committee, due to begin in Cairo at the Tahra Palace on 19 January 1978. We worked extremely hard in the Joint Planning Branch since only two weeks remained before the opening of negotiations. The material had to be completed, brought up for final discussions called by the Minister of Defence and afterwards sent for approval to the Prime Minister.

The preparation of this material was based on the peace plan presented to Sadat and took into account the informal talks I had held with the Egyptian generals at the Cairo Conference in mid-December. At this stage, however, problems arose from an unexpected quarter. While I was completing plans for security agreements, based on the return of all Sinai to Egypt, General Mordechai ('Motta') Gur, the Chief of Staff, requested the General Staff to prepare a plan for security arrangements based on the evacuation of the IDF forces only up to the El Arish–Ras Muhammad security border. He opposed the Likud peace plan on this question and thoroughly prepared his case to show why it was preferable for Israel to withdraw to the El Arish–Ras Muhammad line, in exchange for a non-belligerency pact, rather than to the international frontier for a peace treaty. He maintained that it would only be possible to determine the permanent border with Egypt after a comprehensive and stable peace settlement with all Israel's neighbours had been achieved. I was in a paradoxical position because what Gur proposed was identical with the recommendation I had made to Shimon Peres in 1976. However, the new Likud Government was firmly opposed to surrendering more territory for another interim agreement and was insistent that the next step should be a full peace treaty. It was on that premise that my present plan was drawn up.

I asked Ezer Weizman to present both plans – mine and Gur's – to the

Prime Minister so that the latter might make a decision. Begin called a special meeting to discuss the two plans and, at the close of an exhausting session, concluded that the security plan I had drafted accorded with the Government's policy; it was this which should constitute the basis for negotiations with Egypt.

On 19 January 1978, the Israeli delegation, led by Weizman, flew to Cairo for the meeting of the military committee. The delegation included the Deputy Minister of Defence, Mordechai Zippori; the Chief of Staff, Motta Gur; the head of the Intelligence Branch, Shlomo Gazit; a member of the Foreign Ministry, Ambassador Moshe Sasson (who spoke fluent Arabic and had, in the past, served as Ambassador to Turkey and Italy); and myself. I also took my three chief assistants who had prepared the material for the negotiations: Colonel Yaakov Heichal, the head of the Military–Strategic Planning Section in my Branch; Zalman Einav, the map expert; and Joel Singer, our international law expert.

This was the third time in a month that a plane-load of Israeli passengers had landed on Egyptian soil. As this had not happened for thirty years, there was still a sense of incredulity about it. Like the two earlier flights, this one was also full of pressmen and television crews. At Cairo Airport, Weizman was received with full military honours by Minister of War Gamasi, the Chief of Staff, the heads of General Staff sections and commanders of the air, sea and land forces. Strict security measures were taken around the airport and along the route to the Tahra Palace, which was also heavily guarded.

We ate lunch with our hosts, and Weizman, as is his wont, succeeded in creating an open and friendly atmosphere during the meal. Facing each other across the table, which was laden with typical Egyptian dishes, sat senior officers in command of troops who had been fighting on opposing sides for more than three decades. The main subjects of conversation were past wars and the historic turning-point about to take place in relations between the two countries. One got the impression that the Egyptians saw the October 1973 War (the Yom Kippur War) as a great victory. They had initiated the war, crossed the Suez Canal, gained control of territory several miles to the east of the Canal and succeeded, as they stressed, in attaining their three main objectives: the shattering of Israel's hopes of maintaining unchallenged its gains in the Six Day War; the creation of a sense of international crisis, thus putting political pressure on Israel to withdraw; and the implementation of the first stages of an Israeli withdrawal from Sinai and the restoration of Egyptian control along both sides of the Suez Canal.

The two wars preceding the Yom Kippur War were presented by our hosts as the failures of inept Egyptian regimes: King Farouk had not needed to invade Israel in 1948 and Gamal Abdul Nasser could have avoided the Six Day War. They spoke of the Sinai Campaign as a defensive war aimed at preventing the return of British and French imperialism to the African continent. 'And you, the Israelis, they added, 'hitched a ride on the Franco–British war train. If you had not done so, you would not have succeeded in taking most of Sinai at the time.'

The first official discussions between the delegations was fixed for that evening. We used the free time to tour Cairo and its antiquities.

Talks continued for two days on the security arrangements for Sinai following Israel's withdrawal. Weizman allowed Motta Gur to present his opinion that it was preferable to accept a non-belligerency pact, in which Israel would withdraw only to the security border, than to sign an Israeli–Egyptian peace treaty based on an IDF withdrawal from all of Sinai – a treaty which would not constitute a stable peace as long as it was not part of a comprehensive settlement. The Egyptians angrily rejected his views, which came as no surprise to me. They already knew, from the talks Moshe Dayan had held in Morocco with Tuhami, and from the Israeli peace plan presented to Sadat by Begin in Ismailia, that Israel was prepared to concede all of Sinai for a peace settlement.

I asked Weizman why he had allowed Gur to speak, as the Prime Minister had already decided that the Chief of Staff's recommendations would not serve as a basis for negotiations. Weizman replied: 'It's better that he reach his own conclusions as to the feasibility of his recommendations, in direct argument with the Egyptians, than that he should continue to remain unconvinced by Israeli policy. What matters is that there be a relaxation of tension and the building of sincére and friendly relations between the senior officers of the two armies. They must get to know each other's thinking and learn to live together in peace. If we manage to achieve this, we will have made a great contribution to the future.'

During the talks, it became clear where the main gaps lay. The Egyptians maintained their objection to any continued Israeli presence in Sinai after the return of the area to Egypt. They also demanded that limited Egyptian forces be stationed up to a line about fifteen miles to the west of the international border, while we insisted that they be deployed up to approximately thirty miles east of the Suez Canal and the Gulf of Suez (about 100 miles west of the border), so that the Egyptian army would not cross the Gidi and Mitla Passes. There was also a difference of opinion regarding the time period required for Israel's withdrawal from all Sinai. The Egyptians demanded that it take place within a year, while we maintained that it should take place over a three- to five-year period.

After a series of inconclusive talks, it was decided that I should remain in Cairo to try to reduce the existing gaps before the opening of the second meeting of the military committee, due to take place at the beginning of February.

In Cairo, I held discussions with senior Egyptian officers for about eighteen days, from 13 January to 1 February. I stayed in the Tahra Palace with Egyptian bodyguards. In the adjacent building, Colonel Heichal and Zalman Einav stayed with Israeli security staff and media crews.

Every day, except for Fridays and Saturdays, I met with a group of Egyptians in the luxurious Palace. Besides General Magdoub, they included the Secretary of the Egyptian National Security Council, the official responsible for strategic planning in the Egyptian Ministry of War, the head of Army Intelligence in the Egyptian General Staff, and Magdoub's assistants.

I met with General Gamasi a number of times. He came to visit me at the Palace and I learned from him how negotiations were developing in the political committee, which met in Jerusalem on 17 January with the participation of the Foreign Ministers of Israel, Egypt and the United States.

On several evenings I was entertained by Magdoub at his home, or at an Egyptian restaurant in the Old City of Cairo, or on the banks of the Nile in the Mahdi area. I started to feel at home in Cairo and my knowledge of different sectors of the Egyptian population grew from day to day. It was a strange and uncomfortable feeling for me to be alone, except for the security guards, in a palace with many large halls and rooms. I was accommodated on the third (top) floor in a large bedroom, furnished in the style of Louis XIV, and a reception dining-room, where I ate breakfast and lunch with my assistants from the adjoining building. The Palace was situated in the Heliopolis quarter, where wealthy Egyptians and members of the diplomatic corps had their homes. From my room, I could hear the sounds of the muezzin from the nearby mosques. Surrounding the Palace was a well-kept garden criss-crossed by paths where I would go for walks with my assistants when we wished to talk about matters better not discussed in our rooms, for they were without doubt fitted with bugging devices. I was in direct telephone contact with Ezer Weizman and I knew that the Egyptians listened to all our conversations. I therefore used the telephone for unclassified calls only and for conversations I felt the Egyptians would be pleased to hear. I had other means at my disposal for transmitting classified reports and for receiving instructions.

One evening, Magdoub took me to dine in a fish restaurant on the banks of the Nile, and there I fell in love with a salty cheese that had a very special taste. When I returned to the Tahra Palace, I suddenly became extremely thirsty. I did not dare to drink from the tap in the bathroom (which was decorated in pink Italian marble) because the Chief Medical Officer of the IDF had issued special instructions to those of us travelling to Egypt that we were not to drink undistilled water there for fear of contracting bilharzia. The refrigerator in the reception-room was empty and the kitchen on the second floor of the Palace was locked. I decided to leave the Palace and find something to drink in the adjacent building where my assistants were staying. The Egyptian bodyguards on the first floor were snoring loudly. I approached the Palace gate but, before I could open it, I remembered that I did not know the Egyptian password to give the guards if I was stopped on the way back, and I would run the risk of being shot. I returned to my room in the grip of a terrible thirst. I could not sleep all night. Only in the morning, after the Egyptian cooks had opened the restaurant, could I quench my thirst with bottled soft drinks. That morning I told Magdoub the whole story and he burst out laughing. 'Why didn't you drink from the tap?' he asked. 'In Cairo, the water from the Nile intended as drinking water has been distilled for the past twenty years.' I was afraid to insult the Egyptian national pride by telling him about the Chief Medical Officer's instructions. From that day on I was not afraid to drink directly from the tap, and I found the water from the Nile very pleasant.

In talks with the Egyptians, and especially with General Gamasi, I became well-acquainted with their attitudes on the terms of a peace settlement. I was able to inform Weizman that Egypt would take an extreme opening position, expressing hard-line Arab views, i.e. that Israel withdraw to all the pre-1967 armistice lines and that a Palestinian Arab state be established in the West Bank and the Gaza Strip. But in the course of negotiations, Egypt would be prepared to make a separate peace with Israel on condition that a declaration of principles be agreed providing for self-determination for the Palestinian Arabs after a period of autonomy under Egyptian and Jordanian supervision. They would also want acceptance by us of an obligation to honour the statement in the preamble to Security Council Resolution 242, regarding 'the inadmissibility of the acquisition of territory by war'. They would remain opposed to continuing Israeli presence in Sinai or any adjustment of the international border. However, they would eventually accept our proposal for the security arrangements in Sinai.

On another evening, Magdoub invited me for dinner at the Sheraton Hotel night-club. I arrived with my bodyguards to find that elaborate arrangements had been made in advance. The best table had been reserved for us next to the stage; Egyptian security men were stationed at the entrance and around our table, and a large number of pressmen were present. Magdoub asked me to sit in the place of honour, the chair closest to the stage, but I managed to persuade him to sit there himself, while I sat next to him. My instinct was not mistaken. As was the custom, when the famous belly dancer, Najha Fuad, had finished her act, she approached the person sitting in the place of honour, embraced him and began stroking his chest. I thanked heaven that it was Magdoub and not I who appeared in all the press photographs of this intimate event. I could just imagine how a picture of me in the embrace of a belly dancer would have been received in Israel. It would have been said, 'This is how the Egyptians are softening up Abrasha to get concessions out of him.'

At this meal, Magdoub spoke freely for the first time. He told me about the tough problems facing Gamasi in his negotiations with Weizman. 'Gamasi desires peace,' said Magdoub. 'He is quite willing to be flexible concerning the continued presence of some of the Israeli settlements in Sinai, and of the Etzion airfield as an Israeli base for a period of up to ten years after Israel's withdrawal. He is extremely impressed by Ezer Weizman and stresses that many Egyptians would place their trust in Israelis like him.'

This led me to ask why, if what he said was true, Gamasi had been so rigid at the military committee negotiations on issues about which, Magdoub said, he was willing to be flexible. His reply was that Gamasi had many enemies among the Egyptian army elite, his main adversary being Deputy President Hosni Mubarak. Magdoub and others saw Gamasi as a staff officer who had gone far because Sadat liked him and admired him as an expert strategist, whereas Mubarak saw him as his most dangerous rival for the presidency after Sadat. Gamasi believed that Egypt's major interests should be seen as those of a state lying at the most vital, strategic cross-roads between Africa and Asia, and between the Mediterranean and the Indian Ocean. Egypt's interests did not coincide with those of an Arab world split between power centres which refused to allow their unification into a single, political and strategic entity. Furthermore, among the power centres of the Arab world there were those whose traditional policy was to prevent Egypt, the largest and strongest of the Arab states, from exercising leadership. In this context, Magdoub mentioned Iraq and also Saudi Arabia, for whom an Arab world split between opposing centres of power was preferable to a united Arab world. The Saudis considered that Egyptian leadership was liable to endanger their monarchical regime. Even today, they could not forget the situation in which they had found themselves prior to the Six Day War, when Egypt, under Nasser, controlled Syria, created the eastern front, influenced Libya, became involved in a war in the Yemen and had ambitions to solve Egypt's economic problems by gaining control of the oil resources of the Arabian Peninsula. Israel's victory in the Six Day War, said Magdoub, had saved Saudi Arabia, because since then Egypt's strategic efforts had been concentrated on the Israeli–Arab arena.

The impression given to me during this conversation was that Gamasi's position was being undermined. I did not know whether or not to believe this. As far as Weizman was concerned, Gamasi was one of the key people in Egypt capable of advancing the peace process in which he so deeply believed. I returned that evening to the Tahra Palace, my mind astir with all I had heard.

A few months later, when I accompanied Weizman to his meeting with President Sadat in the Austrian city of Salzburg, Sadat and Weizman had a private talk lasting several hours. Gamasi, Kamel, Magdoub and myself were left to wait on the balcony overlooking the lake with its lovely colours. We passed the time in routine conversations and eating delicious strudel. By then, I had already come to the conclusion that Gamasi no longer held an influential position in Egypt. Here the Egyptian President was meeting with the Israeli Minister of Defence, while Weizman's Egyptian counterpart waited outside on the balcony. Weizman came to the same conclusion, and sadness showed on his face when he met Gamasi afterwards to report on the meeting.

Later, at the Camp David Summit Conference, Gamasi was not included in the Egyptian delegation, despite the fact that he still held the position of Minister of War. After the Camp David Accords were signed, Kamal Hassan Ali replaced Gamasi and headed the Egyptian delegation to the Israeli–Egyptian peace talks held in Washington.

On the second day of the political committee meeting in Jerusalem, Gamasi paid me a surprise visit at the Tahra Palace. He looked very tense. We exchanged greetings and he said that he wanted me to pass on a message to Prime Minister Begin. He told me that on that day a crisis had developed in the political committee. The Egyptian delegation was on the point of breaking off negotiations and returning to Egypt, in accordance with a decision taken by President Sadat. The reasons behind the Egyptian decision, given to the public, would be the negative Israeli position regarding a declaration of principles on the Palestinian issue. In addition, the delegation maintained that Prime Minister Begin and Foreign Minister Dayan had insulted Egyptian honour in speeches and declarations they had made during the negotiations. Gamasi, however, gave me other explanations to pass on to Begin.

The Saudis were exerting pressure on Egypt to break off the Jerusalem negotiations, threatening that if it did not do so, it should expect the moderate Arab states to sever relations and join the anti-Egyptian boycott. It was extremely important, therefore, to endorse a declaration of principles on the Palestinian issue. This would allow the Egyptians to continue bilateral negotiations for an Israeli–Egyptian peace settlement. The declaration could serve as a basis for Jordan and the Palestinians to negotiate separately with Israel on the future of Judea, Samaria and Gaza, 'so that they and not we will deal with the Palestinian problem on the basis of these principles'. The military committee talks would continue despite the many pressures on Egypt and the suspension of the political committee. Gamasi added that Sadat had great trust in Weizman and believed that in the military committee gaps could be bridged not only on security arrangements in Sinai, but also on other issues.

That night the Egyptian delegates to the talks in Jerusalem packed their bags and flew home. The short, unhappy life of the political committee had come to an abrupt end.

The military committee, presided over by Weizman and Gamasi, held its second session on 30 January and 1 February 1978. Weizman did not take Motta Gur or Mordechai Zippori to this meeting. The delegation was small: apart from Weizman, it included the Director of the Intelligence Branch, Shlomo Gazit, Ambassador Moshe Sasson and myself.

At this meeting, we achieved agreement in principle on security arrangements in Sinai concerning the limitation of Egyptian forces and the division of the area into demilitarized and limited-forces zones. There was no Egyptian agreement, however, to a continued Israeli presence of any kind in Sinai. They would not even agree to the continued operation of the Etzion airfield as a civilian base.

Dayan had originally promoted military development and civilian settlements in Eastern Sinai. He assumed that these developments would strengthen the Israeli claim that the planned security border along the El Arish–Ras Muhammad line should become the final peace frontier between Egypt and Israel. Then in 1977, when Dayan had become Foreign Minister in the newly elected Likud Government, he had the secret meetings in Morocco with Tuhami, which preceded Sadat's historic visit to Jerusalem. Dayan came away from these preliminary contacts persuaded that there would be no peace with Egypt unless Egyptian sovereignty was reaffirmed over the whole of Sinai. However, he and Begin reckoned that Egypt might agree to Israel retaining its military and civilian presence in the area between the El Arish–Ras Muhammad line, while the peace negotiations were in progress. This step provoked a crisis in the negotiations and tension with Washington. The Egyptian position became more rigid. In the end, Israel had to accept the total removal of all its military installations and all its civilian settlements, as a major part of its price for peace. In the debate in Israel after the Peace Treaty, the nagging question arose whether these concessions had really been necessary. From my own talks with both Egyptian and American representatives, my feeling was that the Egyptians might have agreed to the Israeli settlements remaining under Egyptian sovereignty and UN supervision in the Northern Sinai area between Rafah and El Arish (the Yamit sector). On the other hand, there was no Egyptian willingness to have any Israeli settlements remain in Southern Sinai, because of Egypt's political sensitivity to an Israeli presence in the vicinity of the Gulf of

Akaba and the Straits of Tiran. But they were angered by what they saw as an Israeli attempt to create new facts on the ground while the talks were in progress. After that, they refused to agree to civilian settlements remaining in any part of Sinai after the Israeli military evacuation.

The military committee did not meet again because the political negotiations had, meanwhile, reached a complete deadlock.

Against this background, the United States became increasingly involved in the conduct of the negotiations. From February 1978, it took on the task of mediator by means of shuttle diplomacy between Israel and Egypt. The 'shuttle' was carried out by Secretary of State Vance and Ambassador Ray Atherton.

During the period between the second meeting of the military committee at the beginning of February and the meetings of the political committee at Leeds Castle in England in July, Ezer Weizman met with Sadat in Cairo and again in Salzburg. We continued to maintain members of my staff in Egypt until after the Salzburg meeting. At first they stayed in the Tahra Palace, and afterwards at Jenklis. It was through this staff that we maintained contact with the Egyptian Ministry of War.

These contacts made it possible to organize meetings between Weizman and Sadat and gave us a kind of 'direct line' to the top, enabling us to prevent incidents between Israeli and Egyptian forces in Sinai. Weizman used the direct line more than once to convey greetings to Gamasi and the Egyptian generals on such occasions as promotions or birthday celebrations.

At Weizman's meetings with Sadat in Cairo and Salzburg, it was made clear again that Sadat was willing to reach a separate peace settlement provided it was accompanied by a general set of principles which would serve as a basis for a comprehensive peace. At these meetings Sadat stressed the importance of reaching a speedy conclusion to the negotiations before a Rejection Front capable of blocking peace could be organized against Egypt.

During these talks, ideas arose for the first time regarding a possible federation or confederation between Israel and a Palestinian entity in the West Bank and the Gaza Strip. This would follow a transitional period of autonomy administered by a joint Israeli–Jordanian–Palestinian council. The suggestion was even made that two transitional, autonomous entities be established – one in the Gaza Strip, to be administered by a joint Israeli–Egyptian council, and the other in the West Bank to be administered by a joint Israeli–Jordanian council – in both cases with representatives of the local Arab population.

It was also proposed that Israel have the right of veto over decisions taken in the joint council or councils, so that it would be impossible to pass a majority resolution to which Israel was opposed. However, the day after Gamasi made this proposal he rescinded it, due to a meeting between Sadat and dignitaries from the Gaza Strip. It was clear, however, that this was not the real reason; it was, in fact, the Saudis who had again exerted pressure.

At the Salzburg meeting with Weizman, Sadat suggested that Israel make a gesture to Egypt. The latter could then claim that progress had been made at the negotiating table. Sadat wanted to instil in Egyptian hearts a belief in the importance of reaching a peace settlement with Israel, even a separate one, since it was impossible to reach a comprehensive agreement owing to the policy of the other Arab states. The gesture requested by Sadat was the return to Egypt of El Arish and of the area in Southern Sinai including the Santa Caterina monastery on the slopes of Mount Sinai (Jebel Mussa), which is also a Moslem holy place. The Israeli Government would not agree to make such a gesture. Sadat's request was leaked to the media. Angrily, he gave instructions that the Israeli military staff, who were at that time residing in Jenklis, should return to Israel. Thus the direct line between the Israeli and Egyptian Ministries of Defence was severed, only to be reopened with the signing of the Camp David Accords in September.

In his book *Breakthrough*, Moshe Dayan defined the political committee meeting at Leeds Castle in July 1978 as 'a milestone in the peace negotiations and a moment of truth'. Dayan pointed out that at Leeds Castle, the Egyptians, for the first time, presented us with a detailed, six-point proposal for the administered territories, called 'The Proposal for Withdrawal from the West Bank and Gaza and for Security Arrangements'. It comprised the following principles:

1 The establishment of a just and durable peace in the Middle East required a just solution to the Palestinian problem in all its aspects based on the legitimate rights of the Palestinian people and taking into consideration the legitimate security needs of all the parties to the agreement.
2 In order to ensure an orderly and calm transfer of authority, the transitional period would not exceed five years and, at the end of this period, the Palestinian people would decide their own future.
3 Talks would be held between Egypt, Jordan, Israel and representatives of the Palestinian people, with UN participation, with the aim of reaching agreement on the following:
- The details of government during the transitional period.
- The timetable for Israel's withdrawal.
- Mutual security arrangements for all parties during and after the transitional period.
- Implementing the UN resolutions concerning Palestinian refugees.

4 Israel would withdraw from the West Bank (including East Jerusalem) and the Gaza Strip. The withdrawal would include the evacuation of settlements established in these territories. The Israeli troops in these territories would be replaced by a United Nations force.

5 The Israeli military administration on the West Bank and in the Gaza Strip would be dismantled at the beginning of the transitional period. During that period the administration of the West Bank would be Jordan's responsibility and that of the Gaza Strip would be Egypt's. Jordan and Egypt would co-opt on to the administration elected representatives of the Palestinian people who would have direct authority within the West Bank and Gaza. The UN would supervise and facilitate Israel's withdrawal and the return of Arab sovereignty to these areas.

6 Egypt and Jordan would guarantee that the agreed security agreements would continue to be honoured in the West Bank and Gaza.

There were some points in common between the Egyptian proposal and the autonomy plan Israel had put forward – particularly the concept of a five-year transitional period of autonomy for the Arab inhabitants. But, as Dayan made clear, other features in the Egyptian proposal were wholly unacceptable to Israel, such as complete withdrawal, the dismantling of Israeli settlements, and deciding in advance what should happen after the transitional period.

3

CAMP DAVID

Since the negotiations had remained deadlocked after Leeds Castle, President Carter again took the initiative. He invited Sadat and Begin to join him in a summit conference at Camp David, the presidential mountain retreat, in September 1978.

Begin appointed me to head an inter-ministerial staff group set up to prepare assessments and recommendations for Camp David. The staff included the Director-General of the Prime Minister's Office, Eliahu Ben-Elissar, the Director-General of the Ministry of Justice, Mayer Gabay, and the Foreign Office Legal Adviser, Meir Rosenne.

We prepared a document which included recommendations on all controversial issues. I presented the conclusions to the Prime Minister in a meeting at his home in Jerusalem. He instructed government ministers to study the document so that they could refer to it at a special Cabinet meeting to be called before the Israeli delegation set off for Camp David.

The Cabinet met, but there was no discussion on the staff's recommendations. The Cabinet decided to base Israel's position on the draft Declaration of Principles presented on 22 March 1978 during Begin's visit to Washington. This Declaration was Israel's response to the Egyptian demands made at the ill-fated political committee meeting in Jerusalem on 18 January. Thus, the Government decided that the Prime Minister and the Foreign and Defence Ministers could, on the basis of that Declaration of Principles, agree to changes which did not affect the spirit of Israeli policy. More fundamental changes would require Cabinet endorsement.

On the El Al flight to the United States, Moshe Dayan asked me why, on some issues, the inter-ministerial staff had made proposals which deviated from the Declaration of Principles. Among other things, he asked, 'Why did you present possibilities of Israeli settlements and IDF bases in Sinai and also the possibility of making changes in the principles regarding a solution to the Palestinian problem?' I replied, 'Moshe, I am a staff officer. As head of the inter-ministerial group, in accordance with the mandate given me by the Prime Minister, my job was to present all the alternatives available for reaching a settlement and to recommend specific ones. You, on the political level, can decide what to accept and what to reject, and the negotiations will be held on the basis of your decisions. Negotiations involve the art of compromise in the areas between the opening positions and the "red line" beyond which there can be no more concessions. In my opinion, the staff's recommendations are in line with these principles. We'll meet after Camp David and see which recommend-ations have served as the basis of a settlement.' As it turned out, most of our proposals were eventually adopted.

The Israeli delegation consisted of the Prime Minister, Dayan, Weizman, Attorney-General Aharon Barak (later Supreme Court Judge), Simcha Dinitz, our Ambassador in Washington, Meir Rosenne and myself, together with a group of assistants and staff. Apart from President Sadat, the Egyptian delegation included the Foreign Minister Ibrahim Kamel, Butros Ghali, Minister of State for Foreign Affairs, Osama el-Baz, the Presidential Adviser, and Deputy Premier Hassan Tuhami. With President Carter in the American delegation were Vice-President Walter Mondale, Secretary of State Vance, Secretary of State for Defence Harold Brown, National Security Adviser Zbigniew Brzezinski and Ambassador Harold Saunders, the State Department's Middle East expert.

The delegations arrived at Camp David on 6 September and spent thirteen days secluded there until 17 September.

We lived in scattered wooden cabins. The weather was cold and rainy most of the time. In breaks between meetings and discussions we would look at movies, ride bicycles and wander from cabin to cabin in electric golf carts. When the weather permitted, there were games of tennis. Begin and Brzezinski (both originally from Poland) had grim encounters across the chess-board. Moshe Dayan, always the loner, took long solitary walks.

In spite of the beautiful wooded surroundings, the invigorating mountain air and the informal atmosphere, it was difficult to relax. The mood in our delegation was pessimistic. Over nine months had gone by since Sadat's dramatic visit to Jerusalem. During that period there had been a series of negotiations between the Egyptians and ourselves, and much American shuttling between the two Governments, without agreement being reached on basic issues. What grounds were there for believing that the wide gaps in the positions would be bridged at Camp David?

Our fears were borne out the day after our arrival. The three leaders met in President Carter's cabin without their delegations. When Begin returned, we gathered anxiously in his cabin to hear his report. He produced an eleven-page document that Sadat had handed to him as a 'framework' for a comprehensive peace. It was totally uncompromising, containing all the maximum Egyptian demands we had found unacceptable at previous meetings, especially at Leeds Castle in July. The essence of the document was a total Israeli withdrawal, military and civilian, from all the territories taken in 1967, including the West Bank, the Gaza Strip and East Jerusalem; and the creation of a Palestinian state, possibly linked with Jordan, after a transitional period supervised by Egypt in the Gaza Strip and Jordan in the West Bank, with a United Nations force responsible for security. At a resumed meeting of the three leaders the following day, Begin rejected the Egyptian proposals point by point.

In its role as mediator between the two parties, the US delegation sought to break the impasse with a compromise proposal of its own covering seventeen pages. To our dismay, the American proposal tended in important respects to support Egyptian positions we had rejected. Clearly, the talks were in for a rough passage, with a good deal of tension and frustration for all concerned.

The discussion focused on producing two Framework Accords. The first was called 'A Framework for Peace in the Middle East'. In fact, it set out a few very general principles for peace between Israel and its four neighbouring Arab states, then concentrated on measures concerning the West Bank and the Gaza Strip. The second Framework Accord was to lay the basis for concluding a peace treaty between Egypt and Israel.

I was surprised to find that the Egyptian delegation did not include any military representative. Later, at the Peace Treaty negotiations in Washington, I asked General Magdoub what the reason was. He replied that they believed Camp David would constitute no more than another attempt to reach agreement on a declaration of principles concerning the Palestinian problem. They did not believe that such an agreement could be reached and they certainly did not expect Camp David to discuss security matters.

Thus, I found myself in an odd position as the only military representative in any of the delegations, although the talks dealt with the security arrangements in the proposed Israeli–Egyptian Peace Treaty, as well as in the West Bank and the Gaza Strip.

On the fourth day of the Conference, I accompanied Ezer Weizman to a meeting with President Carter, who wanted to get from us Israel's views on security matters. The meeting took place in the President's study. Weizman asked me to explain our ideas. I spread out the appropriate maps and began by pointing out how vital the West Bank and Gaza were to Israel's survival and why we had to maintain a military presence in these areas as long as the dangers to our security persisted. We had to be able to defend the country from attack by Arab states lying to the east of the River Jordan and to fight organized terrorism.

The President asked me if our security could be based on a number of locations where troops would be stationed, with movement to and from these locations along defined routes and in co-operation with the autonomy authorities. I told him that security could not be maintained under such conditions. The elements of an effective security presence, able to counter external attack and internal terrorism, had to include:

- a system of patrols and deterrent fences along the River Jordan;
- a security zone to a depth of approximately twelve miles from the Jordanian border, containing the necessary infrastructure for preventing surprise attacks, with fortifications, artillery and tank deployment areas, control systems and maintenance facilities;
- military deployment at major cross-roads to prevent seizure by the enemy in a co-ordinated air and armour strike;
- the installation of early-warning stations on mountain peaks and in locations where anti-aircraft weapons were concentrated;
- the strategic supply dumps for the rapid equipping of reserve forces in the event of war;
- camps for the regular troops stationed in these areas;
- freedom for Israeli air-force planes to overfly the areas;
- freedom for the Israeli navy to use the western half of the Dead Sea, up to the median line, and the shore of the Gaza Strip to prevent terrorist infiltration.

In concluding my remarks on security arrangements for the West Bank and the Gaza Strip, I asked: 'Mr President, do you really think that our defence needs should be conditional upon our co-ordinating our military movements with the Arab autonomy council? Would we need its approval to leave or enter the army bases we would maintain in these areas?' The President listened and made notes of the major points, but did not react. I had the unhappy feeling that I was not getting across what might be called the proximity factor. The maps I produced showed that the country was less than fifty miles wide from the Mediterranean to the River Jordan. The Sharon coastal plain, the most densely populated part of Israel, was ten to fifteen miles wide. Between that and the River Jordan lay the central hill region of the West Bank. From these hills every household in Israel was within artillery and rocket range. The deep trough of the Jordan Valley was the only natural defence line against another attack from the Arab countries to the east, which were in a state of war with us. Hostile aircraft could be over Israel's urban and industrial centres within minutes of take-off and early-warning stations on the hilltops were essential for us. This hill terrain in the wrong hands could also be an ideal base for terrorist operations. In fact, the PLO still clung to the dream of organizing guerrilla warfare from there, on the Vietnamese or Algerian models.

Yet here Weizman and I sat talking about these security concerns to the leader of the mightiest nation on earth, with a country 3,000 miles wide, bounded by great oceans to the east and west and peaceful neighbours to the north and south. The President's home state of Georgia was five times as broad as the whole land of Israel. It would need an extraordinary feat of imagination for him to see Israel's national security through our eyes. Later, during the discussions on autonomy, I learnt that the American viewpoint regarding security arrangements in the territories discounted the opinions I had expounded and wanted the Israeli military presence during the transitional period restricted in the way the President had hinted in his question to me – namely, troops in specific localities with their movements confined to defined routes. That was also the Egyptian position. It was wholly unacceptable to Israel.

Our discussion with the President moved on to security arrangements in Sinai. He was very surprised when I told him that we had already reached an understanding with Egypt on such arrangements except for the question of an Israeli presence in Sinai after its restoration to Egypt – that is, the civilian settlements, air bases and early-warning stations. We did not have an official document signed by the parties, and I was sorry that General Gamasi and General Magdoub were not present at Camp David to confirm what I said. I could, however, report accurately on the agreed points, which were the result of long and exhausting discussions. I then explained in detail to the President what the agreed security arrangements were.

The gist of it was that after the evacuation from Sinai had been completed, there would be security zones in which forces would be stationed as follows:

1 No more than one division (mechanized or infantry) of Egyptian armed forces would be stationed within an area lying approximately fifty kilometres east of the Gulf of Suez and the Suez Canal (Zone A).

2 Only United Nations forces and civil police equipped with light weapons to perform normal police functions would be stationed within an area lying west of the international border and the Gulf of Akaba, varying in width from twenty to forty kilometres (Zone C). (Later, in the Peace Treaty, the breadth was fixed at twenty to thirty kilometres.)

3 In the area within three kilometres east of the international border, there would be Israeli limited military forces not to exceed four infantry battalions and United Nations observers (Zone D). (Later, in the Peace Treaty, the breadth was fixed at four kilometres.)

4 Border patrol units, not to exceed three battalions, would

supplement the civil police in maintaining order in the area not included above (Zone B). (Later, in the Peace Treaty, the number of battalions was raised to four.)

United Nations forces would be stationed (in Zone C): (a) in part of the area in Sinai lying within about twenty kilometres of the Mediterranean Sea and adjacent to the international border, and (b) in the Sharm el-Sheikh area to ensure freedom of passage through the Straits of Tiran; and these forces would not be removed unless such removal was approved by the Security Council of the United Nations with a unanimous vote of the five permanent members.

Carter noted my comments and asked me to leave him the map on which the security zones were marked. The next day, Carter told Weizman that Sadat had confirmed my report. Carter then passed it on to Secretary of State Vance so that the principles for security arrangements in Sinai could be drafted for the Framework Accord.

The President's discussion with Weizman and myself on security arrangements was characteristic of the way he worked. He obviously had great powers of concentration and reserves of stamina. Between meetings he talked to individual delegates, studied documents and maps, followed the intricate drafting exercises and made copious notes. He seemed intent on mastering the details of complex issues that were imbedded in history, geography, defence strategy, national sentiment and decades of mutual distrust.

The day before the signing of the Framework Accords, I heard at the morning meeting of our delegation that Dayan had agreed that in Zone D, the limited-forces zone on the Israeli side of the border, only three Israeli border guard battalions would be deployed, corresponding to the Egyptian deployment in Zone B. As I had told President Carter, we had already agreed with the Egyptians that we would have four mechanized infantry battalions in Zone D. I explained to Begin why I objected to the change Dayan had made. The IDF had no border guard battalions at all; our border guard was part of the national police force. Before the Six Day War, we had stationed infantry in demilitarized zones and pretended they were border guard battalions, and senior army officers had dressed in civilian clothes when they entered the zones. I recalled how, when I headed the Interservice Command and Staff Academy in the 1960s, we used to wear mufti when we carried out course exercises in the demilitarized zone along the Syrian and Jordanian borders. I saw no point in perpetuating this transparent and undignified pretence in the new arrangements now being worked out with the Egyptians. I suggested to the Prime Minister that we inform the Egyptians and the Americans that we were retracting the change made by Dayan and would revert to the four infantry battalions in Zone D that had been agreed earlier between General Magdoub and myself. I asked Begin whether Weizman and I could not approach Sadat directly and explain the matter to him. Begin agreed.

Weizman and I went to Sadat's cabin early in the morning. His top bodyguard was standing in front of the door; he told us that Sadat was busy shaving and ushered us into the reception-room, where we were served sweet tea from Sadat's kitchen. A few minutes later, Sadat came in wearing a coloured dressing-gown and smelling of Aramis 5 lotion. He embraced Weizman and asked him what the problem was. I repeated to him what I had said to Begin. He immediately agreed to the change and asked me to let him have it in writing, so that he could approve it before it was submitted to Carter.

The security arrangements for Sinai as agreed between Magdoub and myself were included in the second Framework Accord. They found their way into the later Peace Treaty, where they were spelt out in greater detail and precision.

Carter had laid down that the Camp David summit meeting had to end by 17 September. It turned out to be a real cliffhanger, and the last days of the talks almost came to grief on two extremely touchy topics: Jerusalem and Israeli settlements in the territories.

The Jerusalem issue produced an atmosphere of crisis and a sense that the talks were about to collapse. Since there was no hope of reaching any agreed form of words on this topic, it was finally decided to leave it out of the Framework Accord and to let Begin and Sadat state the positions of their countries in simultaneous letters to Carter. Before this was done, the Israeli delegation was shown the text of a letter that Carter was about to deliver to Sadat, at the latter's request, stating the United States' own position on Jerusalem.

Even before 1967, the United States had not recognized West Jerusalem as the capital of Israel and had kept its embassy in Tel Aviv, in company with a number of other foreign embassies. (After the Six Day War, the United States regarded East Jerusalem, including the Old City, as Israeli-occupied territory, which had the same international status as the West Bank or Gaza, and whose final destiny was to be decided in further negotiations. Meanwhile, the Arab residents of East Jerusalem should be associated with the autonomy regime in the West Bank.) We maintained that the function of the American delegation at Camp David was to harmonize the positions of Egypt and Israel and not to assert its own position. The Israeli delegation, therefore, objected strongly to Carter's letter on Jerusalem, but Carter refused to go back on his promise to Sadat. In the end, Cyrus Vance and Aharon Barak sat down together and drafted a modified text for the letter; the Israeli objection was then withdrawn. During this tense episode, Begin was further incensed by being told that Sadat demanded the flying of an Arab flag over the El Aksa mosque on the Temple Mount in Jerusalem. The demand was dropped.

Begin's letter to Carter on Jerusalem, dated 17 September, reads:

Dear Mr President

I have the honour to inform you, Mr President, that on 28 June 1967 Israel's Parliament [the Knesset] promulgated and adopted a law to the effect: 'The Government is empowered to apply by decree the law, the jurisdiction and administration of the state to any part of Eretz Israel [Land of Israel–Palestine], as stated in the decree.'

On the basis of this law, the Government of Israel decreed in July 1967 that Jerusalem is one city indivisible, the capital of the State of Israel.

Sincerely,
Menachem Begin

Behind his brief, matter-of-fact statement lay 3,000 years of a unique Jewish attachment to Jerusalem, from the time when King David made the city his capital.

Sadat's letter of the same date read:

Dear Mr President

I am writing you to reaffirm the position of the Arab Republic of Egypt with respect to Jerusalem.

1 Arab Jerusalem is an integral part of the West Bank. Legal and historical Arab rights in the city must be respected and restored.

2 Arab Jerusalem should be under Arab sovereignty.

3 The Palestinian inhabitants of Arab Jerusalem are entitled to exercise their legitimate national rights, being part of the Palestinian people in the West Bank.

4 Relevant Security Council Resolutions, particularly Resolutions 242 and 267, must be applied with regard to Jerusalem. All the measures taken by Israel to alter the status of the city are null and void and should be rescinded.

5 All peoples must have free access to the city and enjoy the free exercise of worship and the right to visit and transit to the Holy Places without distinction or discrimination.

6 The Holy Places of each faith may be placed under the administration and control of their representatives.

7 Essential functions in the city should be undivided and a joint municipal council composed of an equal number of Arab and Israeli members can supervise the carrying out of these functions. In this way, the city shall be undivided.

Sincerely,
Mohammed Anwar el-Sadat

On the evening of 16 September (our last evening in Camp David), Carter convened a meeting of American and Israeli representatives in his cabin, to discuss outstanding issues. Secretary of State Vance was present and, on the Israeli side, Begin, Dayan and Barak. The discussion went on until 1.30 a.m. Much of it concerned the controversial subject of the Israeli settlements in the West Bank and the Gaza Strip. (The US had maintained all along that these settlements were illegal and undermined the peace process. Every Israeli Government since 1967 had rejected this thesis.) Carter pressed Begin to give him a written undertaking that there would be a freeze on any new settlements during the coming negotiations.

Carter claimed afterwards that Begin had agreed to a freeze for the duration of all the negotiations, including those on autonomy. Begin understood that they were only talking about the pending negotiations for a peace treaty with Egypt, to be concluded within three months; and he maintained that he had agreed only to think over the proposal.

Obviously there had been a genuine misunderstanding between two honourable but tired leaders during arguments lasting well into the night. But the relationship of trust between the two was seriously impaired. Incidentally, Barak took meticulous notes of the discussions and, according to his record, Begin's recollection was correct.

Before we left Camp David, Begin made his first visit to Sadat's cabin to pay his respects. Sadat then paid him a reciprocal visit. An atmosphere of friendship and optimism prevailed. The next day all the delegations were flown by helicopter to Washington for the signing ceremony.

Each of the parties had sacrificed cherished principles to reach the agreement in which Carter had invested so much effort. It had been touch and go to the end. Carter was clearly anxious to have the Framework Accord signed at once, fearing that more last-minute obstacles might crop up.

We landed on the lawn of the White House and were ushered into the East Room. Administration heads, American Jewish leaders and other important figures were gathered there. In spite of the festive air, I was already asking myself searching questions about the next round of negotiations. The doubts applied especially to the Palestinian problem. The principles for a solution evolved at Camp David rested on distinctly shaky foundations.

After the ceremony, we travelled from the White House to the Hilton Hotel. It was raining hard. The Israeli Embassy staff were waiting to greet Begin and everyone was excited. I was extremely moved when Begin embraced me and thanked me for my contribution to the talks. I did not share his ideological outlook, but I respected him as a leader and a man of vision; on the human level, he was a courteous and considerate person. I could not sleep that night and sat down to list the issues that would have to be formulated for the autonomy negotiations.

The two Framework Accords concluded at Camp David and signed in Washington represented a great move forwards in the peace process, but left a number of basic questions unresolved. However, the Camp David Summit Conference could not be allowed to end in deadlock and failure because of the remaining disputes. It was the most intensive effort yet made, and at the highest possible level, to break through to a settlement of the Israeli–Arab conflict – at least between Israel and the largest and most important of its Arab neighbours. Admission of defeat at Camp David would set back the cause of peace for years, maybe decades. The consequences would be incalculable for Israel, Egypt, the Middle East region and international peace and security. Too much was at stake for both parties. In addition, the prestige of the United States as a peacemaker, and of the President himself, was committed to the success of Carter's bold initiative in personal diplomacy. Consequently, Camp David ended with a flourish of trumpets, and was rightly hailed as a major international achievement. This was accomplished by stressing the areas of agreement. Some of the unresolved issues were glossed over with vague and ambiguous formulations that left each party maintaining its position. Certain other issues were left out of the Framework Accords and dealt with in separate letters to President Carter from Begin and Sadat.

These unresolved issues would have a marked impact on the further course of the peace process. They were overcome on the road to a peace treaty with Egypt, but have not been overcome to this day regarding the West Bank and the Gaza Strip.

On the projected peace treaty, the first issue left unsettled arose from Israel's insistence that Egypt's obligations under the treaty should take precedence over any obligations that Egypt had as a member of the Arab League. Our main concern was that Egypt was a signatory to a joint defence pact between the Arab states. We maintained that should Israel find itself at war again with other Arab states, Egypt would be committed to remaining at peace with Israel regardless of the terms of the inter-Arab mutual defence pact.

Another point that was not mentioned in the Framework Accord was the Arab League's economic boycott of Israel, to which Egypt was a party. Article III(3) of the Peace Treaty reads: The parties agree that the normal relationship established between them will include 'termination of economic boycotts and discriminatory barriers to the free movement of peoples and goods. . . .'

The fourteen Israeli civilian towns and agricultural settlements in Sinai – the Yamit area in North-eastern Sinai and the Sharm el-Sheikh area in Southern Sinai – were a major stumbling-block at Camp David. For both Begin and Sadat, this was an extremely sensitive and emotional issue. Israel wanted the settlements to remain in Sinai even after it was returned to Egyptian sovereignty for a number of reasons. Yamit and the surrounding settlements contributed to Israel's security. The Israeli presence at Sharm el-Sheikh was needed to safeguard the sea-lane to Eilat through the Straits of Tiran and the Gulf of Akaba. Evacuation of these settlements might set a precedent regarding the settlements in the West Bank, the Gaza Strip and the Golan Heights. In principle, citizens of one country should be able to live in a neighbouring country, when the countries are at peace with each other.

But on this question, the Egyptians were unyielding. Their position throughout the negotiations was: no settlements or no peace. Members of the Egyptian delegation said to us unofficially that they would not mind Israelis settling in Egypt west of the Canal, but not in Sinai. 'Why?' we asked. They replied: 'During the peace talks, when you were in a hurry to establish new settlements along the El Arish–Ras Muhammad line, we learnt that for you settlement is a tool for expansion, as it was with the imperial powers in the past.'

On the El Al plane taking us from Israel to the Camp David talks, Moshe Dayan was angry with me for raising the possibility of evacuating the settlements in return for peace. He changed his mind when he and Ezer Weizman became convinced that the Egyptians would not budge on this question. The two of them then made every effort to persuade Begin. Weizman asked me to get in touch with General Ariel ('Arik') Sharon, then the Minister of Agriculture, and persuade him to accept that the settlements had to be evacuated for the sake of peace; he should then put this to Begin. Sharon was the great promoter of settlement in the occupied territories and served as Chairman of the Cabinet Committee on Settlement. Weizman and Dayan reckoned that if Sharon of all people was willing to give up the settlements in Sinai, this would carry great weight with Begin. Accordingly, I put a call through from Camp David to Sharon in Jerusalem. He told me later that he had spoken to Begin on the phone on this matter.

In the end, Begin yielded to the extent that he was willing to bring the matter before the Knesset. The settlements were not mentioned in the text of the Framework Accord, but were the subject of separate letters addressed by Begin and Sadat to Carter just before the Accords were signed. Begin's letter undertook that, within two weeks of his return, he would submit to the Knesset the question of whether the Israeli settlers in Sinai should be removed if all other outstanding issues were settled in the peace negotiations between Egypt and Israel. The letter stated that each Knesset member would be free to vote according to his conscience without party discipline. Sadat's simultaneous letter was a blunt ultimatum. Agreement by Israel to withdraw all its settlers from Sinai was a prerequisite for the start of negotiations for a peace treaty. 'If Israel fails to meet this commitment, the "Framework" shall be null and invalid.'

The Israeli Cabinet was unwilling to have a separate vote in the Knesset on the settlement question. It was tacked on to the motion requesting approval of the Camp David Accords in general. On 27 September, after a lengthy and at times stormy debate, the motion was carried by eighty-four votes in favour, nineteen against and seventeen abstentions. The decision to remove the settlers would lead three years later to a turbulent and painful episode.

Another dispute concerned the 'linkage' between the two Framework Accords. For entirely different reasons, both the Israelis and the Egyptians wanted the principles for a peace treaty to be accompanied by principles concerning the West Bank and the Gaza Strip. For the Israeli Government, withdrawal from Sinai was to be balanced by retaining control of the territories, while offering autonomy to their Arab inhabitants. However, once the principles were agreed, the implementation of a peace treaty should not be tied to carrying out the proposals for the territories.

Sadat, for his part, had to face the charge that he was making a separate peace with Israel in order to regain Sinai, even if that meant betraying the Arab cause and abandoning the Palestinian people. Egypt was already isolated in the Arab world, and within Egypt there was considerable domestic opposition to Sadat's peace policies. Consequently, the Egyptian position was that peace with Egypt had to be regarded as part of a comprehensive peace based on Resolution 242, and had to be linked with the end of Israeli occupation of the territories and their reversion to Arab rule. The initial Egyptian stand was that a formal peace treaty with Israel could be signed only after Israel had evacuated not only Sinai but also the West Bank, Gaza and East Jerusalem.

The Egyptian proposals assumed that Jordan would have to be a party to any solution for the West Bank and would have to be responsible for supervising a transitional period for it. Yet Jordan had not been drawn into the peace process and was not represented at Camp David. In the earlier talks between Weizman and Sadat in Cairo and Salzburg, Sadat had undertaken that if an agreement was reached between Israel and Egypt, Jordanian co-operation would not be made a condition: 'If he [Hussein] wishes, it can participate; if not, then we will blaze the trail.'

The interconnection between the Israeli–Egyptian component of an agreement and the Palestinian component was bypassed in the Camp David Accords. The problem would come close to wrecking the later negotiations on a peace treaty.

Whatever issues were left unresolved at Camp David, the Framework Accord for an Israeli–Egyptian peace was fulfilled, in that a treaty was concluded six months later. That cannot be said for the other Framework Accord.

The preamble to this Framework Accord, which was for 'Peace in the Middle East', declared that,

> After four wars during thirty years despite intensive human efforts, the Middle East, which is the cradle of civilization and the birthplace of three great religions, does not yet enjoy the blessings of peace. The people of the Middle East yearn for peace, so that the vast human and natural resources of the region can be turned to the pursuits of peace and so that this area can become a model for coexistence and co-operation among nations.

The document invited Israel's other Arab neighbours – Jordan, Syria and Lebanon – also to negotiate peace treaties with Israel based on Resolution 242 and to establish normal relations with it. To this day, no other state has accepted this invitation.

The main theme of this Framework Accord concerned what it called 'The West Bank and Gaza'. The Begin Government saw the future of these territories as lying within the State of Israel, with local autonomy for their Palestinian Arab inhabitants. What Egypt wanted was that they should form a Palestinian political entity linked to Jordan in a federation or confederation. This was also the United States' position, which was later to be made public in the 1982 Reagan plan. One attitude Carter, Begin, Sadat and Hussein had in common was that none of them wanted these territories to become a separate, independent PLO state, which would make trouble for all concerned and would be a base for Soviet penetration.

Since under existing circumstances there was an unbridgeable gulf between the aims of Egypt and Israel for the future of the territories, the only course open was to play for time. Hence a consensus emerged that there should be a five-year transitional period of autonomy, leaving all the options open for a permanent solution in the future. This was easier said than done. The parties disagreed sharply on what should happen during the period of transition, on the nature and powers of the autonomy regime, and on security arrangements.

The initial Egyptian proposal was that Israel should withdraw all its armed forces and civilian settlements from the territories. During the transitional period, Jordan would supervise self-rule in the West Bank and Egypt in the Gaza Strip. A United Nations force would be responsible for security. This extreme position could not possibly be a basis for discussion with Israel. Since the overriding purpose of the Camp David talks, and of the US delegation in particular, was to seek agreement, the Egyptian proposal was untenable as it stood. In a modified position, the idea of a transitional period supervised by Jordan and Egypt was abandoned, as was the introduction of a UN force. It was now proposed that the autonomy authorities would be responsible for internal security and public order through a strong police force. Israel's security concerns could be met by allowing it to maintain, as a safeguard against external attack, security locations in the Jordan Valley and along the boundary between the Gaza Strip and Sinai. Access to these camps would be along specified routes. This proposal was completely at variance with our security needs in the territories as I had explained them to President Carter. Our unyielding position was that the Israeli army would remain responsible for overall security in the territories during the transitional period.

As finally drafted, the Framework Accord outlined the following programme:

- Egypt, Israel and Jordan would agree on the modalities for establishing an elected, self-governing authority (administrative council) in the West Bank and Gaza and define its powers and responsibilities. The Egyptian and Jordanian delegations might include local Palestinian Arabs.
- A transitional period of up to five years would start when the self-governing authority was established.
- A withdrawal of Israeli forces would take place and there would be a redeployment of the remaining Israeli forces into specified locations.
- A strong local police force would be set up.
- Within three years of the start of the transitional period, negotiations would take place between Egypt, Israel, Jordan and the elected representatives of the Palestinian inhabitants to determine the final status of the West Bank and Gaza and their relationship with their neighbours.
- Related negotiations would take place between Israel, Jordan and the local elected representatives (but not Egypt) on an Israeli–Jordanian peace treaty, which would take into account the agreement reached on the final status of the territories. Negotiations would deal, among other matters, with the location of the boundary and with security arrangements.

The programme had some far-reaching implications concerning the Palestinian problem. The text states in a general way that 'the legitimate rights of the Palestinian people and their just requirements' should be recognized. The road to determining the future status of the territories is through agreement between the four parties: Israel, Jordan, Egypt and the elected representatives of the inhabitants of the territories. Since all four parties must agree, Israel retains a right of veto over any proposed solution even if it is supported by the three Arab parties to the negotiations.

Undoubtedly, the adoption of this first Framework Accord was an historic step forward in the peace process. For one thing, Israel and Egypt could not have gone ahead with a peace treaty unless there existed some agreement in principle on the Palestinian problem. But the very general provisions of the Framework Accord were open to such widely different interpretations by the parties that the subsequent negotiations on autonomy would run into a dead end.

The Framework Accord tied Israel's hands in two respects. First, the original twenty-six-point proposal submitted by Begin at Ismailia regarded autonomy as a permanent arrangement: by the Framework Accord, it had become a temporary one, for five years. Second, by making the final status subject to agreement between the parties concerned, it debarred a unilateral annexation by Israel. In the absence of agreement, the autonomy regime would presumably continue after the five years, though the Accord does not deal with this possibility.

On 12 October 1978, the talks intended to finalize the Peace Treaty began in Washington, with Dayan heading our delegation. He and Weizman predicted that the Treaty would be concluded within two or three weeks, an expectation shared by the State Department. The negotiations took place officially at Blair House, the presidential guest-house. The delegations stayed at the Madison Hotel and it soon became the norm to hold discussions there. It was simply more comfortable to remain at the hotel than to travel each day to Blair House, which was a beautiful, historic building but had poor services and food.

The Americans had prepared a draft peace treaty based on the Camp David Framework Accord. The negotiations soon ran into trouble. On the security arrangements in Sinai, the Egyptians made several new demands: they wanted the arrangements to be reviewed after five years; and the withdrawal to the interim El Arish–Ras Muhammad line in nine months to be divided up into sub-phases, with the town of El Arish and the coastal strip of Eilat returned to Egyptian sovereignty within three months. We rejected these demands and insisted that the Camp David arrangements should stay as they were. On the political level, the Blair House Conference became bogged down on two basic issues left open at Camp David: the priority of Egypt's treaty obligations, and a link between the peace treaty and autonomy for the West Bank and Gaza. On the first matter, we maintained that Article VI in the American draft did not dispose of the question that was crucial for us: where would Egypt stand in the event of another Israeli–Arab war? The Americans defended their compromise formula. Carter became angry when Barak produced legal opinion bearing out doubts given by distinguished professors of international law at Yale University.

The Egyptians continued to insist that the Peace Treaty should be related to autonomy. They proposed that the autonomy negotiations be concluded within nine months, which was the period stipulated for the Israeli withdrawal to the interim line and the beginning of the normalization process. Ambassadors should be exchanged only when the autonomy regime had been established. We argued that if the implementation of the Treaty was tied to autonomy, Jordan and the Palestinians would be able to block peace between Egypt and Israel. (Both of them had rejected the Camp David Accords.) Moreover, Egypt itself might at a later date claim that the Peace Treaty was no longer binding on it because the autonomy plan had not materialized. The Americans acknowledged that these arguments had substance; at the same time, they felt that Sadat was under great pressure and would not be able to sign the Treaty unless it was associated in some way with the Palestinian problem.

During the Blair House meetings, Dayan and Weizman raised with President Carter the need for American aid to meet the staggering financial burden involved in evacuating Sinai. For ten years this desert had been our main military area, containing technologically advanced air bases, fortified positions, army camps, supply and maintenance depots, training areas and an infrastructure of roads, water and electricity networks. To recreate these facilities in the Negev (Southern Israel) would cost an estimated $2.5 billion. In addition, the Israeli civilians evacuated from Sinai would have to be compensated and resettled. There was also the question of the oil fields which we had developed on the Gulf of Suez. Handing them over to Egypt would mean a loss of a third of our oil supply. We had no assurance that the Egyptians would sell us this oil or that alternative supplies would be available from other sources.

On the settlements, the President vehemently recalled that the United States had always regarded them as illegal. Removing them was Israel's concern. The question of special aid for the military installations was referred to the Pentagon, where Weizman later discussed it with Defence Secretary Brown. A committee of American and Israeli experts was set up to study the oil question.

The task of working out a detailed Military Annex to the Peace Treaty was dealt with by a military committee. I headed the Israeli delegation, and we had done our homework thoroughly. The 1974 Disengagement-of-Forces Agreement with Egypt, and even more so the 1975 Israeli–Egyptian Interim Agreement, provided valuable precedents concerning Sinai.

On returning from Camp David, I phoned Joel Singer early in the morning and gave him instructions to prepare a draft for the Military Annex, indicating to him basic principles and headings. He and his assistants worked all day and night. The next day we drew up about ten amended drafts until we were satisfied, and then we received approval for the document from Chief of Staff Gur and Defence Minister Weizman.

At the same time, Zalman Einav prepared a file of maps for the negotiations. The file contained, among others, maps for the proposed Zones A, B, C and D; maps showing possible variations for the El Arish–Ras Muhammad withdrawal line; and maps showing possibilities for mutual border adjustments.

The day we arrived in Washington for the next round of negotiations at Blair House I met General Magdoub, and we agreed that we would simply carry on where we had left off. The security arrangements accepted in principle at Camp David had been worked out by the two of us at the Tahra Palace in Cairo, way back in January 1978. We now had much to do to complete the details for the Military Annex. I did not want to tell him that I had brought a draft with me, for fear of hurting his national pride. When we arrived at an understanding of any particular point, Joel Singer and one of Magdoub's aides would sit together and formulate that point in writing.

Magdoub and I preferred direct talks, without American mediation. At the outset, General Lawrence handed us an American draft for the Military Annex with an accompanying map. Magdoub was not satisfied with the line of Zone A, which he wanted further east; while I was dissatisfied with the interim withdrawal line, which I wanted further west. This balance of dissatisfaction led us to shelve the American draft and work on the appendix by ourselves, with Einav providing maps based on our discussions.

The one matter we could not settle without a fresh political directive was the Egyptian demand that the first stage of withdrawal to the interim line should be broken up into a number of sub-phases. This went beyond what had been agreed at Camp David and written into the Framework Accord. The reason they gave was that it was important to demonstrate to the Egyptian people and the other Arab states that the IDF was withdrawing from Sinai ahead of schedule and that the Peace Treaty was bearing fruit. They wanted each sub-phase to include not just a piece of desert, but some well-known place, such as the town of El Arish, the main oil fields, the Santa Catarina monastery or Sharm el-Sheikh.

Ambassador Atherton, who was in charge of the US delegation in Secretary of State Vance's absence, was not happy with the fact that in the military talks we were bypassing the American mediation role. He complained to Dayan, who asked me to bring the American military representatives into the consultations. However, General Magdoub and I continued as before, as our face-to-face talks were going well. One day, after first obtaining Dayan's consent, Atherton called in Magdoub and myself to give him a review of the remaining points at issue. I said to Magdoub, 'You can speak for both of us.' He told Atherton that we had solved most of the problems and he had no doubt that those still outstanding could be settled to our mutual satisfaction. As time passed, we got to know and like General Lawrence and involved him more in the work.

After one month, the Blair House Conference was suspended on a note of deadlock on the political issues. The political members of the Israeli and Egyptian delegations returned home to report, while the military team was left behind to maintain informal contact. I said to Magdoub that officially our negotiations were also suspended, but that we should use the time to continue work unofficially on the Military Annex; he agreed.

During this period I had an opportunity to talk at length with Egyptian leaders who visited Washington in connection with the stalled negotiations and came to see their military people at our hotel. Among these visitors were the Egyptian Vice-President Mubarak and Mustapha Ghalil, who was both Prime Minister and Foreign Minister. I also became friendly with the Egyptian Military Attaché in Washington, General Abu-Gazala (later Deputy Premier and Minister of Defence). He would bring me the same salty cheese that caused me to suffer pangs of thirst at the Tahra Palace in Cairo. Magdoub had mentioned to him that I liked this cheese, and he had kindly asked his wife to prepare it for me. From these conversations with Egyptians, I learned much about their economic problems and about the attitude of the military elite to the Peace Treaty with Israel.

In January 1979, after three months in Washington, Magdoub and I returned to our respective countries with a draft Military Annex in our luggage, which we had not had the authority to conclude. (It would later be approved by our Governments as it stood.)

After the Washington Conference broke up inconclusively, the prospects of peace seemed to recede. Under increasing Arab pressure, the Egyptians stiffened their demands. In the background was the deteriorating situation in the Middle East in the wake of the Iranian revolution. The United States intensified its efforts to overcome the obstacles to an Israeli–Egyptian peace settlement. But resumed negotiations in Brussels in December, and again at Camp David in February, were unsuccessful. At the beginning of March, Begin came to Washington at Carter's urging, and an understanding was reached on some points, at least between Israel and the United States, though not yet with Egypt. Carter now threw the full weight of his authority and prestige into an all-out bid to break through. Accompanied by Vance and a large retinue of aides, he came on an official visit to Cairo and Jerusalem. With some yielding on both sides, the way was cleared for the signing of the Treaty in Washington on 26 March 1979.

The main elements in the 'package' of concessions were:

- Israel accepted that the first phase of withdrawal in Sinai should be split up into sub-phases as the Egyptians wanted.
- An exchange of ambassadors would take place one month after the withdrawal to the interim El Arish–Ras Muhammad line after nine months.
- Words were inserted into Article VI to the effect that the obligations under this Treaty would take precedence over any other conflicting obligations of either party.
- Simultaneously with the signing of the Peace Treaty, a joint letter from Sadat and Begin would be submitted to Carter concerning the autonomy negotiations for the West Bank and Gaza. These negotiations would be based on the Camp David Framework Accord and would start within one month, with the 'goal' of concluding them within a year. Jordan would be invited to join, but if it did not do so, Egypt and Israel would nevertheless proceed, with the full participation of the United States.
- Egypt would sell to Israel at market prices the oil from the Sinai oil fields.

In signing the Treaty, Israel relied on certain bilateral assurances given to it by the United States and contained in a separate Memorandum of Agreement. The United States would take appropriate action if there were violations of the Peace Treaty which threatened Israel's security or the freedom of navigation through the Straits of Tiran and the Gulf of Akaba; the United States would be responsive to Israel's needs for military and economic assistance; and steps would be taken to prevent American arms supplied to other states from being used against Israel. In a second Memorandum of Agreement, the United States guaranteed that Israel's oil supply would be maintained for the next fifteen years.

At 2 p.m. on 26 March, the Peace Treaty was formally signed at the White House by Begin and Sadat, and by Carter as a witness, before the representatives of the world's media. That evening, in a great marquee on the White House lawn, 1,600 guests sat down to dinner in celebration of an event that was the one notable achievement of the Carter presidency. Begin and Sadat had already been jointly awarded the Nobel Peace Prize.

A joint Israeli–Egyptian Military Commission was set up to deal with the withdrawal from Sinai and the agreed security arrangements in it. The task given to me was to co-ordinate both the security aspects of the Treaty and those that concerned the proposed autonomy plan for the West Bank and Gaza.

In the military sphere, friendly co-operation developed at all levels. The Commission met regularly, and we were well-represented on it by Brigadier Dov Sion, an affable and intelligent officer with years of experience in handling armistice and ceasefire affairs. Ezer Weizman and his counterpart, Kamal Hassan Ali, met every two or three months in Egypt and Israel alternately. I went to Cairo whenever that was thought useful.

A problem arose regarding the United Nations peacekeeping force, the UNEF, which operated in Sinai under the 1975 Israeli–Egyptian Agreement and was to assume a similar role under the Peace Treaty. For this purpose, a new Security Council resolution was required, but the Peace Treaty had not been submitted to the Security Council for endorsement because the Russians would have exercised their veto. This lack of a Security Council mandate led to the departure of the UNEF from Sinai.

We had anticipated that such a situation might arise, since the Soviet Union had supported the Arab Rejection Front against the Camp David Accords and the Peace Treaty. Consequently, when the Treaty was signed in Washington, Begin obtained from Carter a written undertaking that if the UN force called for in the Treaty was not established, the President would take steps to form an alternative multinational force outside the UN framework.

This question came up for discussion between Washington, Jerusalem and Cairo when the first stage of the withdrawal to the interim line had been completed. It was decided that the multinational force would come into operation when the final evacuation from Sinai took place in April 1982. Meanwhile, the security arrangements in Zones A and B (to the west of the interim line) would be supervised by the American Field Mission, which was stationed in Sinai under the 1975 Agreement and operated an early-warning system at the Mitla and Gidi Passes. It was also agreed that for the time being there would be a demilitarized strip five kilometres wide along the whole interim line, under joint Israeli–Egyptian supervision.

About a year before the final evacuation of Israeli forces and settlements from Sinai, negotiations took place for establishing the multinational force. Three delegations took part in these talks, representing Egypt, Israel and the United States. Our delegation was headed jointly by David Kimche, Director-General of the Foreign Ministry, and by myself, as Chairman of the military committee. After exhausting discussions, we agreed on a multinational force of 3,000 men to be provided by countries acceptable to the parties, and including an American army battalion which would be deployed at Sharm el-Sheikh and along the coast of the Gulf of Akaba. The force would have a military command which would be responsible to a joint Egyptian–Israeli–American political control group – the three countries that would bear the cost of the force. The head of this political group would be an American Director-General with the status of a senior ambassador, while the commander of the force would be a three-star general chosen by Israel and Egypt. The multinational force thus constituted has operated successfully up to the present day.

4

THE 'COLD PEACE'

While the security arrangements in Sinai developed smoothly, the normalization of relations required by Annex III of the Treaty ran into difficulties. The officials of the Egyptian Foreign Ministry, led by the Minister of State for Foreign Affairs, Butros Ghali, were using delaying tactics in order not to provoke more anti-Egyptian reactions in the Arab world. Defence Minister Ezer Weizman flew to Cairo several times to see Sadat and ask him to throw his full weight into removing these obstacles. As a result, the exchange of ambassadors took place and progress was made regarding the sale of Egyptian oil to Israel and the opening of a civilian air-link between the two countries.

Sadat decided to put the Minister of Defence, Kamal Hassan Ali, in charge of the normalization process. The Israeli Government responded by appointing Ezer Weizman as Ali's opposite number. I served as Weizman's aide, while Ali's aide was my old friend and negotiating partner, General Magdoub. He had been released from the army and made responsible for the Israeli desk in the Foreign Ministry. A joint ministerial committee presided over by Weizman and Ali was given authority to finalize and sign agreements. A steering committee headed by Magdoub and myself had to prepare the drafts, assisted by technical subcommittees on specific topics – trade, cultural exchange, communications, land and sea traffic, civil aviation, police co-operation and oil supply. These committees met alternately in Israel and Egypt. After four months of tough bargaining, we succeeded in concluding all the agreements. The implementation of some of them, however, especially in the fields of trade and culture, remained unsatisfactory.

It was very helpful to us during the implementation of the Treaty that the Egyptians felt such affection and respect for Weizman. As a person he is forthright, sincere and possessed of much of the charismatic charm that marked his famous uncle, Dr Chaim Weizmann, who led the World Zionist Movement for a generation before the state and became its first President. Weizman dealt with the Egyptians as equals, without a trace of condescension, and sought compromises that would be tolerable for them as well as for us.

The particular problem we had with the Egyptians was national pride. (I think this is the case with many states established after a struggle against a foreign occupier.) We had to bear in mind that we could not appear to be dictating a victor's terms. In the negotiations, some Israelis behaved as though, since we were conceding Sinai to them, it was up to the Egyptians to yield on other points. But the Egyptians felt no reason to be grateful for this concession. Sinai was Egyptian soil; Israel had occupied it by force, and it was up to Israel to return it in exchange for peace. Furthermore, the Egyptians did not accept that they were meeting us as a defeated nation. In fact, the Yom Kippur War was for them a great victory which had restored Egyptian pride. They had broken through the vaunted Bar-Lev Line on the Suez Canal, crossed to the eastern side of the Canal and engaged our forces in a tremendous battle. The fact that we later turned the tables on them did not change this Egyptian perception. What is more, they saw our successive withdrawals in Sinai – under the 1974 Disengagement-of-Forces Agreement, the 1975 Interim Agreement and the 1979 Peace Treaty – as political achievements flowing from their surprise assault on Israel in the Yom Kippur War.

While Weizman was assured of a spontaneous welcome in Cairo, this was not necessarily so with other Israeli leaders. When Moshe Dayan paid his first official visit to Egypt after the signing of the Peace Treaty, I was sent to Cairo a few days before to make the arrangements. The programme I worked out with Defence Minister Ali included, apart from official talks, visits to the historical sights in Cairo and Upper Egypt and a tour of the Khan el-Khalil souk – Cairo's oldest and most central market. This market is always teeming with people, and I assumed that Dayan would be greeted by a big crowd. He himself was looking forward to this chance to meet the Egyptian man-in-the-street. Ali objected for security reasons, and I had to persuade him to agree. When Dayan and his entourage reached the market, I was dismayed to find that the Egyptians had emptied it of crowds, closed most of the shops, cleaned up the area and stationed in it hundreds of security men who cheered loudly and shouted, 'Moussa Dayan, Moussa Dayan!' (Moussa is the Arabic equivalent of Moshe). Dayan was not taken in by this display.

When Begin made an official visit to Cairo about a month after the signing of the Treaty, his staff were extremely anxious about the way he might be received. Would the Israeli national anthem be played? Would the Israeli flag be hoisted? What would be the reactions of the crowds in the street?

In fact, the Egyptians observed strict protocol and laid on the type of reception normally accorded to a head of government. Vice-President

Mubarak welcomed him at Cairo Airport, where he inspected a guard of honour; an Egyptian band played the national anthem of both countries; President Sadat hosted a state dinner on the lawn of the Kubbeh Palace, with a performance by an Egyptian dance troupe; and visits were made to the Pyramids and to the Cairo Museum.

On the way from the airport to the Tahra Palace, where Begin was to stay, very few Israeli flags were to be seen, and waving crowds were conspicuous by their absence along the route of the convoy. I took this up with General Lavib, head of Military Intelligence, who had been put in charge of the arrangements. (We had become friendly during the peace negotiations.) He said, 'Don't draw any conclusions from what you saw on the road from the airport. It goes through an affluent area that never has many people in the street anyway. Tomorrow, when your Prime Minister goes to the Pyramids and the Museum, the convoy must pass through the centre of the city and I assure you there will be a popular welcome on a large scale.' 'And what about the flags?' I asked him. He replied, 'Our factory that makes flags is not yet organized to produce the Israeli one. We have hoisted all the ones you brought us.' (He was referring to the 200 flags I had brought for Weizman's visit.)

Next morning our expectations were again dashed. The convoy was taken to the Pyramids and the Museum through back streets where few people saw it. Fortunately, when the Prime Minister drove to the Kubbeh Palace for the official dinner, he was cheered by the crowd that had gathered along the road. Begin was extremely moved by the cheers. He stopped the car and shook hands with people on the pavement while reporters and photographers hurried round to transmit this historic scene to the outside world. At the Palace dinner, I left the head table to sit with Lavib and Magdoub. Lavib said to me with a grin, 'This time I did not leave it to chance. I saw to it that a few hundred of our Defence Ministry staff were in the street.'

When General Sharon, then Minister of Agriculture, came to Cairo, his Egyptian counterpart asked me what he liked apart from the army. I replied, 'Fields, animals and food.' I hope these words were not responsible for the fact that the function for Sharon was held in the Cairo zoo (which happened to fall under the Ministry of Agriculture).

The main purpose for my trips to Egypt was to talk to Egyptian officials, especially Defence Minister Ali, on questions that arose in connection with carrying out the Treaty.

In winter, an Israeli air-force plane would bring me to Cairo, and in summer to Alexandria, since the Egyptian elite would be staying at their holiday villas on the Mediterranean coast. General Lavib would meet me and take me to an oriental restaurant for a meal. Over food, he would bring me up to date on the mood in Egypt and the latest gossip in the regime. On one such trip, I had to settle with Ali the arrangements for his first visit to Israel. I went to see him at his home in Cairo during the Ramadan fast period. He suffered from severe back pains and was stretched out on a bed with a hard board. When the day's fast ended at sunset, we shared a simple meal ending up with honey cakes and dessert. Weizman had told me that it was politically important to include Jerusalem in the itinerary, but Ali did not want to do this for fear of provoking Arab reactions, especially from Saudi Arabia, in its role as guardian of the Moslem holy places. I argued that Egypt should help to overcome the growing doubts in Israel about the Peace Treaty instead of trying to placate criticism in the Arab world, which would only undermine Egypt's own 'peace strategy'. As a compromise, we agreed that Ali would be flown over Jerusalem and the West Bank by helicopter, which would touch down at various observation points that were not close to Israeli settlements. The visit was carried out according to plan. The helicopter circled several times over Jerusalem while Weizman explained various points of interest. The aircraft touched down in the West Bank and the party was briefed on security problems by the GOC Central Command, General Moshe Levy (later Chief of Staff).

The sensitivity had worn off when Ali made a subsequent visit, this time as Egyptian Foreign Minister. He called officially in Jerusalem on the President, the Prime Minister and the Israeli Foreign Minister.

Throughout this period, discussions on autonomy and normalization, as well as meetings of the joint Military Commission set up by the Peace Treaty, took place as usual. But in Israel, a gloomy atmosphere began to take root as a result of the fading of expectations regarding peace with Egypt. This atmosphere helped more extreme elements to influence Israeli Government decisions. It also caused the total destruction of the town of Yamit, where, according to the agreement with Egypt, we were supposed to leave complete any building not transported to Israel and not classified as serving security purposes. Negotiations were being held on the sale of these buildings to Egypt, which was willing to pay $120 million for them and was about to sign the agreement.

Israel's disappointment with the peace derived from a number of causes. One reason was Egypt's policy regarding the implementation of the normalization agreements. Egypt linked the development of its relations with Israel to the progress of the talks on autonomy for the West Bank and Gaza. We had returned, therefore, to the problem of the connection between the Peace Treaty and the remaining aspects of the Israeli–Arab conflict, which had caused us such difficulties from the very beginning of the peace negotiations. Whatever the text of the Treaty and the accompanying letters might say on this point, normalization of relations was bound to be influenced by the Palestinian problem and by the level of confrontation between Israel and other Arab countries.

Israelis saw the peace with Egypt in entirely different terms. In their eyes, this was the first example of peace with an Arab state after thirty years of war, in which thousands of Israelis had fallen in Sinai. In return for peace, Israel had given up the strategic depth of Sinai, its control of the Straits of Tiran and the Gulf of Suez oil wells. The Israeli public had assumed that, in return, we would have the normal relationship spelt out in the Treaty itself. The Israeli media also added fuel to the fire by stressing the difficulties that were occurring.

The Egyptian Foreign Ministry seemed to be obstructing the agreements and promises given by Sadat to Begin at every summit meeting between the two, at Beersheba, Haifa, Cairo, Aswan and Alexandria. We wondered more than once whether they were employing a deliberate tactic of speaking with two voices: the 'calm' voice of Sadat, intended to give the impression that peace was uppermost in his mind in order to ensure that Israel would evacuate Sinai without a hitch; and the 'harsh' voice of Butros Ghali, meant to assure the Arab world that Sadat's 'peace strategy' constituted the only lever capable of forcing Israel to accede to the 'Arab consensus' (return of all the occupied territories and Palestinian statehood), which the Arab states had not managed to achieve in the past and which they would not be able to obtain through war in the future.

While the pendulum swung between these two voices, the good and the bad, it was necessary to convince the Israeli public that peace would develop gradually; that the most important component of peace was the renunciation of hostilities; that Egypt had tough problems with the Arab world and, therefore, that we should wait patiently until it could overcome them.

We could clearly see what contribution peace had made to our national security during Operation Peace for Galilee in Lebanon in May 1982 (see Chapter 10). When Israel was on the brink of war with Syria, the situation on our southern front remained calm and Israeli tourists continued to visit Egypt. Egypt's reaction to the IDF invasion of Lebanon came only after the massacre in the refugee camps of Sabra and Shatilla (carried out by the Christian Phalange militia). The Egyptian Ambassador was recalled and some normalization activities were halted. At the same time, the reaction of European states, who were officially at peace with Israel, was much stronger: they imposed political and economic sanctions.

If there had been no state of peace with Egypt and no security arrangements in Sinai, I am convinced the IDF would have had to deploy considerable forces in the Negev during the Lebanese war, and quite possibly would not have had freedom of action to occupy all of Southern Lebanon and lay siege to Beirut.

* * *

56

At one of my meetings with Kamal Hassan Ali, when he invited me to his home during the autonomy talks, I remonstrated with him about the 'cold peace'. I said to him: 'You won't be able to bring a comprehensive peace to the area by such means and you will remain isolated in the Arab world. With your own hands you are felling the tree you planted. A peace treaty in writing is not sufficient. Peace has to be felt; it has to be built. This can only be done when Egyptians *en masse* come to visit Israel and Israelis, in turn, visit Egypt. Normalization must take place between peoples and not only between governments. If the people of Israel do not feel that such mutual relations have come about, they will not continue to support the peace process.'

During this period, I asked myself whether it would not have been better to adopt the idea of peace in two stages, as I had recommended to the Labour Alignment Government in 1976. If there was no chance of reaching a stable and normal peace with Egypt as long as there was a state of war between Israel and the rest of the Arab nations, would it not have been preferable to seek a first-stage agreement just on an Israeli withdrawal to the security border (El Arish–Ras Muhammad) in return for a non-belligerency pact? A permanent border on this international frontier could then have been made conditional upon a peace treaty with all the Arab confrontation states.

The United States usually supported Egypt's 'cold peace' policy. It did not wish Egypt to feel isolated within the Arab world; only the Soviets could gain from that. US Ambassador Atherton said to me in Cairo: 'There is no alternative. The only way to get out of the woods is by broadening the basis for peace. The involvement of other Arab states in the peace process will bring Egypt out of its isolation and give it the freedom to develop peaceful relations with you to your mutual advantage.' The involvement of other Arab states had a price, of course – a price that Israel was not prepared to pay.

The second factor that led to Israel's disenchantment with the peace process were the changes in the political–strategic situation in the area. These brought renewed risks and created a feeling that a region as prone to change as the Middle East had no chance of sustaining a stable peace between Israel and its neighbours. The main changes were as follows:

- Soon after the Treaty was signed, an Arab summit conference in Baghdad reaffirmed the organization of the Arab states into a Rejection Front opposed to the Treaty. They imposed political and economic sanctions on Egypt, recalled ambassadors and severed diplomatic relations.
- An alliance was formed between the USSR and Syria increasing the military strength of the latter both quantitatively and

qualitatively so that Syria might achieve 'strategic parity' with Israel – in other words, the capacity to fight Israel on its own, without other Arab states.

- The fall of the Shah and the rise of the Khomeini regime turned Iran into an indirect confrontation state against Israel. Iranian volunteers joined PLO terrorist organizations.

- Iraq was bogged down in the Gulf War with Iran, but the tripling of Iraqi arms in the war increased the potential threat to Israel in the future.

- The attempted development of nuclear weapons in Iraq obliged Israel to destroy Iraq's nuclear reactor by an air strike in 1981.

- There was a deterioration in the border situation between Israel and Lebanon as a result of the growing strength of PLO terrorist organizations in Southern Lebanon and West Beirut. This led to Operation Litani in 1978, even before the Peace Treaty was signed with Egypt, and would eventually lead to Operation Peace for Galilee in 1982.

This was not the only period of national disillusionment in Israel. One had occurred with the Yom Kippur War, when the assumption had collapsed that the Arab states would be deterred from further attack and the status quo created by the Six Day War would remain unchanged until peace was attained. Another period of public frustration would occur over the Lebanese war.

The central question was, how far had Egypt committed itself to peace? Its policy towards Israel resembled more a state of non-belligerency than a system of normal relations characteristic of true peace.

Many in Israel had believed that the Peace Treaty would solve, once and for all, the Israeli–Egyptian conflict, regardless of what happened concerning other aspects of the Camp David Accords – namely, a comprehensive Israeli–Arab peace and Palestinian autonomy in the West Bank and Gaza.

The Egyptian Government believed that the peace with Israel constituted only the first stage in a settlement of the Israeli–Arab conflict on conditions acceptable to the Arab world. Furthermore, Egypt felt entitled to take any political measures at its disposal – including a freeze in the normalization process, a suspension of agreements already signed and the recall of the Egyptian Ambassador to Israel – in order to put pressure on Israel over autonomy, or as a reaction to Israel's policy with regard to other Arab states, or as sanctions imposed upon Israel in reaction to the IDF invasion of Southern Lebanon in Operation Peace for Galilee.

In my opinion, our expectations from the peace were too rosy and even, to some extent, naïve. Despite the enormous gain of having signed a peace treaty with the strongest of the Arab states, it could have been anticipated that we would be obliged to live in the shadow of a 'cold peace' as long as other Arab nations continued to live with us in a state of war.

Within the context of a peace agreement, we could determine with precision the security arrangements to be implemented by the parties – for instance, the depth of demilitarized zones, limitation of forces and weapons, and supervisory machinery. However, we could not fix exact dimensions for normalization because that depended on a system of relationships affected by domestic problems, by inter-Arab relations and by political changes within the region and globally.

In tough arguments which I had with various people while I was co-ordinating the negotiations on normalization, I claimed that the Peace Treaty's most important achievement was the fact that force would no longer be used to solve problems between Israel and Egypt. It was preferable for the people of Israel to come to terms with political pressure, or even deadlock in political and economic relations, than to go to war. I expected our relations with Egypt to be more or less similar to those obtaining between Israel and countries such as Turkey or Romania, which maintain relations with Israel, but for reasons of national interest give priority to contacts with the Arab states.

In trying to make a balanced assessment of the strength of Egypt's commitment to peace, it is as well to consider what its reasons were for turning to the peace option. First and foremost, it saw no hope of solving the Arab conflict with Israel through military means. This conclusion was based on the very heavy price it had paid in both lives and equipment during the thirty years of war with Israel (1947–77) and on its estimate of Israel's future strength.

Second, Egypt's severe economic situation, arising mainly from the growth in population (nearly a million a year), required it to concentrate its resources on improving the conditions of life for its people, before internal unrest swept away the regime.

Third, Egypt had other external security problems which had obliged it to transfer strategic forces to the borders with Libya and the Sudan. Colonel Gaddafi's Libya was trying to topple the Egyptian Government, through the exploitation of extremist factions in Egypt. The assassination of President Sadat in 1981 was the highlight of such activity.

Dangers also threatened Egypt as a result of Soviet strategic installations in Libya, Ethiopia, South Yemen and Madagascar. These countries constitute Egypt's strategic back yard. They are mainly countries through which the Nile (Egypt's means of survival) flows, or countries which provide the sea- and air-links between the Gulf of Suez and the Indian Ocean. Furthermore, Egypt's main oil resources are located in the Gulf of Suez. These security problems brought about strategic co-operation between the US and Egypt with the aim of containing Soviet expansion in North and East Africa, the Arabian Peninsula and the Persian Gulf. Egypt granted the United States air and naval bases for the purpose of military intervention in the Persian Gulf in an emergency.

Egypt's strategic, economic and political links with the US have had a stabilizing and moderating influence on the Egyptian Government, and encouraged it to co-operate in the peace process. President Carter was a signatory to the Camp David Accords and the Israeli–Egyptian Peace Treaty, and the US is a full partner in the implementation of these agreements. It provides a vital security umbrella over the two parties to the peace, both of whom are in great need of American aid.

Fourth, the security arrangements in Sinai prevented the establishment of an infrastructure which could be used by Egypt to launch an offensive against Israel. If Egypt were to disobey these restrictions, it would be tantamount to abandoning the Peace Treaty and making a declaration of war. Egypt knew that such action would impose an intolerable burden on the country. For one thing, it would wipe out the Egyptian development plan for Sinai and the rehabilitation of the towns in the Canal zone. Furthermore, during the three-year period set by the Treaty for the Israeli evacuation of Sinai (till April 1982), any outbreak of hostilities would end the withdrawal and find the IDF still deployed in the centre of Sinai, while it would take time for Egyptian forces to reach that area.

Thus, however cold the peace might be, it rested on a foundation of objective factors. In spite of this, it seemed to hang precariously in the balance after President Sadat was assassinated on 6 October 1981. From the beginning, his peace policy had encountered much domestic opposition. Would Egypt, in the post-Sadat era, be willing and able to maintain the peace against national and pro-Arab pressures? The answer was fraught with doubt.

Begin, too, had had to contend with domestic resistance to the Camp David Accords and the Peace Treaty from right-wing elements within his own party and with those further to the right of it in the political spectrum. This opposition now reasserted itself strongly, led by Professor Yuval Ne'eman, leader of the small ultra-nationalist Tehiya Party, and Professor Moshe Arens, a prominent member of the Likud who was Chairman of the Knesset Foreign Affairs and Defence Committee (he later served as Ambassador in Washington and then as Minister of Defence). This group of people wanted to revoke the Treaty before Israel had to withdraw the IDF forces and evacuate the civilian settlements between the interim El Arish–Ras Muhammad line and the international frontier. They tried every means to persuade the Israeli public that, with

Sadat gone, the Egyptians would wait until all Sinai was in their hands, then abandon the Peace Treaty and come to terms again with the rest of the Arab world.

The Israeli delegation to Sadat's funeral included Prime Minister Begin, Cabinet Ministers Yitzhak Shamir, Sharon and Dr Yosef Burg, Directors-General David Kimche and Chaim Kubersky, and myself.

The funeral took place on Saturday. The day before, the Prime Minister and the Israeli Cabinet Ministers moved to a military camp close to the funeral route so that they could walk there and not break the Sabbath. On the Saturday in the early afternoon, we joined the crowd of representatives from all over the world who had gathered in a large marquee erected next to the funeral route. A gun carriage harnessed to six black horses was already in position; on it lay Sadat's coffin draped in a black shroud bearing his official emblems and decorations. On either side of the carriage and behind it serried ranks of unarmed soldiers, representing the various Egyptian armed forces, stood to attention. Among the mourners were several heads of state, present and past, including President Carter and ex-Presidents Richard Nixon and Gerald Ford.

The sun was beating down. An ominous silence pervaded the scene, which was enveloped in clouds of yellowish-brown dust blown from the eastern desert. The carriage and soldiers began to move towards the burial place situated at the lower part of the area allocated to the tomb of the unknown soldier. Behind, the hundreds of guest dignitaries trudged slowly to the beat of drums and the wail of funeral dirges.

The parade which was to bring death to Sadat had passed along this very road, and his grave was across from the platform on which he had been killed while watching it.

I marched along wearing my IDF uniform and surrounded by representatives of Arab countries who were wearing traditional dress, some carrying swords inlaid with diamonds. Until he came to Jerusalem to launch his peace initiative, Sadat had appeared to us as an uncompromising enemy with whom we had no chance of reaching peace during our generation. Now, by a strange turn of events, the Israeli people grieved deeply over his untimely death. And here I was taking part in his funeral as a representative of the Israeli army, which had been at war with his country for thirty years.

When we arrived, hot and weary, at the stadium behind the parade platform, a great crush formed as hundreds of people rushed forward to assure themselves a seat. The Egyptian security guards, who were extremely nervous for fear of further killings, rudely pushed back distinguished guests who tried to make their way forward. Fortunately for me, some of the guards recognized me from my previous trips to Egypt and they helped me to reach the platform. I was shocked to see next to me the British heir to the throne, Prince Charles, being pushed aside by Egyptian guards, even though he stood out in his white naval uniform with his many decorations and a long sword at his side. I took his hand and pulled him after me to the platform. That was my first, and probably also my last, meeting with the future King of England. We did not see the actual burial ceremony. Only members of the family and close friends took part. After the ceremony was over, we entered a nearby room to present our condolences to the family. Beside them stood the next President, Mubarak, and President Numeiry of Sudan. I was surprised and touched when Mubarak greeted me by name when we shook hands.

After the Sabbath, Begin and his entourage met with US Secretary of State Alexander Haig and his aides in Begin's guest-room at the Holiday Inn hotel to discuss two major issues.

The first concerned the American proposal that Israel carry out a partial withdrawal from the El Arish–Ras Muhammad line before the prescribed date in April 1982. The purpose was to help the new President Mubarak strengthen his position in Egypt and the Arab world. (The general assumption was that an unstable situation could develop in Egypt after Sadat's death.) Begin opposed such a gesture, saying that the Peace Treaty had stipulated a timetable for the evacuation of Sinai only after lengthy discussions. Israel would remove its troops and settlements in accordance with the Treaty and there was no reason to make any changes in that respect.

The second issue concerned the means whereby progress could be made on autonomy for the West Bank and Gaza. Most of those present at the meeting supported the view that before Israel finally evacuated Sinai, there should be agreement at least on the principles of autonomy in a more specific manner than the Camp David Framework Accord. The only aspects which it was necessary to formulate in detail at that stage were those dealing with the autonomy council and the institutions, and its election system. For the rest, turning the general principles into detailed agreements could be negotiated after autonomy had been initiated.

The discussion which took place in Cairo with the Americans on the day of Sadat's funeral did not reach any conclusions and it was decided that talks would continue during the forthcoming visit to Israel of Secretary of State Haig. Thus, a few weeks later, Haig visited Israel and Egypt in an effort to bring about a breakthrough in the autonomy negotiations. These efforts were based on ideas suggested at the Cairo talks.

Arik Sharon surprised most of those present at the talks with Haig when he declared that he needed only another ten settlements in Judea and Samaria in order to complete the settlement plans. Both the

Americans and the other Israelis breathed a sigh of relief. A major obstacle to the autonomy negotiations had been removed. I could almost read what was passing through the minds of the Americans: 'We will allow Sharon to build another ten settlements and then it will be possible to announce openly that the building of new settlements has been frozen.' However, all those who entertained such hopes did not know how Sharon's impulses could swing back and forth.

After the Knesset elections the previous June, Sharon had become Minister of Defence in the new Begin Government. After Sadat's funeral, and before our meeting that evening with the Americans, I went with Sharon to call on his opposite number, Marshal Abu-Gazala, in his office in Cairo. He received us very warmly. He looked tired and his hand was bandaged due to shrapnel from a grenade which had hit him when he was standing beside Sadat on the parade platform. 'My blood was mixed with his,' he said. 'But I stayed calm, kept my head, and gave instructions which helped us gain control of the situation.' He gave a full account of Egyptian security forces' attempts to find the assassins and prevent any further attacks.

We had become very friendly at an earlier period when he was serving as Military Attaché in Washington, and I was there working on the Military Annex to the Peace Treaty. He did not then expect that his next position would be Egyptian Chief of Staff following the death of General Badwin in a helicopter accident, while visiting troops stationed on the Libyan border. He certainly never dreamed that he would be the Egyptian Minister of Defence. At one of the breakfasts we had had together at the Madison Hotel in Washington, he had told me that he had been offered the position of head of Military Intelligence but had no urge to accept it. He intended to serve another year as Military Attaché and then obtain his discharge from the army. We greatly admired his talents. During the Yom Kippur War, he had commanded the artillery division of the Second Army, which had fought against Sharon's division on the Suez Canal front. As deputy to Sharon, I had travelled with him in an armoured troop carrier, and we were more than once obliged to make a quick dash away from Abu-Gazala's line of artillery fire. When I told Abu-Gazala this, he laughed and said, 'I was the one who had the most luck. I once got out of my command car to urinate, and before I got back, it was struck by a direct artillery hit of yours and all those inside were killed.' He admired Sharon as a military leader and spoke to him with respect. This was the second meeting between the two men. The first was when we were in Cairo for the Begin–Sadat summit and had dined with Abu-Gazala at a renowned fish restaurant. Afterwards, we had had a full discussion in his office on how to strengthen contacts between the Israeli and Egyptian General Staffs. Abu-Gazala promised to consider our suggestion in a positive light and to give us final replies at a later date. At the meeting held after Sadat's funeral, we indeed received positive responses to all our proposals. These included arrangements for Abu-Gazala to visit Israel, reciprocal visits by the Chief of Staff, and an agreement to have regular meetings between the heads of Military Intelligence.

When we left the Egyptian Defence Minister's office, I said to Sharon, 'Who knows how many of the Egyptian top brass were involved in the attack on Sadat? It is difficult to believe that an assassination carried out by participants in the parade could have succeeded without co-operation from higher up.'

The peace came under further strain, especially after Sadat's murder, due to two sources of friction over the Sinai provisions in the Treaty. One concerned the demarcation of the international border; the other concerned alleged breaches by Egypt of the limitation-of-forces restrictions. These difficulties were exploited by those Israeli elements who were not reconciled to the peace and would welcome its collapse before Israel had to evacuate Eastern Sinai, with its military installations and civilian settlements.

The border dispute mainly concerned Taba, a tiny strip of shoreline at the head of the Gulf of Akaba, adjacent to the Israeli port and resort town of Eilat. Sharon caused consternation in Cairo by threatening to halt the evacuation of Sinai unless the Egyptians gave up their claim to Taba (see Chapter 6).

In terms of the Treaty, a joint Commission had been set up to supervise the Israeli withdrawal and the security arrangements in Sinai. One of its express functions was to deal with reported breaches of the arrangement. But what was actually happening was that the complaints of Egyptian violations were being sent to the Prime Minister, the Foreign Minister, the Minister of Defence and others, before they had been properly examined by the head of the Israeli military delegation to the Commission, Brigadier Dov Sion, or discussed in the Commission. On one occasion, Professor Arens called a meeting of the Knesset Foreign Affairs and Defence Committee to consider the unchecked reports, which he took at their face value. Premier Begin, who at that time still held the Defence portfolio as well, appeared before the Committee and asked me to be present to comment on the allegations. To Professor Arens' obvious chagrin, I explained that some of the complaints were not borne out by the actual text of the Military Annex to the Treaty, while others had been magnified and would be dealt with in the normal course by the joint Commission.

The complaints mainly concerned the composition of the mechanized infantry division the Egyptians were allowed to keep in Zone A, which stretched to a depth of about thirty miles to the east of the Suez Canal and the Gulf of Suez. I pointed out that, whereas the division could consist of up to 22,000 men, the Egyptians had only about 12,000 in Zone A, and fewer tanks and armoured personnel carriers than the numbers specified in the Military Annex. In concluding my comments, I asked Professor Arens whether he had made any attempt to check his information with Dov Sion, the officer officially responsible for dealing with such complaints. There was no response.

While Ezer Weizman was Minister of Defence, and Begin after Weizman's resignation, complaints of breaches by Egypt of the restrictions in the Military Annex were dealt with through the proper channels, without much fuss. That changed after Sharon became Minister of Defence, during 1981, when he saw to it that alleged breaches were made the subject of public agitation in Israel and when he took a well-publicized trip to Cairo to confer on the matter with President Mubarak and his Foreign and Defence Ministers. The prominence given to the issue in Israel, together with Sharon's threat over the Taba dispute, caused the Egyptian leadership to fear that Israel was trying to back out of the obligation to evacuate all Sinai. The Egyptian Foreign Minister, Kamal Hassan Ali, accompanied by the Secretary of State for Foreign Affairs, Butros Ghali, came to Jerusalem to see Premier Begin and Foreign Minister Shamir in order to obtain a reaffirmation that Israel would withdraw to the international border in accordance with the timetable laid down by the Treaty. Begin gave them a firm assurance on that score.

Washington was sufficiently concerned over these strains for Secretary of State Haig to send his Deputy, Walter Stoessle, to deal with them on the spot. He moved between Jerusalem and Cairo and helped to calm the crisis atmosphere which had developed.

During this period, the peace could have been in real danger of collapse if it had not been for Begin's insistence that the Treaty he had signed be implemented in full. For all the risks it involved, peace with Egypt was an historic turning-point in the Israeli struggle, and the one outstanding achievement of the Begin era. He was not prepared to let the peace be obstructed even by his own followers, who had given his peace policy far less support than the Labour Alignment opposition party had done.

The final phase of the evacuation in April 1982 was a grim experience for the Government and the country. The settlers in the Yamit area refused to leave their homes and fields, and the army had to be sent in to remove them. The soldiers met with stiff, though unarmed, resistance and had to drag away the people by force. Hundreds of sympathizers with the settlers, from the right-wing Tehiya Party and the nationalist–religious Gush Emunim (the bloc of the faithful) movement, rushed south to help put obstacles in the way of the army in carrying out its unpalatable task. But the evacuation was completed on time, and was accompanied by generous compensation to the persons displaced and extensive plans for the resettlement of all those who wanted it.

On Sharon's orders, the coastal town of Yamit was destroyed after it was evacuated, instead of its being surrendered intact to the Egyptians as stipulated in the Peace Treaty. While smoke and dust were still rising from the ruins of Yamit, the dark clouds of another Israeli–Arab war were already gathering over Lebanon. Six weeks after the evacuation of Sinai was completed, Operation Peace for Galilee was launched.

The pessimists in Israel, and the opponents of the Treaty, had predicted that once Egypt had regained possession of all Sinai by April 1982, it would abandon the peace with Israel. That did not happen. On the other hand, the normal interstate relations called for by the Treaty did not happen either. Agreements signed by the parties for economic ties and cultural exchanges remained virtually frozen. Many Israelis visited Egypt, but Egyptians were discouraged from visiting Israel, and very few did so. The tone of the Egyptian press remained hostile or at least cool towards Israel, even verging at times on the anti-Semitic. Early in the Lebanese war, after the massacre of Palestinians by the Christian Phalange in the Sabra and Shatilla refugee camps, the Egyptian Ambassador to Israel was recalled and the Embassy remained under a Chargé d'Affaires. The reasons given by the Egyptians concerned Israel's settlement drive in the West Bank and the Gaza Strip; criticism of Israel's treatment of the Arab inhabitants of these territories; the application of Israeli law to the Golan Heights; and the IDF invasion of Lebanon. The Egyptians claimed that all these developments created the impression in the Arab world that Egypt had signed a Peace Treaty which gave Israel a free hand to annex territories captured in the Six Day War or to attack another Arab state.

Israel's position was that it had fully carried out its obligations under the Treaty, and Egypt had to do likewise. Egypt was not entitled to link its Treaty obligations to Israel's policy in the territories, or to Israel's security actions concerning other Arab confrontation states which still maintained a state of war with it.

The 'cold peace' would begin to thaw only after the National Unity Government was formed in Israel in October 1984. Prime Minister Shimon Peres launched an effort to improve relations with Egypt on the basis of a 'package deal', which would include the Taba dispute, the implementation of the normalization agreements, the return of an Egyptian Ambassador to Israel and the revival of the peace process.

5

AUTONOMY

Soon after the signing of the Israeli–Egyptian Peace Treaty in March 1979, negotiations began on autonomy for the West Bank and Gaza.

The parties were once again Egypt, Israel and the United States, Jordan having rejected the invitation to participate. It was indeed an unusual forum, in that the two Arab parties most directly concerned – Jordan and the inhabitants of the territories – were not represented at the negotiating table.

Both the Egyptian and the Israeli positions hardened in advance of the negotiations. Egypt was being even more ostracized in the Arab world after the Treaty. Moreover, it had no mandate from the Jordanians or the Palestinians to speak on their behalf. Egypt thus gave an extreme interpretation to the Camp David Accords, in an effort to persuade the Arab world that it was genuinely safeguarding the future of the Palestinian people. In Israel, the Likud Government faced its own domestic 'Rejection Front' drawn mainly from Begin's Herut Party and the religious parties. They had voted in the Knesset against the Camp David Accords and the Peace Treaty and were pressing for the annexation of the West Bank and Gaza to show that the aim of eventually incorporating these territories in a Greater Israel had not been sacrificed at Camp David. It proved impossible to reach agreement between the two parties that gave such conflicting interpretations to the principles of autonomy, a term which in any case has no precise meaning in international law. The main points of dispute were:

The Concept of Autonomy

For Egypt, the concept was territorial, applying to the areas of the West Bank and Gaza as bounded by the pre-1967 armistice lines. For Israel, autonomy did not apply to the territories as such but to a community, the Palestinian Arabs residing in them.

The Autonomy Council

Egypt understood that the 'self-governing authority' should be a large elected body exercising full legislative and executive powers except for external defence and foreign policy. In Israel's view, no more was called for than a small elected council of fifteen or twenty persons to administer certain limited functions, while the rest of the powers of government would remain vested in Israel.

The Source of Authority

Egypt considered that the basic source of authority in the transitional period should be the elected autonomy council, under the general supervision of a joint committee composed of Egypt, Israel and the United States (and Jordan, if it joined). For Israel, the basic source of authority would be the Israeli Government.

IDF Deployment

Israel was willing to comply with the Camp David requirement that part of its forces should be withdrawn and the remainder redeployed into specified security locations. But the extent of the withdrawal and the locations of redeployment were for Israel to decide in accordance with its security needs, with freedom of movement and action. Egypt and the United States would be kept informed. If and when a peace treaty with Jordan was concluded, the deployment would be reviewed according to the terms of that treaty. According to Egypt, the provision in the Camp David Accords on this point would be met by the IDF having several Israeli camps in the Jordan Valley, with access to them along specified routes.

Jerusalem

The parties maintained their positions as set out at Camp David in separate letters from Sadat and Begin to Carter. Egypt's position was that East Jerusalem was part of the autonomy region. Israel's position was that the whole of the city was permanently under Israel's jurisdiction, and East Jerusalem with its Arab residents was thus excluded from the autonomy region.

Settlements

While this sensitive question had been omitted from the Camp David Accords, Egypt demanded that Israeli settlements in the territories be frozen during the transitional period while Israel claimed the right of the Government to continue settlement on state-owned lands with individual Israeli citizens permitted to purchase and reside on privately owned Arab land.

Future Status

The Camp David Accords had deliberately refrained from suggesting what should be the final status of the West Bank and Gaza at the end of the five-year transitional period, leaving this to be negotiated between Egypt, Israel, Jordan and the elected representatives of the local inhabitants. Egypt maintained that the decisive factor should be the wishes of the inhabitants, i.e. self-determination. Israel made clear that at the end of the autonomy period, it would press its claim to sovereignty over the territories.

The American position on autonomy inclined towards that of Egypt on such issues as the source of authority (a joint committee of the parties to the negotiations); the legislative powers of the autonomy council; responsibility of the autonomy council for internal security; control of state lands and water resources; and a freeze on new Jewish settlements. On all these points, American proposals were rejected by the Israeli Government. Clearly, the basic reason for disagreement was the very question which the Camp David Accords had left open for the future: the final status of the territories. For the Likud Government, the point of departure regarding the autonomy arrangements was the eventual incorporation of the territories into Israel. Both the Egyptians and the Americans held that Israel would have to withdraw to the pre-1967 lines, subject to minor changes, while in the West Bank and Gaza, a Palestinian Arab national entity would be established, linked with Jordan in a federation or confederation.

Some useful work was done on the staff level by a working group of Egyptian, Israeli and American officials. Our team was headed by the Director-General of the Ministry of the Interior, Chaim Kubersky, an exceptionally able and experienced cjvil servant. It included representatives of the Foreign and Justice Ministries and myself as the adviser on national security. Our negotiations made good progress on some practical issues, such as elections to the autonomy council, the judicial system and a division of autonomy functions. But these areas of agreement remained on paper, since the questions of principle had to be settled at a higher political level.

In our main delegation, I put forward a set of proposals to overcome the stalemate in the autonomy talks. I did so in the spirit of Camp David, where it was accepted that a partial agreement was better than total failure. The Framework Accords had reflected points of agreement and left points of disagreement for later negotiations.

Accordingly, I proposed dividing all the autonomy issues into groups:

1 Points to be agreed upon before the establishment of autonomy:
   • The election of the autonomy council, its composition and its institutions.
   • Those powers to be granted the autonomy council on which there was general agreement so that the council could begin to function.
   • The establishment of joint Israeli–autonomy council committees which would function after the establishment of autonomy, in order to discuss certain of the issues left open.
   • The source of authority could be vested for the time being either in a joint committee of the parties to the negotiations or in a joint committee composed of Israel and autonomy council representatives.

2 Issues connected with autonomy which could be discussed and agreed upon by means of the joint committees mentioned above, after the autonomy council had started functioning. These issues concerned the legislative and executive powers of the executive council that had not been agreed in advance.

3 Issues which could be postponed to the negotiations on the final status of the West Bank and Gaza. (By the Camp David Accords those negotiations were to start three years after the beginning of the autonomy period.) These issues would include:
   • The status of the Arab residents of East Jerusalem.
   • The future of Jewish settlements in the West Bank and Gaza.
   • Economic relations.
   • Control of state lands and the water sources in these areas.
   • Permanent responsibility for internal security.

This 'Camp David approach' did not commend itself to my political masters. The reaction was that there was no point in starting the autonomy regime unless and until all the issues concerned were settled.

As I have mentioned, the same idea came up in the talk we had in Cairo with Secretary of State Haig and his aides on the evening after Sadat's funeral. A few weeks later Haig visited Jerusalem and Cairo, in a personal attempt to reach some agreement on autonomy. That visit was followed by more shuttling between the two capitals by Walter Stoessle and by special envoy Ambassador Richard Fairbanks. But the US mediation efforts failed to produce any real progress. The Americans were trying to find compromise solutions between two Governments, each of which was locked in a situation that did not leave it any room for manœuvre.

Egypt was in no position to be flexible. It had no mandate from the Arab League, the PLO or Jordan to represent them. Its hope was that in due course Jordan and the Palestinians would join in the autonomy negotiations, and Egypt could let them bear the responsibility for accepting compromise solutions. Moreover, Egypt claimed that the negotiations were serving as a smokescreen for an Israeli policy of *de facto* annexation, as evinced by the continued Jewish settlement of the territories, the dismissal of pro-PLO mayors and the annexation of East Jerusalem. For all these reasons, Egypt stuck firmly to its interpretation of the Camp David Accords, which was that autonomy was a stepping-stone to the change from Israeli rule to Arab rule, preferably in a Palestinian–Jordanian framework.

Equally, the Begin Government did not budge from its own interpretation, which was that autonomy was a stepping-stone to the eventual incorporation of the territories into Israel. In a way, the position of the Government was paradoxical. The autonomy plan that Begin had originally presented to Sadat at the Ismailia Conference in December 1977 had been based on the premise of permanent Israeli rule over the territories. The autonomy plan Begin had signed after Camp David was quite different. It was a transitional stage to a future for the territories to be settled by negotiation and agreement. Jordan and the representatives of the local Arab inhabitants were granted key roles both in setting up the autonomy regime and in deciding the final status. Yet an Israeli Government pursuing an annexationist policy could not share power and influence in the territories with Jordan nor agree to give extensive autonomy to an autonomy council elected by the local inhabitants, none of whom wanted to remain under Israeli rule. In these circumstances, the Government preferred the status quo to any agreement that might be reached with Egypt and the United States on the principles of autonomy.

The hard-line position of the Government was reinforced by the shift in its policies and its membership. After the signing of the Peace Treaty, the influence of Dayan and Weizman on the Government and on Begin had waned. Attention had shifted to the Palestinian problem with the autonomy negotiations as its focus. On that issue Dayan and Weizman increasingly found themselves a dissident minority in the Cabinet. The gap between their views and those of the majority in the Government came to a head when the official policy statement on the principles of autonomy was stiffened so as to place greater emphasis on Israel's claim to sovereignty. As a concession to Weizman and Dayan, and to Deputy Prime Minister Yigael Yadin, the revised policy statement was not published. (It was a strange fact that the leading 'doves' in the Cabinet had all three been top army generals.)

Soon after the signing of the Peace Treaty, a Cabinet Committee had been appointed to supervise the autonomy negotiations and the work of our group under Kubersky. Its chairman was not Dayan but Dr Yosef Burg, the Minister of the Interior and the head of the National Religious Party. The Committee of Six turned out to be an impotent body. It had no authority to take decisions and was unable to reach a consensus. Dayan was a member but did not attend the meetings, and Weizman, also a member, soon resigned from the Committee.

Dayan was apt to say sarcastically at this time, 'We have four Foreign Ministers. The Prime Minister serves as the Foreign Minister for the US and the Jewish people. The Minister of Defence is the Foreign Minister for the Arabs. The Minister of the Interior is the Foreign Minister for autonomy. As the official Foreign Minister, I serve as an administrator for the other Foreign Ministers.'

Although Dayan and Weizman were not opposed in principle to settlement in the administered territories, they were very unhappy about current settlement policy. As Chairman of a Cabinet Committee on Settlement, Arik Sharon was vigorously directing a programme of creating facts on the ground, designed in the long run to lead to annexation.

In October 1979, six months after the signature of the Peace Treaty, Dayan resigned from the Government. He explained to the Prime Minister that since the Six Day War he had devoted himself to developing a pattern of co-existence with the Arabs in the administered territories. He disagreed with the Government's existing approach to this question and felt that the autonomy negotiations would be fruitless. His job had become frustrating. 'The things that interest me I do not handle; and what I deal with holds no interest for me,' he told Premier Begin.

Weizman also felt unable to go along either with the hard-line policy reflected in the revised statement of principles on autonomy, or with the settlement drive in the territories. Together with Israeli leaders of all parties, Weizman rejected the assertion by the Carter Administration that these Jewish settlements were illegal. Whatever the final political status of these territories, they could not be made 'Judenrein'.

But Weizman maintained that Jewish settlement had to be carried out in practice in a way that did not harm the local Arab population, or frustrate good-neighbour relations with them. Small, scattered settlements that imposed an economic burden on Israel should be discouraged. Priority should be given to a few larger centres or settlement clusters, which would be economically and socially self-contained, and which would not encroach on Arab population centres. Arab-owned lands should not be expropriated for alleged 'security reasons'; there was sufficient unpopulated land available for this purpose in key strategic areas. The Jewish settlements should be integrated into the general defence system and their protection should include the means of self-defence.

As for a long-term solution, Weizman favoured autonomy for the Palestinian Arab inhabitants of the territories within an Israeli framework only if this was done with their consent. A willingness on their part to consider such a solution could only evolve during an interim period of full civilian self-rule for them, in conditions which would foster friendly relations and co-operation between them and the Jewish settlers.

At Weizman's request, I converted these general principles into a detailed settlement plan, on which I marked existing settlements, the areas of state-owned land and seven projected settlement clusters which would conform with Weizman's criteria.

But there was a widening gap between Weizman's approach and government policy, which was more and more influenced by right-wing nationalist and religious elements headed by Gush Emunim. Like Dayan before him, Weizman felt himself unable to serve any longer in a government with which he was out of step, and in the summer of 1980 he resigned. He felt deeply about Israeli–Arab peace and co-existence. A little while before his resignation, he wrote in his book *The Battle for Peace*: 'I believe that if we do not find a way to live in peace with the Arabs, we will have to live with them with missiles and laser beams. When my son, Shaul, went to the Suez Canal front, I wrote to him, "When you were born, I told your mother I hoped you would not need to go to war. Now, as you leave for battle, I ask myself what the mistakes were that we made." '

With the resignation of Dayan and Weizman, followed by the retirement of Yigael Yadin, Arik Sharon gained greater power in the Government. The Egyptian leadership came to fear his influence on Israeli policy, particularly in the period between his appointment as Minister of Defence, after the Knesset elections in June 1981, and the final Israeli evacuation of Sinai in April 1982. The Egyptian Foreign Minister, Kamal Hassan Ali, made great efforts to find a common language with Sharon and to reach an understanding with him on matters in dispute.

Ali knew Sharon from before, when the latter was still Minister of Agriculture in the first Begin Government. During the summer of 1980, while the autonomy talks were in progress, Ali played host several times to Weizman or Sharon at his summer beach house near Alexandria, and as a rule I accompanied them. The talks would be concluded at a fish restaurant in the town of Abukir, which was situated between Alexandria and the Gulf of Abukir. The western fork of the Nile flows into the Gulf at this point, which is famous as the site where Admiral Nelson sank Napoleon's fleet after his invasion of Egypt.

On one of Sharon's visits to Ali's summer home, he presented his host with a settlement map for Judea, Samaria and the Gaza Strip. It was a truly outrageous map, which I saw then for the first time and knew did not have Cabinet approval. Whoever drew it had emphasized in blue those areas vital to Israel's security. There was so much blue that the original colour of the map was hardly visible. The impression given was that this was a map intended to show not so much settlements as Israel's control over ninety per cent of Judea and Samaria. Sharon had hoped to leave this meeting with greater Egyptian understanding of our position, but actually left his host in a state of shock.

At the internal discussions of the Israeli autonomy delegations, I expressed the opinion that it was preferable to reach an agreement based on compromises, which would not endanger Israel's interests in the West Bank and Gaza, than to be party to the collapse of the negotiations. I argued that as long as the IDF was deployed in the territories, there was no chance of any change undesirable to Israel taking place in their political and security status. The reality, however, was otherwise. The deadlock was no longer due to disagreement over Camp David; rather, it put an end to Camp David as a basis for negotiations altogether. Today, negotiations are based on the Reagan plan, which contains additional principles to those included in Camp David, the most important of which stipulates that the permanent solution to the West Bank and Gaza must be worked out in conjunction with Jordan.

In my opinion, if we had been prepared to accept the following compromises, it would have been possible in 1981 to reach agreement on the basic principles for autonomy, which was due to be established in 1982:

1   Not to build new settlements during the autonomy period but to concentrate on the growth of existing ones.
2   An agreement that a joint committee including Israel, Egypt, Jordan and the United States, or just Israel and Jordan, would constitute the source of authority for the autonomy administration, provided that decisions taken by this committee would be unanimous.
3   An agreement to establish the autonomy regime in stages (as I have already outlined).

But by 1982, the circumstances were not propitious for any compromises. There was a deadlock over the demarcation of the international border at Taba, in the vicinity of Eilat. Tension had arisen over alleged breaches by Egypt of the security arrangements in Sinai. The situation in the north with Lebanon and Syria was deteriorating and would soon slide into war. And on 1 September of that year the Reagan plan was proclaimed in Washington. It went far beyond the Camp David Accord, which had left the future of the territories an open question, the subject of negotiations at a later stage. The Reagan initiative put on public record an American position which pre-empted the results of those future negotiations. It ruled out both a separate Palestinian Arab state in the West Bank and Gaza, and their annexation by Israel; instead, the territories should be linked to Jordan in a confederation or federation. The Begin Government rejected the plan outright.

In this atmosphere, the autonomy negotiations petered out and have not been resumed to the present day. The West Bank and the Gaza Strip have remained under the Israeli military government, with a civilian administration functioning under it. What their future may be is a matter on which the people of Israel are deeply divided. East Jerusalem has been absorbed into the reunited city, and nobody thinks seriously of dividing it again as part of any political settlement.

6

WHOSE TABA?

It sometimes happens between states, as between individuals, that a dispute over some relatively minor matter acquires symbolic and emotional overtones out of all proportion to its intrinsic value, and becomes the touchstone of a relationship. That is what happened between Egypt and Israel over Taba, a tiny strip of sand at the head of the Gulf of Akaba, less than a square kilometre in area.

Article 2 of the Peace Treaty states that 'the permanent boundary between Egypt and Israel is the recognized international boundary between Egypt and the former mandated territory of Palestine. . . . The parties recognize this border as immutable.' The joint Commission set up by the Treaty was made responsible for organizing the demarcation of the border. For this purpose, Israeli and Egyptian survey teams were used.

The Commission instructed them to check the locations of the border markers that existed since the British Mandate. Where these had disappeared during the Mandatory period, the Commission was required to fix their locations on the basis of the documentary evidence relating to the original demarcation of this border in 1906. Egypt was then nominally still part of the Ottoman Empire but actually under British control, with Lord Cromer, the Consul-General, as the virtual ruler of the country. The British were determined to push the Turks as far east of the Suez Canal as possible. They sent troops into Sinai and forced the Turks to accept a border line between Egypt and Turkish Palestine that ran from Rafiah to the vicinity of Bir Taba (the Well of Taba), a distance of 135 miles. The whole British-occupied Sinai thus became an effective buffer between the Canal and Turkish-held territory. Since Sinai was still technically subject to Turkish sovereignty, the border had the status of a 'separating administrative line' and not a political frontier. After World War I, it became the frontier between Egypt and Mandatory Palestine, and by the Peace Treaty of 1979 the frontier between Egypt and Israel.

In demarcating the border, the Israeli–Egyptian Commission found fourteen points of dispute, all of them insignificant except for Taba. The key question on Taba was the location of border marker no. 91, which no longer existed. That was the easternmost marker of the 1906 border and was located at what was called Ras Taba on the Gulf of Akaba shore. The Egyptians maintained that the original marker 91 was located where remnants of the Mandatory marker could be discerned. The Israelis claimed that the original 91 was located at one of two alternative positions further south than the point identified by the Egyptians.

The Taba dispute became more complicated when the Israeli authorities issued a permit for the construction of a privately owned luxury resort hotel, the Avia Sonesta, and also a holiday beach camp run by a bearded character called Rafi Nelson. When the joint Commission began demarcating the border in this sector, the building of the hotel was in its final stage. The Egyptians demanded that the work be stopped. In spite of this protest, the work was completed and the hotel and holiday camp opened.

By the Egyptian claim, the whole site is Egyptian territory. In rejecting this claim, Israel relies, among other grounds, on the principle laid down by the 1906 agreement that 'boundary pillars' should be situated 'at intervisible points' – i.e. that marker no. 91 should be within a line of sight from marker no. 90. This test would rule out the location for marker 91 according to the Egyptian contention. Israel's contention suggests a grove of palm trees or, alternatively, an outcrop known as the 'granite knob'.

In December 1981, while I was at the Mena House hotel in Cairo in connection with the autonomy negotiations, Defence Minister Sharon telephoned me on an ordinary line (as he usually did when he wanted the call to be overheard) and told me to inform the Egyptian Foreign Minister, Kamal Hassan Ali, that the IDF would not withdraw from the El Arish–Ras Muhammad interim line if Egypt did not drop its claim to the Taba area and other disputed points along the international frontier. 'Tell him', said Sharon, 'that I am not prepared to withdraw to a disputed border and we will remain along the El Arish–Ras Muhammad line until the dispute is settled.' I did not carry out his instructions because I knew he had no approval from the Prime Minister for such an ultimatum; I also did not want to be the 'bad guy' and pass it on to the Egyptians. I did contact Ali and made an appointment to see him that night at his home. I asked Ambassador Sasson to accompany me. We talked into the night. I stressed that Israel's position derived from the belief that the Taba area belonged to Israel in the light of old Turkish and German documents and maps of 1906 and after. I said: 'Do you think that, having agreed to evacuate air bases, settlements and all other camps and facilities in Sinai, we then decided to build an hotel in Taba simply in order to create a *de facto* annexation of an Egyptian area by Israel? Up to now the issue of the border demarcation has been dealt with at the level of the military officers in the joint Commission. Each party has come with its documents, maps and photographs, but had no authority to change his Government's stand. The time has come for your Minister and Defence Minister Sharon to meet, examine the border area yourselves, and settle the dispute before we evacuate Sinai. Nobody understands why you want to force your view on us and why you portray us as if we wish to deceive you into making border adjustments. There is hardly anywhere in the world where frontiers are unquestionably accepted by both sides. This is the first time that Israel and Egypt are demarcating a common frontier. Therefore, it is up to us to guarantee its accuracy in accordance with all the sources at our disposal. I suggest you meet Arik Sharon at Taba tomorrow. If you can resolve the problem there, you can continue to examine and agree on other disputed marker positions along the border.' He accepted my suggestion.

The visit began at the Etzion air base near Eilat. It was the first time that an Egyptian military plane had landed at this base, which we had tried so hard during the peace negotiations to keep under Israeli control. Kamal Hassan Ali arrived with his entourage of mapping assistants, advisers and military personnel. Sharon and his staff received him. They began to argue as soon as we had eaten breakfast.

The two Ministers were not prepared to budge. I knew from my contacts with the Egyptians that they might be willing to consider a Solomonic judgment – dividing Taba. At that time, the issue of paramount concern to them was that the evacuation of Sinai be completed, and for that purpose they would be flexible on issues of less importance. Dividing Taba into two would leave the Avia Sonesta Hotel and Rafi Nelson's camp under Israeli sovereignty. But Sharon was not prepared to listen when I suggested this possibility to him. He stuck to his attitude that either the Egyptians would agree to leave the whole of Taba in Israel's hands, or there would be no withdrawal from the El Arish–Ras Muhammad line. The meeting at the Etzion air base came no nearer to agreement.

Nevertheless, the rest of the Egyptian visit proceeded as planned. We flew by helicopter to Taba, and from there northwards along the border to Rafiah, stopping along the way where there were disputed points. From Rafiah we flew to Sharon's farm for lunch, and then the Egyptian party returned to Cairo.

A few weeks later, Kamal Hassan Ali led a high-level Egyptian delegation to Jerusalem and discussed the Taba problem with Prime Minister Begin and Foreign Minister Shamir. At this meeting, Begin did not utter one word about the possibility of Israel's refusing to withdraw from the El Arish–Ras Muhammad line. There were several positive results to the talk. It was agreed that there would be no further construction in disputed areas; and that the multinational force in Sinai would have an observation post at Taba. The Taba dispute would be settled in terms of Article VII of the Treaty, which read:

1 Disputes arising out of the application or interpretation of this Treaty shall be resolved by negotiations.
2 Any such disputes which cannot be settled by negotiations shall be resolved by conciliation or submitted to arbitration.

Pending a settlement, the question of sovereignty over Taba would remain open.

The Taba dispute remained dormant until the beginning of 1985, when Shimon Peres, as Prime Minister of the newly formed National Unity Government in Israel, launched a determined effort to improve relations with Egypt.

For the next twenty months, I was engaged in tough negotiations with the Egyptian leadership on a 'package deal' of outstanding issues, which included the Taba dispute. The key to progress lay in the Taba talks. They were beset by crises in Israel, which could have led to the break-up of the National Unity Government. The reason was that the Likud ministers in the Inner Cabinet were not prepared to agree to international arbitration. Since in Article VII of the Peace Treaty 'conciliation' is mentioned before 'arbitration', it was their opinion that the former method should first be put to the test in the search for a solution. However, the Egyptian Government was not prepared to accept conciliation. Due to strong internal opposition to its peace policy, it had no desire to give the impression that it was ready to compromise over any part of 'sacred' Egyptian soil. Egypt insisted that four wasted years (1981–4) had shown that there was no hope of solving the problem by means of bilateral negotiation and agreement, and the only course was to turn to international arbitration.

It was only when agreement was reached on a formula for the Taba arbitration that it became possible to hold a summit conference at Alexandria between Peres and President Mubarak, and reach an understanding on the whole package of issues. At Alexandria, the Taba 'compromis' was signed by Nabil el-Arabi, Legal Adviser to the Egyptian Foreign Ministry, myself for Israel and Assistant Secretary of State Richard Murphy for the United States.

As finally agreed, the Arbitration Tribunal consisted of five jurists: three of them 'international' and two 'national'. The international members were Judge Gunnar Lagergren of Sweden as President of the Tribunal, Judge Pierre Bellet of France and Professor Dietrich Schindler of Switzerland. The national members were Professor Hamit Soultan of Egypt and Professor Ruth Lapidoth of Israel.

By Article IX of the 'compromis', the President, together with the Israeli and Egyptian members, would form a chamber to 'explore the possibilities of a settlement of the dispute'. Only if this effort at conciliation failed would the arbitration take its course until the Tribunal handed down its binding decision. In that case, it was estimated that the proceedings would take one and a half to two years, at a cost to the parties of some $3 to $4 million. (Such a process seemed rather like using a steam-hammer to crack a nut.)

After the 'rotation' in October 1986, when Shimon Peres became Vice-Premier and Foreign Minister, I was appointed Director-General of the Foreign Ministry. In this capacity I left on 5 December 1986 for Geneva with a team of Israeli lawyers. Our purpose was, together with Nabil el-Arabi, the head of the Egyptian delegation, to sign the ratification documents of the arbitration 'compromis', which had been approved by the Israeli and Egyptian Governments. On 9 December, we participated in a ceremony by which the Tribunal commenced the arbitration process.

After the opening ceremony, I met Nabil el-Arabi at the Continental Hotel in Geneva and said to him: 'We have succeeded in transferring the Taba issue from difficult, vexing and complex political negotiations between our two Governments to settlement by five arbitrators, three of whom do not even know where Taba is. I cannot but regret the loss of so much time already spent over Taba. During that time, we could have held a number of summit meetings which would, in my opinion, have been able to advance the peace process. By the beginning of 1985, we could have reached an agreement over Taba reflecting a proper balance between sovereignty over the area and what would in practice be within the area – the nature of the tourist facilities and access to them. I hope that by the end of arbitration we will, in fact, have such an agreement.'

By the end of September 1987, some ten months after the start of the arbitration proceedings, this was the position. Each side had submitted its memorial (detailed written case) and each was about to submit its counter-memorial replying to the other. The United States had made a compromise proposal, which was unacceptable to Israel. The next step would be the effort at conciliation called for by the 'compromis'.*

* A Chamber consisting of the Egyptian and Israeli members together with the President of the arbitration tribunal would try to reach an agreed solution by February 1988. If that failed, the arbitration would proceed until the final verdict was handed down.

7

PACKAGE DEAL

The process which led to a thaw in the 'cold peace' between Israel and Egypt began after the National Unity Government was formed in Israel in October 1984. This Government was based on the two main parties – the left-wing Labour Alignment and the right-wing Likud (which included Herut and the Liberals). The 1984 Knesset elections had produced a stalemate, with neither of the two major parties able to form a government that could rest on even a bare Knesset majority (sixty-one out of the 120 members).

Ezer Weizman had decided to return to active politics and formed a new party, 'Yahad' (Together), which submitted a separate list of candidates for the elections. At his insistence, I resigned from public service and accepted the post of Secretary-General of his party. Weizman and the next two candidates on his list were duly elected.

(By Israel's proportional representation electoral system, voting is done for a party list and not for an individual candidate. The number of members elected from each party is in proportion to the percentage its list gets of the total national vote.)

The Likud, which had the backing of the small religious parties, needed the additional support of Yahad's three seats to gain a slight Knesset majority and set up a government. I accompanied Weizman to several meetings with Yitzhak Shamir, Prime Minister in the outgoing Government. At these meetings it was suggested that Weizman return to the Likud and serve as Deputy Prime Minister, also as Foreign Minister or Minister of Defence. In either case, he would be number two in the Likud.

In talks with Yitzhak Modai, Chairman of the Liberal Party faction in the Likud, it was proposed that Yahad and the Liberals should form a bloc within the Likud under Weizman's leadership. This bloc could have obtained a majority within a Likud movement united into a single party. But Weizman decided against rejoining the Likud, in spite of these tempting offers. His overriding urge was to revive the peace process, to which he had already made so signal a contribution. In his view, Likud policies had become an obstacle in the path of peace, which was why he had resigned five years earlier. Instead, Yahad threw in its lot with the Labour Alignment. Even then, Labour could not form a government without at least some support from the various religious parties, which it was unable to gain.

During this time of political dickering, there was a growing public demand for the major parties to join forces in order to tackle two critical national problems which neither party had the strength to solve on its own. One was to extricate the army from Lebanon (where it was bogged down after Operation Peace for Galilee – see Part Two) while maintaining the security of the northern border areas; the other was the grave state of the economy, marked by galloping inflation.

This was the background to the Likud–Labour agreement, in September 1984, to form the National Unity Government. The agreement held an exact balance between the two parties which was reflected in two novel factors. First, an Inner Cabinet was formed comprising ten members – five from the Likud and five from Labour. Its function was to take decisions on foreign, defence and settlement policy, in which areas it would function as a 'government within a government' with neither side able to get policy decisions adopted against the wishes of the other. The second feature was a 'rotation' between Peres and Shamir half-way through the Knesset term. One would serve as Prime Minister, the other as Vice-Premier and Foreign Minister; after two years (in October 1986), they would exchange posts.

The affiliation of Weizman and his Yahad Party to Labour gave the latter a slight numerical edge over the Likud, with the result that Peres became Prime Minister for the first half of the 'rotation'. Weizman went into the Government as a Minister without Portfolio, occupying one of the five Labour seats in the Inner Cabinet. He was attached to the Prime Minister's Office and given special responsibility for the affairs of Israel's Arab minority. He was also on occasion sent on special political missions – especially to Egypt, where he remained the most liked and trusted of Israel's leaders.

When Peres became Prime Minister of the National Unity Government, he appointed me Director-General of the Prime Minister's Office and National Security Adviser to the Prime Minister. In this dual capacity, I was drawn into the active pursuit of a policy objective to which Peres and Weizman attached prime importance – namely, to halt the deterioration in our relations with Egypt, to bring about a thaw in the 'cold peace', and to reach an understanding with Egypt on the renewal of the Israel–Arab peace process in general. Later I co-ordinated this work as Chairman of a committee of Directors-General of the Prime Minister's Office and the Foreign and Defence Ministers.

This was at a time when the Egyptians held Israel responsible for the deterioration due to our policy in the West Bank and the Gaza Strip (Jewish settlements and restrictions imposed on political freedom of expression), the annexation of East Jerusalem and the Golan Heights, the bombing of the Iraqi nuclear reactor, the invasion of Lebanon and the massacres in the Sabra and Shatilla Palestinian Arab refugee camps.

On the other hand, Israel claimed that Egypt was responsible for the worsening relations since it had not implemented the normalization agreements signed by both parties on the basis of the Peace Treaty, and had recalled its Ambassador to Israel. The Likud insisted that the Taba dispute be dealt with in this broader context.

In February 1985, Premier Peres decided that I should go to Cairo and initiate talks with the top echelon of the regime on the matters in dispute. There were two aspects to these matters. One related to bilateral issues which were a hangover from the Peace Treaty – Taba, normalization and return of the Egyptian Ambassador. The other aspect was a renewal of the stalled peace process, involving the Palestinian Arab problem, an Israeli–Jordanian peace and movement towards a comprehensive Israeli–Arab peace, to which all Israel's Arab neighbours would be parties. Before leaving for Egypt, I had to clarify what the guidelines were for these talks. On aspects other than the bilateral relations with Egypt, I drew up a position paper on the basic principles of peace strategy and received the Prime Minister's approval to sound out the Egyptian leadership about them (they are set out more fully in the next chapter).

Armed with this brief, I proceeded to Cairo and outlined our views in a private meeting with President Mubarak. (I was to have six further talks with him before the Alexandria Summit took place.) I also held many discussions with Kamal Hassan Ali (now Prime Minister), the Deputy Prime Minister and Foreign Minister, Dr Abdul Meguid, the previous Prime Minister, Dr Mustafa Kalil, the Minister of Defence, Marshal Abu-Gazala, and the political adviser to President Mubarak, Osama el-Baz. In addition, I had several confidential meetings in Cairo with representatives of other Arab nations. In these talks I suggested a series of procedures to promote simultaneously a thaw in Israeli–Egyptian relations, negotiations between Israel, Jordan and the Palestinians, and movement towards a comprehensive and stable peace. I proposed that official talks should be opened between the Israeli and Egyptian delegations, with US participation, on a 'package deal', leading up to a summit conference between the Egyptian President and the Israeli Prime Minister. At the same time, there should be secret contacts between Israel, Egypt and a Jordanian–Palestinian delegation, which should lead to preparatory meetings aimed at resolving outstanding issues concerning an international peace conference. These talks would be at the level of senior officials. The initial informal contacts between the Israeli and the Jordanian–Palestinian delegations would be under the auspices of the United States and Egypt. At the stage of preparatory meetings, the auspices might also extend to Britain and France, and maybe Morocco.

In February 1985, when I discussed all these matters with President Mubarak, I received the following impression regarding Egypt's basic policy:

1   Egypt's highest priority was to bring the Taba dispute to arbitration. No summit or thawing of relations would take place before this was agreed and implemented.
2   The improvement of mutual relations would be contingent upon IDF withdrawal from Lebanon and on a change in Israeli policy in the West Bank and the Gaza Strip as regards settlements and freedom of political expression for the Palestinian population of these areas.
3   Negotiations aimed at finding a solution to the Palestinian problem could not be held if the PLO did not participate as the sole representative of the Palestinians.

Thus, plans should not be made on the assumption that the PLO could be replaced, for such a premise had no basis in reality. However, plans could be made in anticipation of a change in PLO policy as a condition of their participation in the political process. As a result of a change of policy, the PLO leadership was also likely to change and Egypt was ready to accept developments in this direction.

Osama el-Baz was the architect of Egyptian policy in all matters connected with relations with Israel. His planning policy derived from one central belief: that Egypt must regain its lead in the Arab world, and that this aspiration should be based on a peace strategy. On the basis of this strategy, Egypt had so far succeeded in bringing about an agreement between King Hussein and the PLO leader, Yasser Arafat, and in renewing political contacts with Jordan. It must, therefore, continue to maintain its major political tactic, i.e. its policy of ensuring correlation between the development of the peace process and the development of mutual relations with Israel.

In my meetings in Egypt between 28 February and 3 March, I succeeded in reaching agreement on the opening of official negotiations between Israeli, Egyptian and American delegations on the package of issues. Heading the list was the Taba dispute.

Prime Minister Peres accepted my recommendations to set up a committee of Directors-General for the negotiations. This committee included myself as Chairman, the Director-General of the Foreign Ministry, David Kimche, and the head of the Planning Branch of the General Staff, General Menachem Einan. When Einan left for the US, he was replaced by my dear friend, the late Brigadier-General Uri Talmor, who died when we were on the verge of completing the Taba 'compromis'.

The head of the Egyptian delegation was Deputy Foreign Minister Abdul Halim Badawi. After he was appointed Egyptian Ambassador to the United Nations, he was replaced by the extremely able Legal Adviser to the Foreign Ministry, Nabil el-Arabi. The US delegation was headed by Alan Gretzco, a specialist on Middle Eastern affairs, a young lawyer of imposing stature who radiated charm, intelligence and humanity.

The talks lasted approximately twenty months and took place alternately in Israel and Egypt. They worked their way through a three-stage obstacle course.

In the first stage, there were exhausting arguments without any result on whether to resolve the Taba dispute by means of conciliation or arbitration. It was clear even before talks began that there was no chance of Egypt agreeing to conciliation. This stage lasted six months, from March to August 1985.

The second stage began when I gained Egyptian consent that the negotiations should continue in two directions: first, agreement on the principles of the 'compromis'; and, second, an effort to reach an agreed compromise over Taba. This was the point of breakthrough that enabled the talks to deal simultaneously with arbitration and conciliation.

The third stage was initiated when the Israeli Cabinet approved a decision, on 13 January 1986, that the Taba dispute could be submitted to arbitration, within the context of the whole 'package'. This decision became possible after I had obtained President Mubarak's agreement that the arbitration process should itself include an attempt at conciliation between the parties. Another eight months went by, however, before the text of the 'compromis', setting out the exact terms of the arbitration, was finally agreed and signed.

The turning-point in the talks with Egypt (what I have called the second stage) came about in a meeting I had on 26 August 1985 with President Mubarak and Osama el-Baz. It took place at the President's residence in the Cairo suburb of Heliopolis. At Cairo Airport I was met by the general in charge of presidential security, the Egyptian Chargé d'Affaires in Israel, Mohammed Bassiouni, and a presidential aide. We drove to the presidential guest-house adjacent to his own home, and I was shown my apartment on the second floor. I was happy to find a good after-shave in the bathroom and a video in the bedroom with films on terrorism, detective stories and sex. I returned from my talks after midnight and I enjoyed watching the films until the early hours of the morning. The next day I discovered that the night before my arrival, Yasser Arafat had stayed in the same room, slept in the same bed, asked for films and left his favourite after-shave in the bathroom. Osama el-Baz said to me with a broad smile, 'Some sort of common denominator has at last been found between you.'

In my meeting with the President, at which Osama el-Baz was present, I made the following opening remarks:

'Prime Minister Peres greatly admires the path along which you are leading Egypt towards economic growth and to a key position in the establishment of peace and stability in the region. The Prime Minister is convinced that this is the only way. A process leading to the establishment of a stable peace is an absolutely vital goal. If it fails, there may be a grave deterioration in the situation.

'The Prime Minister is convinced that the peace process depends on co-operation between himself, yourself, King Hussein and President Reagan, so that the Palestinian problem may be solved within a Jordanian–Palestinian framework and by means of direct negotiations with a Jordanian–Palestinian delegation. You can regard the Prime Minister as a partner in this process. Taba is a problem which can be solved on the basis of one of the two possibilities I am about to present to you. But the main problem is the renewal of the peace process and there is no doubt that a summit meeting can contribute in this respect.

'The Prime Minister asked me to remind you of the message I brought from you to him after my visit here in February 1985. You stressed that you are striving to renew the peace process and that we must wait and see what happens with the PLO – whether it finally splits or not. But because the PLO does not wish to split, it sabotages any renewal of the peace process by carrying out terrorist action.' (Here I described various actions, stressing acts of terrorism on the high seas, which had been approved by Arafat and his deputy, Abu Iyad.)

At this point, the President interrupted me and said: 'Arafat was here two days ago. I remonstrated with him to stop his terrorist activities since he is destroying the whole political process, but he swore that he did not give instructions to carry out such acts, and would have been crazy to do so.'

I rejoined: 'Believe me, I know what I'm talking about. We have definite information.'

The President continued: 'Tell Peres he must understand that the main danger lies with the Shi'ites and not with the Palestinians. They are a danger to all of us – to you, me and to all the moderate nations in the region. Arik Sharon invaded Lebanon; he destroyed the PLO infrastructure and replaced it with a Shi'ite infrastructure whose aim is to turn

Lebanon into a Shi'ite country. Tell Peres that I want to meet him but I have domestic problems which prevent me from doing so if the Taba dispute remains unsolved, even though it is very important for me to talk with him on the possibilities of advancing the peace process. Tell him that we have secret information concerning an agreement between Syria and Iran according to which Iran will send a million Shi'ites to Lebanon and Syria will receive large sums of money. We will all suffer. We must, therefore, push towards a solution of the Palestinian problem. Peres must believe me that the PLO will do as it is told.'

I responded: 'Mr President, the ideas you have expressed here serve to stress how important it is that you voice them directly to Peres and not through envoys. Talk and consult, and I am sure each will contribute to the thinking of the other. Peres is doing all he can to maintain an open-door policy. The problem is that every time he makes a declaration in favour of the peace process and of an open-door policy, appalling terrorist acts are perpetrated. This creates a difficult atmosphere in Israel and internal problems for Peres, which are as difficult to deal with as yours. You both remind me of air pilots who must reach their objectives by penetrating an air-space riddled with ground-to-air missiles.'

The President said: 'Peres must believe that the moment the US recognizes the PLO after they, for their part, recognize Israel in accordance with 242 and 338 and declare a halt to terrorist operations, they will come under the American umbrella. They will then be influenced by the US and not by the Soviet Union. Syria will not participate in an international conference. Assad is crazy. He gets under your feet and has no vision. They will not be present at the conference and direct talks will take place between you and the Jordanian–Palestinian delegation which will include representatives acceptable to the PLO. I don't know what is happening with the Americans. Why aren't they taking any initiative?'

I resumed: 'Allow me now to present the principles involved in each of the possibilities open to us for reaching a solution to the Taba dispute. I will then meet afterwards with Osama el-Baz and go into greater detail. It would be advantageous if I could return tomorrow with an answer.'

On this, the President pointed out that Abdul Meguid, the Foreign Minister, was coming back the following week, and he would like first to consult with him. He added: 'I have difficult domestic problems because you did not withdraw from Sinai to the British Mandatory border as was stipulated in the Peace Treaty. You have been arguing over Taba and the opposition accuses me of being willing to surrender Egyptian soil.'

I answered: 'Those of us who took part in the Peace Treaty negotiations believe that Israel has the right to examine where the border markers were originally located when the border between Egypt and the Ottoman Empire was first delineated in 1906. We have the right to come and check that the border between Mandatory Palestine and Egypt, which was designated by the Peace Treaty to be the Israeli–Egyptian border, has not been changed over the years by adjusting the border markers.

'You, Mr President, and Mr Peres both have domestic problems; but you do have one common belief, and that is the absolute necessity of removing the obstacles on the path to peace. I will now go into detail regarding the possibilities open to us regarding Taba. I came here with a mandate to conclude an agreement on the basic principles of a "compromis". Peres will convene the Cabinet and, on the basis of the agreed principles, a decision will be taken one way or another regarding arbitration. However, last night I could not sleep and I decided, on my own responsibility, to suggest another possibility which, in my opinion, can constitute a viable basis for agreement. This is because I don't believe that the Israeli Cabinet will agree to arbitration. I am quite convinced of your firm belief that there is no need for the Israeli Government to fall for the sake of Taba.

'But, Mr President, I ask you not to be angry and stop listening, because I am about to suggest an alternative possibility which includes an attempt at conciliation.'

The President smiled and said: 'Please continue. I would like to hear what you have to say.'

I went on: 'I suggest that negotiations on the Taba dispute and the thawing of mutual relations continue to be conducted by means of three subcommittees. One will prepare the foundations of an arbitration "compromis". A second will try to reach a compromise which is, in fact, the process of conciliation. The third committee will discuss bilateral relations. In October 1985, a summit conference will be held and, if no compromise solution is reached by then, the summit will decide whether to refer the issue to arbitration based on the foundations of the "compromis" as settled in negotiations.'

The President asked: 'Which option, in your opinion, is favoured by Peres?'

I replied: 'I have no doubt that he favours the second possibility because that would allow him to obtain a Cabinet decision before the summit meeting takes place. If no compromise is reached, the only remaining option would be arbitration.'

The President said: 'Go and meet Osama now in the next room and discuss the two options. I will have an answer for you in a few days after we have discussed the matter with Abdul Meguid and the Deputy Prime Minister.'

Osama el-Baz and I met in the adjacent room; for six hours we not only discussed the two Taba options I had presented, but also exchanged opinions and ideas on the world situation, the situation in the Middle East and the possibilities of renewing the peace process.

Following this meeting, I devoted much thought to Mubarak's personality and politics and gave the following assessment on my return home:

He claims credit for the Hussein–Arafat agreement of February 1985. He will not agree to a peace process which excludes the PLO as long as he believes there is a chance of the PLO accepting Resolution 242. If he definitely feels that there is no chance of that, he is likely to support negotiations without PLO participation but which leave the door open to them to join later, if they accept 242. The reason is that he does not want to remain with a separate Egyptian–Israeli peace treaty in conditions of deadlock, which might lead to deterioration and extremism.

He will give top national priority to finding a solution to Egypt's economic problems.

He prefers to deal with the opposition in a democratic manner and out in the open rather than drive their leaders and activities underground. But he will continue with his supporters to maintain full control of the security forces (the army, the police and internal security) and with their aid he will prevent the opposition executing a coup.

He will base his policy regarding Israel on a broad national consensus. He has conducted matters in this fashion on the Taba negotiations. He has incorporated representatives of the more democratic opposition parties, such as the Wafd, within the consultative council formed to deal with the talks on the issue.

Mubarak needs the support of Jordan, Iraq and the PLO in order to take an initiative on the Palestinian issue. In his opinion their agreement will also lead to agreement on the part of Saudi Arabia. It is better to recruit Saudi support by such indirect means. He assumes that Saudi Arabia is wary of Egypt as a power centre in the Arab world, following Abdul Nasser's attempts to take over the Arabian Peninsula. It is for this reason that Saudi Arabia, contrary to Egyptian hopes, has so far taken no action to assist Egypt's return to a leading position in the Arab world.

Mubarak's relationship with Israel will be influenced by developments within the Arab world and by Israel's policy regarding other Arab nations.

He is a clever man who is proud yet modest, while also being suspicious and closed. He is very cautious of taking any initiative unless he feels the conditions are ripe for success. He works with a small group of trusted persons, especially Osama el-Baz and the Foreign and Defence Ministers.

About a week after my visit to Cairo, the Egyptian Chargé d'Affaires in Israel, Mohammed Bassiouni, brought me the Egyptian response to my proposals. Mubarak accepted the second possibility, i.e. negotiations aimed at preparing the fundamentals for an arbitration 'compromis' while attempting at the same time to reach a compromise solution.

But this conciliation attempt also ran aground. A compromise was not achieved because the Egyptians were unwilling to accept a division of the Taba area between the parties, with the Avia Sonesta Hotel and Rafi Nelson's beach camp in the Israeli part. Israel, on the other hand, refused to accept the Egyptian proposal that the whole of Taba be transferred to Egyptian sovereignty and that suitable agreements be made with Israel as regards entry to it and the administration of the facilities in it. Since no compromise was achieved, the Likud ministers again voiced their opposition to arbitration.

Against this background of renewed deadlock, in December 1985 I met with President Mubarak, Abdul Meguid and Osama el-Baz. I put forward a proposal agreed by the Israeli Cabinet, which the Egyptians approved. The proposal included two principles. One involved an arbitration process including a conciliation phase. The second provided that, whatever the outcome of the arbitration, the two parties would agree in advance on access to the area where the hotel and other facilities were located.

On 12 January 1986, the Israeli Cabinet convened and, after about fourteen hours of discussion, a comprehensive decision was taken. Its main provisions were:

1 The Taba dispute and other disputed points along the international border between Israel and Egypt would be settled through arbitration.

2 The full and complete formulation of the 'compromis' would be agreed. This would include the identity of the arbitrators, the number of arbitrators and the length of time designated to the arbitration process. The 'compromis' would enable each party to make its full claim and present evidence on the various issues in dispute.

3 During the first stage of the arbitration process, in accordance with Article 1 of the 'compromis' (about eight months), the arbitrators would act to bring about a conciliation regarding the Taba issue.

4 Agreements would be reached to take effect in Taba after arbitration was concluded. These agreements would include free access to the area, security arrangements and arrangements regarding existing facilities in Taba.

5 Egypt would return its resident Ambassador to Israel.

6 A timetable would be agreed upon for implementing the agreements signed between Israel and Egypt in the fields of commerce, tourism, transport, civil aviation, culture and political dialogue.

7 Egypt would present Israel with a report on the murder which took place in Ras Burka and the question of compensation to the bereaved families would be discussed. [On 4 October 1985, an Israeli family party was having a picnic on the beach at Ras Burka on the Gulf of Akaba, when an Egyptian soldier wantonly opened fire on them from a nearby outpost, killing three adults and six children and wounding two more children. The soldier was convicted of murder and committed suicide in gaol. The Egyptian

Government undertook to pay compensation to the families, but two years after the tragedy the level of compensation and the method of fixing it were still unresolved.]

8 The return of a resident Ambassador, the signing of the 'compromis' and the process of normalization would take place simultaneously. The commitments regarding the above agreements were one entity and the implementation of each part of these commitments was connected with the implementation of the whole 'package'.

9 The two parties would reaffirm their willingness to remain faithful to the Peace Treaty, and to those parts of the Camp David Accords that were relevant to the relations between them. In particular, they would fulfil the obligations set out in Article III of the Peace Treaty, and would prevent any terrorist presence or activity in one country directed against the other country and its citizens.

10 The parties would work to prevent hostile propaganda against each other, and would allow free access to each other's media representatives.

After the Cabinet decision was taken, the Israeli, Egyptian and American delegations began negotiations which led, in September 1986, to the signing of the Taba 'compromis' and to the summit meeting between President Mubarak and Prime Minister Peres at Alexandria. That meeting eased Israel's relations with Egypt in various ways. Taba had been submitted to the judgment of neutral third parties. Mohammed Bassiouni was appointed as the new Ambassador. The Egyptian press and media became more restrained in tone concerning Israel. There were a few cases of scientific exchanges – for instance, in February 1987, officials from the Egyptian Energy Ministry toured Israeli facilities. What was of special significance was the understanding reached between the two leaders about reviving the dormant peace process.

8

THE PEACE PROCESS REVIVED (1985–7)

After the failure of the autonomy talks that followed the Israeli–Egyptian Peace Treaty of 1979, the peace process failed. What may well have been a missed opportunity to renew it arose in 1982 out of Israel's war in Lebanon, called Operation Peace for Galilee.

With the wiping out of Arafat's mini-state in Southern Lebanon and the PLO expulsion from Beirut, a weakened and disrupted PLO split into two camps. One of them remained loyal to Arafat and consisted mainly of his own organization, Fatah. It indicated that it was prepared to seek a political solution in a Jordanian–Palestinian framework. Arafat and his followers came under Egyptian patronage. The other camp was more extreme. It included the smaller, radical PLO groups and was led by Abu Mussa, one of Arafat's former lieutenants. It continued to uphold the original PLO aim: an armed struggle which would eventually lead to a Palestinian state on the ruins of the State of Israel. This camp was taken under the wing of Syria, and with the help of regular Palestinian units serving in the Syrian army, it drove the rest of Arafat's followers out of Lebanon.

The United States saw this as a propitious moment to take a fresh initiative on the Palestinian problem. On 1 September 1982, the Reagan plan for the West Bank and Gaza was made public. It ruled out both an independent Palestinian state in these territories and their annexation or permanent occupation by Israel. It proposed that in them there should be a Palestinian national entity linked with Jordan in a federative framework. This proposal was in line with the positions of both Egypt and Jordan, and the Egyptian Government set about promoting an agreement between King Hussein and Arafat that would give effect to it.

But the Begin Government rejected the Reagan initiative out of hand. It protested that Washington had acted contrary to the Camp David Accords, which had left the final status of the territories an open question to be settled by negotiations between the interested parties – Israel, Jordan, Egypt and the representatives of the local inhabitants. The basic reason for the rejection was the intention of the Israeli Government to claim sovereignty over these territories when their future came to be decided.

In the view of Defence Minister Sharon, who prepared the ground for Operation Peace for Galilee, crushing the PLO in Lebanon would neutralize its influence in the West Bank and the Gaza Strip and allow a local Arab leadership to emerge which would be amenable to the concept of autonomy within Israel. In that sense, the war aims in Lebanon concerned Israel's hold on the occupied territories as well.

The Labour Alignment opposition in Israel had a more positive reaction to the Reagan initiative and was willing to regard it as a basis for discussion. Had the Labour Alignment been in government at the time, some momentum in the peace process might have been created concerning two related objectives of the Camp David Framework Accord: a settlement of the Palestinian problem and an Israeli–Jordanian peace. There can be no assurance that this would actually have happened. But the Likud Government, pursuing entirely different policy goals, slammed the door on that possibility.

A more definite move to revive the peace process came about when the National Unity Government was set up in Israel in October 1984. As its first Prime Minister, Shimon Peres took steps to renew the peace process between Israel and its neighbours; first and foremost, between Israel, Jordan and the Palestinian people.

Our broad peace strategy contemplated creating a situation in the area which would pave the way for direct Israeli–Arab political negotiations. These would focus on a peace settlement between Israel, Jordan and the Palestinian people, while also leaving the door open for direct negotiations with Syria and Lebanon.

Activities between 1985 and 1987 completely changed the general context for peace talks. The period from 1982 to 1985 had seen a deterioration in Israel's relations with Egypt; Israel's sinking into the mire in Lebanon due to a massive IDF presence there; Israel's intervention in internal Lebanese affairs; and a cooling of Israel's relations with the US and other nations in the free world.

The steps which changed that picture included the withdrawal of the IDF from Lebanon and the end of Israel's involvement in its internal affairs; a change in policy regarding the West Bank and the Gaza Strip, where the establishment of new Jewish settlements was discontinued and efforts made to improve the quality of life of the Palestinian Arab population; the improvement of relations with Egypt after the Taba issue had been submitted to international arbitration; talks with Arab leaders (including Palestinians) and heads of state; and discussions with leaders of free world nations (the US, Canada and Western Europe), in order to

93

gain their backing for the peace initiative and their willingness to supply economic aid to those countries in the area that required it, so that they might be saved from economic collapse and political extremism.

A major factor in Peres' efforts was his positive style of discourse. He constantly emphasized the possibilities rather than the obstacles, and created a hope and belief in the chance of achieving peace.

The peacemaking efforts under Peres' leadership in the 1985–7 period were to a large extent influenced by the comprehensive peace plan I had presented to him a decade earlier, in 1976, when he was Minister of Defence, and to Ezer Weizman, in 1977, when he served in that capacity in the Likud Government. The plan incorporated the ideas that had crystallized during lengthy discussions in the Joint Planning Branch, which Peres had established the previous year with myself as its head.

The two-stage peace plan I recommended at that time called for direct negotiations taking place separately between Israel and each of its Arab neighbours, within the framework of a revived Geneva Conference.

Israel should resist the revival of the Geneva Conference on the conditions demanded by Syria: i.e. a single united Arab delegation, separate representation for the PLO and the right of the two superpowers to intervene in the negotiations. A pan-Arab delegation confronting Israel across the table would be bound to adopt the extremist, uncompromising positions held by Syria and the PLO, and not the position of more moderate Arab states. The Soviet Union would support the extreme Arab positions. In order to retain its influence and interests in the Arab world, the United States would put pressure on Israel to make concessions. Israel would soon find itself isolated and blamed for the failure of the Conference and the breakdown of the peace process.

Nevertheless, if the Conference did take place, Israel could not refuse to attend; in that case, we should insist that plenary sessions be confined to topics of common interest, such as the definition of the essence of peace, limiting the Israeli–Arab arms race, regional economic co-operation and the refugee problem. The Israeli delegation would negotiate separately with the delegation of each Arab state on matters which concerned Israel and that state, such as borders and security arrangements. Regarding the PLO, Israel had successfully resisted its participation in the first session of the Geneva Conference and should continue to do so. The Jordanian delegation could include Palestinian representation.

Whatever form the negotiations took, I could see no prospect for the conclusion of a comprehensive peace treaty at that stage. Egypt and Syria would demand a full return of their territory lost in 1967 and would not settle for less, while Israel would not accept that demand. The Arab states would insist on the whole of the West Bank and the Gaza Strip becoming an independent Arab state, or one that was linked to Jordan, but this proposal was completely unacceptable to Israel. Given these unbridgeable positions, a comprehensive settlement was not a realistic objective.

There was no room for further partial agreements without peace on the lines of those concluded with Egypt and Syria in 1974 and 1975. Even if one or more Arab states would be willing to negotiate another such agreement (which I considered highly unlikely), they were no longer in the Israeli interest. We would be required to yield more territory vital to our security without gaining a comprehensive and stable peace.

The option worth pursuing was a two-stage peace with Egypt with the intermediate stage based on a non-belligerency pact. Egypt was the only Arab country that had the power to conduct separate negotiations with Israel even in the face of opposition from other Arab states. This fact had come to our notice during the negotiations on the 1975 Interim Agreement, which proceeded despite Syrian and Jordanian opposition. If Egypt was willing to consider such an intermediate non-belligerency pact, the intermediate withdrawal line should be the projected border – that is the El Arish–Ras Muhammad line. I did not expect, however, that Egypt would sign such a pact unless it expressly stipulated that the final peace border would be the international frontier of the British Mandatory period. Moreover, as the leading Arab state, Egypt would not sign a separate peace treaty with Israel which did not include general principles acceptable to the rest of the Arab world concerning a solution to the Palestinian Arab problem, and concerning an Israeli peace with its other Arab neighbours. Even then, a separate peace with Egypt was liable to be unstable and involve the risk of renewed war, as long as Israel's other neighbours maintained a state of war with it. The risk could be minimized by including in the peace treaty with Egypt security arrangements which would prevent another surprise attack on Israel. This could be achieved by means of a demilitarized zone and restricted-forces zones in Sinai. An international force would be stationed in the demilitarized zone and supervise the restricted-forces zones. The security arrangements which had already been devised for the existing Interim Agreement in Sinai could be adapted to a peace treaty with Egypt.

Because of Jordan's weakness in the Arab world, it should be assumed that it was unlikely to negotiate separately with Israel, or to deviate from the Arab consensus on the Palestinian issue. Peace negotiations with Jordan could be held in the framework of an international conference either parallel with those with Egypt or after a peace agreement had been signed with Egypt. An immediate agreement with Jordan would be a functional one – either autonomy for the Palestinian Arab inhabitants of the West Bank and the Gaza Strip, or a system of joint Israeli–Jordanian–Palestinian administration. Under this system there could be areas under Jordanian–Palestinian administration and security areas under Israeli administration. In that case, there could be Jewish settlements which would come under the Jordanian–Palestinian administration, and Arab towns or villages under the Israeli administration. Joint Israeli–Jordanian–Palestinian machinery would be set up to deal with matters that required co-ordination for the territories as a whole.

The most feasible framework for relations of peace between Israel on the one hand, and Jordan and the Palestinian people on the other hand, was one of confederation (community). It could be developed in two stages. In the first stage (transition), the confederation would be based on three factors: Israel, Jordan and a joint Israeli–Jordanian–Palestinian system of administration in the West Bank and Gaza. In the second stage – which would be a permanent solution – the confederation would be based on two factors: Israel and a Jordanian–Palestinian federal state, which would include autonomy for the Palestinian Arabs in a substantial part of the West Bank and the Gaza Strip, though not in East Jerusalem.

Jerusalem would remain united under Israeli sovereignty, but the confederation would facilitate finding acceptable solutions to the status of the Moslem holy places and to the civil, cultural and religious status of the Arab community in East Jerusalem.

Lebanon was a weak and fragmented country divided among various ethnic and religious communities. Lebanon could not risk concluding a peace treaty with Israel which was not part of a wider peace with Israel's other neighbours, or at least with Syria.

For reasons of national security, Israel should on no account give up the existing ceasefire lines with Jordan and Syria until the dangers to Israel's security no longer existed. In the 1967 Six Day War, the Arab armies on Israel's eastern front – Syria, Jordan, Iraq and Saudi Arabia – had consisted chiefly of infantry formations. Since then their armies had become based chiefly on tank and mechanized formations, and they now possessed advanced air forces, long-range artillery and missiles. Such far-reaching changes in the striking power of these Arab states had drastically altered the dimensions of time and place concerning Israel's security. Military control of the West Bank and the Golan Heights had become vital to Israel's defence. Moreover, these fronts held no space equivalent to the Sinai Desert, which could serve as a buffer zone between Israel and Egypt. My conclusion, therefore, was that only a comprehensive and stable peace which eliminated the security threats to Israel could justify substantial territorial concessions in these sectors.

By a 'comprehensive and stable peace' more was meant than the signing of peace treaties. The peace should create a new and positive relationship between Israel and its Arab neighbours (including Saudi Arabia) summed up in the word 'normalization'. It should comprise borders open to the free movement of people and goods, economic co-operation, and cultural and scientific ties – in fact, a strategic and economic bloc.

It was in the context of a peace thus defined that Israel's final borders with Syria and Jordan would be settled. These borders would be of an administrative nature rather than defensive in character – borders such as exist in the Western European community.

When Jimmy Carter was elected President in November 1976, I pointed out that he might launch a political initiative in 1977 in order to give renewed impetus to the Israeli–Arab peace process. The aim would be a comprehensive peace based on Security Council Resolution 242, instead of the piecemeal, step-by-step approach of Dr Kissinger's diplomacy in the 1974–5 period. I urged, therefore, that we should prepare ourselves without delay to meet this challenge.

In 1977, after the Likud Government came to power under Menachem Begin, Israel renewed its agreement to a peace process under the auspices of the Geneva Conference. However, Sadat's initiative led to direct negotiations between Israel and Egypt under American auspices, and to the 1979 Peace Treaty. The idea of an international conference as a framework for direct talks was revived in 1985, chiefly as a concession to Jordan.

In the renewed peace efforts (1985–7), the concepts of the 1976 proposals, as I have outlined above, remained basic to Israeli policy – at any rate, as far as Shimon Peres and his party were concerned. That applied in a two-stage peace based on Resolution 242; the nature of a comprehensive and stable peace – the stage at which the final frontiers with Jordan and Syria could be established; a transitional stage of a functional character for the West Bank and the goal of meeting 'the legitimate rights of the Palestinian people' in the context of a Jordanian–Palestinian federal state. (This last objective was shared also by Jordan, Egypt and the United States. They recognized, as we did, that there was no demographic or security logic in dividing the Palestinian Arab population between Israel, Jordan and a separate Palestinian state – a solution which would constitute a risk to the national security of both Israel and Jordan, and a destabilizing factor throughout the region.)

The peace process during this period did not as yet come to grips with the substance of a settlement, but concentrated on the effort to set up an international conference as a framework for direct Israeli–Arab negotiations on the basis of Resolution 242. Our position on the proposed conference was as follows:

- The conference would at the outset open the direct negotiations, which would then proceed in three 'regional' committees: Israel, with a joint Jordanian–Palestinian delegation; Israel–Syria; and Israel–Lebanon (assuming the participation of Syria and Lebanon).

The parties to the direct negotiations could by agreement among themselves request the conference to reconvene in plenary session in order to receive reports on the talks or to deal with general problems that concerned the economic development of the region and its stability.

- The direct negotiations would be without preconditions, and each party would be entitled to present its proposals.
- The conference would include the five permanent members of the United Nations Security Council (US, USSR, Britain, France and China) on condition that they had diplomatic relations with each of the parties directly concerned. (In practice, this applied to Soviet and Chinese relations with Israel.) In the case of the Soviet Union, an additional condition was a change in policy regarding the emigration of Russian Jews.

(The need to include the five permanent members of the Security Council [on the conditions stipulated above] derived from the view that it would be impossible otherwise to attain a comprehensive peace where some of the parties directly involved in the conflict maintained strategic–political ties with the United States, while Syria maintained similar ties with the Soviet Union. It was hoped that the participation of all five permanent members might lead to understandings between them which would mitigate the confrontation between the two superpowers in the Middle East. This confrontation was a major cause of the instability prevailing in the region and helped to foment its recurrent coups and wars.)

- The Arab parties participating in the conference would be required to recognize Israel's right to exist, accept Resolutions 242 and 338, agree to a state of non-belligerency and oppose terrorist acts.
- Jordan and the Palestinian Arab people would be represented at the conference by a joint delegation.

The peace campaign launched by Shimon Peres had to pick its way through a political minefield which could bring it to a standstill at an early stage. Yet today, the possibilities for progress still outweigh the risks involved. The political readiness of the relevant countries (Israel, Egypt, Jordan and the United States) is still capable, in 1988, of overcoming the obstacles to direct talks between an Israeli delegation and a Jordanian–Palestinian delegation, within the framework of an international conference which would remain open to Syrian and Lebanese participation.

The main problems still requiring solution before such peace talks can get under way are as follows:

1 Jordan must agree that an international conference should

constitute a framework for ensuring direct negotiations while not, itself, having the authority to intervene in this process. There is a strong chance that Jordan will show flexibility and agree to a conference on this basis. In that case, a common denominator will have been created between Israel, Jordan, Egypt, the United States, Great Britain and France regarding the powers of the conference. The USSR and China may then decide to take part in the conference in accordance with the format agreed by the parties directly concerned rather than finding themselves excluded from the peace process altogether. In the talks I held with the Soviet and Chinese Ambassadors to the UN in March 1987, I could already sense a certain flexibility regarding the powers to be vested in an international conference.

2 The USSR must agree to renew diplomatic relations with Israel. It may be assumed that China would then also establish such ties with Israel. The USSR would, furthermore, be required to change its policy on Jewish emigration.

3 All parties to the international conference must agree that a Jordanian–Palestinian delegation and not a Jordanian–PLO delegation would represent Jordan and the Palestinian people at negotiations to establish peace with Israel. This problem still constitutes the main barrier to the opening of peace talks and its source lies in the gap in positions between Israel and all the other parties involved in the peace process regarding the status of the PLO. Israel is not prepared at present to hold talks with the PLO. However, the position of the US, Jordan and Egypt is that it is impossible to find a replacement for the PLO as a Palestinian Arab national movement. Thus, they claim that instead of seeking to bypass this organization, one should try to gain its acceptance of a negotiated solution of the Palestinian problem within the framework of a joint Jordanian–Palestinian federation and not on the basis of an independent Palestinian state. This view influenced King Hussein of Jordan to sign, in February 1985, an agreement with Arafat that called for a joint Jordanian–Palestinian federation which would include the West Bank and the Gaza Strip. Hussein made the execution of this agreement conditional on PLO acceptance of Security Council Resolution 242. It was clear to all concerned that Israel would not agree to the establishment of an independent Palestinian Arab state and negotiations on such a solution were viewed as a 'non-starter'.

The US supports Hussein's position. It may, therefore, be inferred that if the PLO were to accept Security Council Resolution 242, recognize Israel and cease all terrorist acts, then, despite Israel's opposition, the US would recognize the organization as a possible partner to peace negotiations.

The PLO is prepared to recognize Resolution 242 only if it is stipulated that the Palestinian people have a right to self-determination. The acceptance of 242 without a right to self-determination is seen by the PLO as blocking the road to a political solution in the form of an independent Palestinian Arab state. There is no doubt that the PLO, which suffered a serious setback due to the division in its ranks caused by the war in Lebanon, is now undergoing a further split between those who are not prepared to give up the idea of an independent state and those who are willing to accept a joint Jordanian–Palestinian solution.

Egypt did its utmost to prevent a split within the PLO and to encourage its participation in negotiations. Its efforts in this direction included attempts to persuade Shimon Peres to accept the principle of the right to Palestinian self-determination or, alternatively, the national rights of the Palestinians within the framework of a federation, as opposed to two separate states. Peres, however, refused to accept these proposals due to his fears that they would be regarded as preparing the ground for an independent Palestinian state.

The subject of Palestinian Arab participation in the peace process was further complicated by the meeting of the PLO's Palestine National Council, which took place in Algeria in April 1987. The gathering marked a reconciliation between Arafat and the leaders of two radical terrorist groups in the PLO which had broken away – Dr George Habash of the 'Democratic Front' and Na'if Hawatmeh of the 'Popular Front'. To regain this degree of unity in PLO ranks, Arafat accepted that his February 1985 agreement with Hussein be formally repudiated; that the principle of independent Palestinian Arab statehood be reaffirmed; and that the PLO be represented at an international conference by a separate delegation having equal status with other delegations.

The USSR supports the PLO as the sole, legitimate representative of the Palestinian people, but it must be assumed that it would accept a PLO decision to be represented at peace talks, at least during the first stage, by a Jordanian–Palestinian delegation and not through direct representation.

I was closely involved in the effort to find common ground between Israel and Egypt on the problem of Palestinian representation at an international conference. This was a major topic at the Summit Meeting between Mubarak and Peres in Alexandria in September 1986 and at the subsequent Mubarak–Peres meeting in Cairo in February 1987.

I began to prepare the Mubarak–Peres Summit in July 1985 after it had already become clear that we were on the verge of completing the arbitration 'compromis' on Taba.

I travelled with Mohammed Bassiouni in his car from Tel Aviv to Alexandria. We passed places I had not seen for years: the Yamit region, El Arish, the coastal road to Kantara, the Suez Canal ferry crossing Ismailia and Cairo. Throughout the journey we were impressed by the marked growth in development and construction: orchards, roads, electricity and water systems. In Cairo we had lunch at Bassiouni's sister-in-law's home and from there we continued to Alexandria by presidential limousine, accompanied by motorcycles along the road which crosses the Nile Delta. We passed through densely populated areas lush with plants and criss-crossed with water-channels. In the town of El-B'ne we stopped at a mosque because Bassiouni wished to pray there. The driver and the other men accompanying us also entered the mosque, while I remained alone in the car parked in the courtyard, the object of attention of a large crowd of curious onlookers who gathered around. I was not at all worried. The atmosphere was calm. The people looked peaceful and friendly, and it was difficult to imagine that all this was happening in a town notorious for religious ferment and clashes with the authorities.

That night we stayed in the Alexandria Sheraton, which is situated on the seashore by the Monteza Palace – one of the palaces of the Egyptian kings. I had already done my homework for the meeting with President Mubarak, which was due to take place the following day in the beautiful French-style Ras-Aton Palace located in the port area.

Late that night I left the hotel to walk along the beach and I found many others doing the same. The lights were dim and darkness covered the sea. The cool, light, Mediterranean breeze was welcome. I recovered from the long, exhausting journey and felt ready for the next day, which, I knew, would determine the fate of the Summit.

The talks with the President were held on the balcony of his office overlooking the sea. We sat in comfortable chairs and talked for two hours. I stressed the necessity of his reaching an agreement with Peres before the rotation agreement in Israel was due to take effect. I also stressed the need for preparatory talks to solve problems still outstanding regarding an international conference. 'We have two main problems to solve,' I said. 'First, the powers to be vested in the international conference; second, Palestinian representation to the conference.' The preparatory talks, therefore, could not include the five permanent members of the Security Council, though they could send observers. Only the parties to the direct negotiations could be included, as well as Egypt, as host.

In addition, the PLO as such would be unable to attend the preparatory talks. The Palestinians would be represented by a Jordanian–Palestinian delegation and the issue of Palestinian representation at the international conference would be settled at the preparatory talks.

At the Summit Meeting in Alexandria, in September 1986, no agreement was reached on setting up the preparatory talks. Hussein, who had met with Mubarak in Alexandria a few days before the Summit, insisted that the preparatory talks also be held within the framework of the international conference – a position Peres found irrational and unacceptable. Furthermore, Osama el-Baz, Mubarak's political adviser, continued to press him not to widen the split in the PLO as long as the peace process had not yet begun. El-Baz maintained that only the Syrians could gain from such a split. Egypt should persuade Israel to accept the PLO as a partner to the political process if the PLO were to accept the principle of 'the right of self-determination within a confederation' or 'national rights within a confederation'. Such a formulation would make it clear that under discussion were the autonomous rights of the Palestinians within a federative framework, which would have one central authority. The PLO should then be included even in the stage of preparatory talks.

However, some important agreements were reached at the Summit regarding the continuation of the peace process. The main ones among them were:

- The composition and power of the international conference.
- The establishment of the conference would take account of the legitimate rights of the Palestinian people.
- Negotiations would be held without preconditions and would be based on Security Council Resolutions 242 and 338.

At the very end of the Summit Conference, an opportunity arose which was not fully exploited due to lack of time. As a basis for securing Palestinian representation, Mubarak proposed to Peres the objective of a 'confederation based on the agreement between Jordan and the Palestinians'. It was clear that what was intended was the Hussein–Arafat agreement of February 1985. Mubarak said: 'I will suggest that formulation to Arafat. If he accepts, then he will take part in the negotiations; if not, we'll start negotiations without the PLO.'

Peres opposed Mubarak's formula because it could be interpreted in Israel as acceptance of a formula by which the PLO could demand the establishment of an independent Palestinian state. To dispose of this possibility, Hussein publicly declared that his agreement with Arafat would be frozen as long as the PLO did not recognize Resolution 242, agree to negotiations through a joint delegation with Jordan and did not accept the objective of a confederation having a single central authority, as opposed to a confederation between two states – Jordan and Palestine.

Peres suggested the following formula to Mubarak: 'A confederation based on *an* agreement between Jordan and the Palestinians' and not '*the* agreement'. This was because the peace negotiations had to be based on an agreement acceptable to Israel; and, furthermore, Hussein was not prepared to implement the February 1985 agreement with Arafat due to the interpretation given to it by the PLO.

If we could have prolonged the Summit by a few hours, it may have been possible to find a mutually acceptable formula. But it was a Friday and, therefore, a short working day, as we had to return to Israel before the onset of the Sabbath. A good chance of bringing about an historical turning-point had been lost.

In January 1987, after 'rotation', I went to Egypt to prepare for a meeting between Mubarak and Peres (now Vice-Premier and Foreign Minister) which was due to take place in Cairo in February. This meeting would symbolize the continuation of the peace process and lead to the additional understandings required to open peace negotiations.

I had a very long conversation with Osama el-Baz. I reminded him of my suggestion at the Ras-Aton Palace in July 1986 regarding preparatory talks prior to the international conference. The idea of preparatory talks had been dropped because of Hussein's insistence that they take place in the framework of the international conference and because of el-Baz's insistence that the PLO also participate in preparatory talks. I told el-Baz: 'We have two options. There is no third. One option is to get the peace talks going during 1987. For that to be possible, you must give Hussein the green light to start talks with Israel through a Jordanian–Palestinian delegation, the Palestinian component of which will be determined together with Israel and Jordan. The other option is deadlock. I don't believe that the PLO, in its present situation, will give up the idea of an independent state, and of participation in an international conference as an independent organization. If the situation reaches deadlock in 1987, I feel that the chance of renewing the peace process will have been lost for many years to come. If so, who knows what may happen during those years against a background of stalemate which could serve as fertile ground for all the extremist elements in the region. If the PLO does not accept 242, and does not cease terrorist activities, it is unthinkable that you should continue to help them bring the peace process to a halt. If the talks start without PLO participation, the PLO will have the chance during the talks to examine their progress and decide whether they do want to change their policy. Continuation of their existing policy would isolate them from the political process and, as far as Israel is concerned, make them a target for war to the bitter end.'

The meeting between Peres and Mubarak at the end of February 1987 led to further understandings on solving outstanding problems. These understandings included:

- An Egyptian agreement that the Jordanian–Palestinian delegation be based on Palestinian representation acceptable to Jordan and Israel (in accordance with criteria already agreed upon with Jordan).
- An agreement that contacts with all the relevant parties be maintained with the object of starting peace talks during 1987.

Efforts to remove remaining obstacles have continued in this spirit since then. But the idea of an international peace conference has been vehemently and publicly opposed by the Likud, partner in the National Unity Government, and in particular by Prime Minister Shamir. In May 1987, Peres reported to the ten-member Inner Cabinet on his efforts and proposal regarding an international conference. The Cabinet was unable to take a vote for or against the Peres policy, since it was evenly balanced (five Labour, five Likud). Moreover, the Likud was able to block the Labour Party's attempt to muster a majority in the Knesset for early Knesset elections, in which the issue could be submitted directly to the Israeli public. The fateful question which the Government and the people of Israel have to answer is whether to renew the peace process or to continue in a state of deadlock, which will encourage extremist trends in the region and may produce a slide back towards war.

PART TWO
ISRAEL'S WAR
IN LEBANON

9

TROUBLE IN THE NORTH

Israel was sucked into the Lebanese morass by the need to defend its northern border areas against PLO terrorism. Our involvement in that unhappy country culminated in Operation Peace for Galilee (1982–5) – the longest of Israel's wars with its Arab neighbours and the most controversial. In the years before and during this war, my work projected me into the policy-planning process, and then into the protracted negotiations with the Christian Lebanese and the Americans for a treaty which proved stillborn. It was a frustrating experience.

After World War I, when France was given a League of Nations Mandate over the Syrian area, it was instrumental in separating Lebanon from Syria. The aim was to create an independent republic in which the Christians (mostly of the Maronite sect) were the dominant majority. The President of Lebanon has always been a Maronite Christian, and in the Parliament the majority of seats are reserved by the constitution for Christians.

In the course of time, the Moslems came to outnumber the Christians and to challenge Christian hegemony over the country. One basic difference is that the Christians are Western-oriented while the Moslems seek closer integration into the Arab world. That was apparent in the crisis of 1958, when a rebellion of pro-Nasserite Moslem elements was suppressed only with the help of American marines landing on the Beirut beach.

The Lebanese Moslems are divided into three distinct communities: Sunni Moslem, Shi'ite Moslem and Druze. The Sunnis belong to the mainstream of Islam and constitute a Moslem establishment in Lebanon. The Prime Ministers of the mixed Christian–Moslem Cabinets have always been Sunni Moslems. The Shi'ites adhere to a dissident branch and are the largest single community in the country. They form the poorer urban working class and rural peasantry, and have in the past had little political influence. In recent years, though, they have begun to organize and assert themselves. The more extreme Shi'ite groups have come under the sway of the Khomeini regime in Iran, the only Moslem country where the Shi'ites are in power. Shi'ite attitudes have been important to Israel, since the great majority of the local inhabitants in Southern Lebanon are Shi'ites.

The Druze are a telling factor in Lebanese affairs, although they constitute less than ten per cent of the population. They are a mountain people with a fighting tradition and a mystic creed of their own, an offshoot of Islam. Since the nineteenth century, there has been recurrent trouble between them and the Maronite Christians over control of the strategic Shouf Mountain region in Central Lebanon, which both communities regard as their ancestral heartland.

After the defeat of the Arab states in the 1967 Six Day War, the PLO launched its own 'armed struggle' against Israel. That struggle never progressed from terrorism to real guerrilla warfare, as it was supposed to do according to Maoist doctrine. Some of the terrorist raids from Lebanon had provoked reprisal attacks by the IDF. But the main PLO concentration was in Jordan, where several thousand Palestinian terrorists were supported with funds and arms by Egypt, Syria, Iraq and Saudi Arabia. They became independent of Jordanian authority and an increasing threat to the Hashemite regime. The showdown came in 1970–71. In a virtual civil war, King Hussein's army destroyed the PLO's political and military infrastructure in Jordan, and expelled its leadership and fighting men. Crushed in Jordan, the PLO moved its major base of operation into Lebanon. Here the PLO took advantage of the internal strife in the country and the weakness of its central government to develop a 'state within a state' over most of Southern Lebanon, with its headquarters in West Beirut.

After the 1973 Yom Kippur War, with Egyptian and Syrian fronts established, the PLO presence in Lebanon became Israel's most active security problem. It also became the centre of international terrorism, providing training bases, arms, forged documents and asylum for other terrorist groups all over the free world – West Germany, Italy, France, Holland, Spain, Northern Ireland, Greece, Turkey, Japan, Sri Lanka, Argentina, Chile, Eritrea and Southern Africa. (To give one instance, Thomas MacMahon, who was convicted for the assassination of Earl Mountbatten in 1979, had been trained in a Popular Front camp in Lebanon.) Lavish bribes enabled PLO members, visitors, weapons, explosives and supplies to be carried by Arab airlines and pass freely through Beirut's airport and post. Discreet contact was maintained with the Soviet Embassy in West Beirut, and Arafat was made welcome in Moscow, since it was and remains Soviet policy to encourage terrorism as a destabilizing factor in the West. All these facts about the role of the PLO were borne out by the mass of files captured in Lebanon by the Israeli army during Operation Peace for Galilee.

In 1975, full civil war erupted in Lebanon – an outright and bloody arms struggle between the Christian and Moslem camps for control of the country. The Christians were organized into the Free Lebanon Front, whose main military arm was the Phalange, a militia founded by Pierre Gemayel with his son Bashir as its commander. The forces of the Moslem–Druze camp called themselves the Lebanese Rescue Front, which was led by the left-wing Druze leader Kamal Jumblatt. The PLO entered into an alliance with this camp.

In the early stage of the civil war, the Christians found themselves in a desperate situation due to the superiority in men and weapons of their opponents. President Elias Sarkis turned to Syria for help. It was like inviting into one's house a neighbour who wanted to take it over.

Syria has never recognized the independence of Lebanon or abandoned the hope of swallowing it up as part of a Greater Syria. The civil war gave Syria an opening to enter Lebanon with its armed forces and gain control of the country in two ways: by direct military occupation of strategic areas, and by holding the balance between the contending Lebanese factions. The Syrian army in Lebanon was given added legitimacy by Arab League approval of its peace-keeping role, as a so-called Arab deterrent force. Its first act of 'deterrence' was to stop the Moslem–Druze–PLO coalition from overwhelming the Christian militias. When Kamal Jumblatt tried to organize resistance to the Syrians, they had him murdered. He was succeeded by his son Walid.

When the Christians were able to go on to the offensive against Druze areas, Syrian support swung the other way, in accordance with its policy of divide and rule.

Syria was unable to annex Lebanon outright because its major communities – Christians, Sunni Moslems, Shi'ite Moslems and Druze – all preferred a whole and sovereign Lebanon to a country that was partitioned between them, or one that would be incorporated in a Greater Syria. The struggle among the Lebanese factions was over the nature of the regime and their individual share in the institutions of the state. Moreover, there was no likelihood that the Arab League would acquiesce in the annexation of one of its member states; and Syria needed Arab League endorsement for its presence in Lebanon.

In March 1976, the Phalange sent a secret emissary to request aid from the Israeli Government, on the grounds that the Syrians and the PLO were their common enemies. By this time the developments in Lebanon obliged the Government of Yitzhak Rabin to clarify its own policies on three related subjects: concerted measures against PLO terrorism, the Syrian military presence in Lebanon and aid to the Lebanese Christians.

With my Planning Branch in the General Staff, I was called upon to prepare a set of recommendations on these subjects for Defence Minister

Peres. They were debated in the Cabinet and the General Staff, and the policy guidelines in each of the three areas were adopted by the Government.

The anti-terrorist measures included security arrangements in border towns and villages, protection of road transport and the prevention of infiltration across the frontier by electric fences, patrols and outposts. Defensive measures covered reprisal actions by land, air and naval forces, artillery bombardment of terrorist bases and ambushes across the border. In addition, there was full logistic support for a Lebanese force organized and commanded by Major Sa'ad Haddad, which controlled the strip of Lebanese territory adjacent to the Israeli border. This force had come into existence to keep out the PLO terrorists who were a threat to the local inhabitants. It was composed mainly of Christians, but also had a number of Shi'ite Moslem recruits. This Haddad-controlled strip became known simply as the 'Christian enclave' and gave a measure of defensive depth to Israel's border control.

The Lebanese Government and the army command wrote Major Haddad off as a renegade officer working for the Israelis. What we Israelis saw was a stocky, red-faced man who lived austerely and acted not out of personal ambition but out of patriotism. His home was in the village of Marjayoun in Southern Lebanon. The local population from whom his men were drawn (about 2,000) had lived under a brutal and rapacious PLO domination for years and were prepared to fight in order to keep the Palestinian terrorists away from their area. This they could not do without Israel's help. Our relationship with Haddad's militia thus derived from a common purpose. His force had the inestimable value of having an intimate knowledge of the population and the terrain.

Gates were opened at several points along the border so that the nearby Lebanese inhabitants could cross into Israel for employment, trade and medical attention. This policy was dubbed by Peres 'The Good Fence'. Israel also provided the enclave with water after it had been cut off from the north.

The policy determined by the Israeli Government concerning Syrian military intervention in Lebanon was based on the concept of a 'red line', which marked the limits for Syria's deployment of its forces and weapons systems that Israel was prepared to tolerate. The 'red line' was transmitted to Damascus through the good offices of the United States and with its support. This was a period when the United States believed that Syria was fulfilling a positive function in Lebanon by maintaining some stability through its Arab deterrent force. The 'red line' policies, which formed a tacit understanding between Israel and Syria, contained three elements: no Syrian army deployment south of a line running between twenty-five and thirty kilometres north of the Israel–Lebanon border; no stationing of Syrian surface-to-air missiles inside Lebanon; and no Syrian combat planes entering Lebanese air-space. One consequence of this understanding was that the Syrians made no attempt to interfere with Israeli attacks on PLO terrorist bases in Southern Lebanon.

When this policy was being discussed by the IDF General Staff, differences of opinion emerged about the implications for Israel of Syria's intervention in Lebanon. These differences were also reflected in the Cabinet discussions. Several generals, who had at some time commanded the northern front and been responsible for Israel's defence against possible Syrian attacks, opposed Israel's acquiescence in a Syrian military presence in Lebanon on the grounds that it would create an additional front for a potential assault on Israel, and would provide a Syrian–Soviet protective umbrella for the consolidation of a Palestinian terrorist state in Lebanon.

Another school of thought, which became the basis for the policy adopted by the Government, argued that the Syrian forces in Lebanon were not a threat to Israel's national security as long as they were not near Israel's border and were not protected by missiles and planes. Some believed that splitting up the Syrian army between the Golan Heights and Lebanon actually lessened the danger to Israel.

As for the military aid requested by the Phalange, the Government's decision was that such help should be given only to enable the Christians to defend themselves; on no account was Israel to be directly involved in Lebanon's internal problems. Help would be provided primarily for humanitarian reasons, to prevent the Christians from being massacred. Nonetheless, the policy took account of the fact that the Christians were also fighting the PLO. There was the further hope that the Christian leaders might one day be in a position to direct Lebanese policy towards peace with Israel. There had always been a feeling in Israel that Christian Lebanon and the Jewish state were natural allies: both were adjacent to non-Moslem enclaves facing a Moslem world which threatened their survival.

In 1978, there was an increase in terrorist attacks on civilian targets inside Israel and against Jews in other countries. The worst incident took place on 11 March, when a seaborne PLO terrorist group from Lebanon landed on Israel's coast at Kibbutz Ma'agan Michael. They hijacked a bus on its way from Haifa to Tel Aviv, intending to enter Tel Aviv and use the passengers as hostages for the release of fellow terrorists held in Israeli prisons, and for their own safe getaway. The bus was stopped by security forces at a road-block a few miles from Tel Aviv. In the ensuing battle, nine terrorists were killed and two captured, but not before they had murdered thirty-seven people and wounded eighty-one others.

Three days later, the Israeli army entered Southern Lebanon. It occupied and cleared the area up to the River Litani, some twenty kilometres north of the border (hence the name Operation Litani). The UN Security Council called for the withdrawal of Israeli troops and set up the United Nations Interim Force in Lebanon (UNIFIL). Its mandate was to move into the area evacuated by Israel and help the Lebanese Government assert its authority in that area. In withdrawing to its own side of the border, the IDF ensured that the Christian enclave along the border would remain in the sole control of Major Haddad's Lebanese force without allowing UNIFIL to enter. The local Shi'ite population had welcomed the Israeli troops as liberators from the brutal tyranny of the PLO, and many of them joined Haddad's force. For a number of reasons Israel regarded UNIFIL as incapable of serving as a shield against terrorist attacks. It was a UN peace force set up to observe and report, but with no combat function. Its soldiers, drawn from many countries, were allowed to use their arms only in their own defence. To this day, Israel does not rely on UNIFIL as a security buffer.

Operation Litani failed to give the PLO in Southern Lebanon a serious or lasting blow. During the Israeli advance, most of the PLO terrorists had fled north of the River Litani. They soon established new bases between the Litani and the River Zaharani a little further to the north, in the coastal town of Tyre and along the coastal plain right up to Beirut. Several hundred terrorists also infiltrated into the territory south of the Litani where UNIFIL was deployed and began operating against Israel from there.

From 1979 onwards, the nature of the PLO presence in Lebanon underwent a fundamental change. From a conglomeration of lightly armed terrorist groups, it began to develop into something of a standing army with fixed bases, heavier weapons and an elaborate logistic infrastructure. Its terrorist activities became bolder and more sophisticated, with new devices for sabotage and mine-laying and new methods of infiltration, including unsuccessful attempts to cross the border fences at night with hang-gliders. There were also proposals to send in aircraft filled with explosives on suicide missions. (They never actually tried one.) Hundreds of Soviet field guns and Katyusha rocket launchers enabled the PLO to shell Israel's northern towns and villages. The Government was forced to construct shelters and, at times, families had to spend considerable periods in them. The children slept in them most nights.

The PLO went to great lengths to protect its bases against Israeli attack, especially from the air. Wherever possible its positions were located in densely populated areas, especially in crowded refugee camps, exploiting the known reluctance of the IDF to harm innocent civilians. Command posts and arsenals were placed in underground concrete bunkers. Each base was defended by anti-aircraft guns and rockets, including shoulder missiles operated by Libyan units attached to the PLO by Colonel Gaddafi. Soviet T34 tanks were deployed. The area under PLO control was divided into defensive sectors manned by contingents up to battalion or brigade strength.

The principal sources of arms for the PLO were Syria, Iraq, Libya, the Soviet Union and other Warsaw Pact countries, China and Cuba. Payment for this equipment and the maintenance of the PLO forces came largely from Saudi Arabia. Facilities for officer and NCO training and technical courses from specialists were made available in Eastern Europe and China.

From 1979 to 1981, there was an escalating cycle of violence. Acts of terror were followed by Israeli attacks against PLO bases: the air force was mainly used, but Israeli naval vessels also shelled along the Lebanese coast. The PLO would retaliate by opening up with its artillery and Katyushas against Israel's border area. The worst sufferer was the town of Kiryat Shmoneh in the north-eastern tip of the country.

The Syrian forces in Lebanon had remained on the sidelines during Operation Litani, which did not encroach on Syrian-occupied areas. But as Israeli planes attacked PLO concentrations located in or near these areas, the Syrian air force started to react. In July 1979, an attempt by Syrian aircraft to intercept Israeli planes resulted in five of the Syrian planes being shot down without an Israeli loss. In September, there was another brief air battle in which another four Syrian planes were shot down.

The leaders of the Christian Free Lebanon Front were disappointed that Operation Litani had not led to a military showdown between the IDF and the Syrian army in Lebanon. They had little interest in Israel's security problem in the southern part of the country. Their main concern was to restore Christian domination of Lebanon, but for that they needed control of Beirut and of Central and Northern Lebanon. The main obstacle to this ambition was Syria, whom they wanted removed by Israeli military power. When the IDF withdrew again after Operation Litani, the Christian militias tried on their own to expand the areas under their control. This led to clashes between them and the Syrian army, which were particularly serious during the period from July to October 1978. The Syrians pounded the Christian quarter in East Beirut with heavy artillery and captured several Christian strongholds further to the north.

In June 1978, the Christian Front had split, because of the bitter political and personal rivalry between two prominent Maronite families, the Gemayels and the Frangiehs, each seeking leadership of the Front. Suleiman Frangieh's son Tony and his family were murdered by Bashir Gemayel's Phalangists. Suleiman, the leader of the Christian community in the northern Lebanese mountains, took his militia men out of the

Front and went over to the Syrian side, allowing the Syrian army to take over his region. He had come to the conclusion that the Christian position in Lebanon could best be preserved by co-operation with Syria.

In October 1978, a Security Council resolution called for a halt to the fighting between the Christian militias and the Syrian army in Lebanon. Shortly after, the Lebanese Government, now completely under Syrian influence, dispatched an army battalion to the south in order to take over the area controlled by Major Haddad. The battalion was halted by Haddad's men and returned.

By 1981, Israel was sliding into a more serious involvement in Lebanon. This was to some extent due to changes within the Israeli Government itself. The policy guidelines laid down by the Rabin Government in 1976 were designed to deal with the PLO terrorist problem and to help the Lebanese Christians help themselves, without Israeli interference in the internal affairs of Lebanon and without a military confrontation with Syria. After the Begin Government came to power in 1977, this cautious policy was continued for some time, mainly due to the influence of three former generals – Deputy Premier Yadin, Foreign Minister Dayan and Defence Minister Weizman. But Dayan resigned in 1979, and Weizman in 1980; not long after, Yadin retired from politics and went back to his archaeological work. Until the elections in June 1981, Begin kept the Defence portfolio that Weizman had relinquished. Since Begin knew little about modern warfare, he came to rely on the guidance of two men who had both been outstanding field commanders – Agriculture Minister Sharon and Chief of Staff General Rafael ('Raful') Eitan.

One factor that undermined the policy guidelines on Lebanon was Israel's growing commitment to the Christian militias, and especially to the Phalange. Bashir Gemayel and his aides met with Israeli political leaders and with senior army and security officers. The flow of Israeli military equipment was stepped up. Hundreds of Phalange men came to Israel for additional training and Israeli military advisers were attached to the Phalange. Begin became emotionally involved with the fate of the Lebanese Christians and vowed publicly that Israel would not stand idly by if they were faced with 'genocide'.

The 'red line' policy had been concerned only with giving Israel a free hand in its fight against PLO terrorism, without interference from the Syrian army in Lebanon. But the policy now started moving towards the hazardous notion that Israel was the protector of its Christian Lebanese 'ally'. Warning voices were raised in Israel, notably those of General Yehoshua Saguy, head of Army Intelligence, and Mordechai Zippori, the Deputy Minister of Defence. But they were brushed aside.

Unfortunately, the leaders of the Free Lebanon Front were encouraged to believe that by provoking clashes between the Syrian forces and themselves, they could drag the Israeli army into direct conflict with the Syrian army. This is precisely what happened at the end of March 1981, bringing Israel and Syria to the brink of war in a 'missile crisis', which was defused only with the help of the United States.

It was not difficult to work out the geographical areas that Syria regarded as vital to its interests in Lebanon and would fight to defend. They were the Beka'a Valley in Eastern Lebanon, running close to the Syria–Lebanon frontier; the Damascus–Beirut highway; and the high ground that gave strategic domination of Beirut and of the port city of Tripoli in the north.

At the end of March 1981, Bashir Gemayel's Phalangists deliberately challenged the Syrian army's hold on these areas. They seized control of Zahle, the regional capital of the Beka'a Valley, and took up positions on the nearby strategic height of Mount Sanin. This put them in a position to command part of the Beka'a Valley and the Damascus–Beirut highway. The Syrians promptly reacted by laying siege to Zahle and shelling it heavily. Gemayel, together with the veteran Christian leader Camille Chamoun, appealed to Israel for help. After a Cabinet debate, Israeli planes were sent to intervene in the Zahle battle and shot down two Syrian helicopters carrying commandos for an attack on Mount Sanin. As a result, the Syrians for the first time deployed batteries of Soviet SA3 and SA6 surface-to-air missiles inside Lebanon, followed by SA2 missiles brought up on the Syrian side of the border. This Syrian missile deployment was considered by the Israeli Government to be a breach of the 'red line' understanding, which would seriously constrain air attacks on PLO positions and reconnaissance flights. Begin obtained Cabinet approval for the air force to go into action immediately in order to destroy the missile bases. The operation was delayed at the last moment by bad weather – a circumstance that may well have averted an all-out Israeli–Syrian war. That evening, Begin received a message from Washington that President Reagan was sending the veteran US diplomat Philip Habib as a Special Ambassador to try and work out a solution between Damascus and Jerusalem. The danger of war receded, but the Syrian missiles remained in Lebanon.

When the Christian militias realized that Israel was not going to save them from attack, they accepted a ceasefire with the Syrians whereby the situation in the Zahle–Mount Sanin area was restored to what it had been before the Phalange moved in. Bashir Gemayel then hurried to Jerusalem, where he met Begin and Yitzhak Shamir, who had succeeded Dayan as Foreign Minister. Gemayel persuaded them that he had been forced to yield to the Syrians this time, but that he wanted his relationship with Israel to remain intact. Begin assured him that it would.

Syria was aware of the ties between Israel and the Free Lebanon Front, whose ambition was to be the controlling power in Lebanon. The Free Lebanon Front, and particularly Bashir Gemayel, were regarded as inimical to Syrian interests. Punitive action was taken against them at the slightest infringement of the arrangements dictated by the Syrians for separating the Christian and Moslem camps in Beirut and elsewhere. Gemayel's policy became ambivalent. He still hoped that Israel would oust the Syrians from Lebanon and help him gain power. But if that failed to happen, he wanted the Syrians to leave the Christians in control of the areas they still held.

After the June 1981 elections, Sharon was finally appointed Minister of Defence, the post he had been seeking for the previous four years. In July, the air force resumed bombing of PLO positions in Lebanon on a more intensive scale than before. The new policy was that the PLO should be subjected to continuous attack at times and places of Israel's choosing, instead of in reprisal for specific acts of terrorism. The climax of this offensive came on 17 July with an air attack on PLO headquarters and command posts in the heart of West Beirut. The large number of civilian casualties produced strong public reactions in Israel and abroad, and a protest from the US Administration.

What came as a shock to Israel was the PLO reaction to these bombings. Israeli towns and villages in the border areas came under artillery and rocket fire lasting on and off for twelve days, without Israeli counter-barrages being able to suppress the sources of the fire and to silence them. Normal life in the border areas was interrupted and some civilian casualties were suffered. Philip Habib and his aide negotiated a ceasefire between Israel and the PLO.

The conviction grew in the Government and General Staff that another invasion of Southern Lebanon was inevitable. Its objective would be to smash the PLO and destroy its installations, at least up to a depth that would put the population in the northern border areas out of the range of its guns and Katyusha rockets. A further consideration was that a crippling blow to the PLO in Lebanon would diminish its influence in the West Bank and Gaza, and thus strengthen Israel's hold on these occupied territories.

At this time there was a significant shift in United States' policy in Lebanon. The Carter Administration had regarded the Syrian army, in the guise of the Arab deterrent force, as a stabilizing factor in the Lebanese chaos. General Alexander Haig, the Secretary of State in the newly elected Reagan Administration, adopted a different policy. In essence, all foreign forces were to leave Lebanon as a condition for bringing about internal reconciliation and political stability. By 'foreign forces' the US meant the Syrians, PLO terrorist groups and the Israeli military presence in the south. The United States put forward a three-stage plan for this purpose.

In the first stage, there would be a separation of forces between the PLO and Israel to consolidate the existing ceasefire between the two secured by Habib. The PLO would withdraw its artillery to a distance of forty kilometres north of the border, while Israel would pull its soldiers out of the enclave controlled by Major Haddad.

During the second stage, there would be free elections for a new Lebanese President. (President Sarkis' term of office was due to end in the summer of 1982.) Syrian and PLO forces would leave Beirut and its environs so as not to impede the elections. A coalition government would then be formed in which the main communities would be represented.

In the third stage, all Syrian and PLO forces would be evacuated from the whole of Lebanon.

The American plan also called for the employment of an expanded UNIFIL to assist the Lebanese Government in establishing its authority over the whole country in co-ordination with the three stages of the plan.

Washington had reason to believe that through Saudi Arabia and other moderate Arab states, it would be possible to persuade the Syrians and the PLO to accept the plan.

What the Americans failed to understand was that their plan did not satisfy Israel's aims in Lebanon. The Begin Government had no interest in a continued ceasefire and a separation of forces with the PLO, as called for in the first stage of the plan. The Government was determined to fight the PLO until it ceased to be a military factor or a political obstacle to Israeli policy in the West Bank and the Gaza Strip. As for the later stages of the plan, Israeli leaders regarded it as wishful thinking that either the Syrian army or the PLO would ever leave Lebanon of their own accord. Sharon and Eitan had opposed the original ceasefire with the PLO secured by Habib and saw no alternative to military action. They were helped in pressing this view by the PLO itself. It interpreted the ceasefire as applying only to actions across the Lebanese border, leaving it free to continue terrorist attacks through Jordanian territory and against targets in Western Europe.

I was convinced that it was both possible and desirable to go on seeking a political rather than a military solution to our own security problem as part of a solution to the general Lebanese problem. Accordingly, I submitted to Sharon a detailed plan based on the American three-stage plan, with modifications which would make it more acceptable to Israel. But such an approach was out of step with the prevailing mood in the Government and with Sharon's views. My proposals were not put forward for consideration by the Government nor shown to the Americans.

In the winter of 1981–2, the atmosphere in Israel was already one of imminent war. There were those who tried to halt this trend, while others sought to strengthen it.

The military picture was complicated by the law adopted by the Knesset on 14 December 1981, on the initiative of the Government, extending Israeli law to the Golan Heights. This was a formula for quasi-annexation, which followed the precedent of East Jerusalem after the Six Day War. An army intelligence report suggested that the Syrians might react with a sudden invasion of the Golan Heights. The Israeli troops in that section were reinforced. At the same time, increased Israeli forces were deployed along the Lebanese border, poised to advance into Southern Lebanon if that decision was taken. In both sectors soldiers shivered in the exceptionally cold and snowy conditions. Tension rose in the towns and settlements near the border. They had been the sufferers in the artillery exchanges between the IDF and the PLO, and all they wanted was that Southern Lebanon be cleared of the terrorists once and for all. As the IDF General Staff prepared plans for an incursion into Lebanon, two distinct trends emerged. The more ambitious one favoured a large-scale invasion aimed at resolving all the problems – Palestinian, Christian and Syrian. Therefore, the entire southern and central parts of Lebanon should be occupied, including Beirut and the Beirut–Damascus highway. The minimalist approach contemplated a limited operation to drive the PLO out of Southern Lebanon up to the River Zaharani or the River Awali. This school was against Israeli entanglement in the complex internal affairs of Lebanon; against a course which might lead to war with the Syrians; and against the complications which would arise from an attempt to oust the PLO from Lebanon altogether.

The plan that emerged at the beginning of 1982 was a compromise between these two trends. Israeli forces would advance in Western Lebanon up to the approaches to Beirut. The main terrorist concentrations and bases were located in this area – in the coastal cities of Tyre, Sidon and Damour and the adjacent refugee camps – and would therefore be destroyed.

Sharon considered the capture of Moslem West Beirut to be an objective for the Christian militias and not for Israel. He was not prepared at that time to let Israeli troops get ensnared in a densely populated urban centre, and thereby provoke an international outcry. For similar reasons, the plan did not include military action in the central and eastern sections of Lebanon beyond the River Zaharani, for Sharon did not wish to engage the Syrians deployed in that area.

According to this plan, the army would withdraw from Lebanon when an international force could ensure that the destroyed PLO bases would not be restored; and when a security zone had been created to a depth of

The author (right) as a Haganah
commander at Gush Etzion, May 1948

The author (centre, facing the camera) with paratroopers during the capture of the Old City of
Jerusalem, June 1967

The author (second from left) enjoying an early morning jog at the Pyramids during the Mena House Conference, Cairo, December 1977

The Israeli–Egyptian military committee, Cairo, January 1978: second left, Israeli Defence Minister Ezer Weizman; third right, Egyptian Minister of War Abd-el Gamasi; the author is first left

The author staying at the Tahra Palace, Cairo, January 1978

With Egyptian General Magdoub, Cairo, January 1978

Camp David, October 1978: President Carter shows Prime Minister Begin around the grounds. Mrs Carter is in the middle; the author is in uniform on the right

Begin and Sadat share a joke. The author is on the right

(Left)   Prime Minister Begin conducts a meeting of the Israeli delegation at Camp David. Back to camera: Foreign Minister Dayan; facing camera, left to right: Defence Minister Weizman, Ambassador Dinitz, the author, Attorney-General Barak and Legal Adviser Rosenne

At the entrance to the Suez
Canal, Port Said, 1981

At Taba, December 1981: the Egyptian Foreign Minister Kamal Hassan Ali points out a feature to
Defence Minister Sharon (behind him). The author is in the centre foreground

Welcoming Egyptian
Foreign Minister Kamal
Hassan Ali on a visit to
Israel, January 1982

The author during his mission to Egyptian President Mubarak, Alexandria, August 1985

The author (right) and Chief of Staff Eitan (left) studying terrain across the Lebanese border before Operation Peace for Galilee

The Israeli, American and Lebanese delegations before the signing of the Israeli–Lebanese Agreement

Defence Minister Sharon, Bashir Gemayel and the author share a meal, Lebanon 1982

Negotiating the Israeli–Lebanese Agreement, 1983: left to right, the author, David Kimche, Lebanese Ambassador Fattal and US Ambassador Morris Draper (back to camera)

The Yom Kippur War, October 1973: across the Suez Canal with Defence Minister Dayan

The author signing the Israeli–Lebanese Agreement, May 1983

The Yom Kippur War: crossing the Suez Canal with General Arik Sharon

At a White House luncheon in honour of Prime Minister Shimon Peres. On the left: Secretary of State Shultz, President Reagan, National Security Adviser Robert MacFarlane, Assistant Secretary Richard Murphy; on the right: Premier Peres (third right) and the author (second right)

forty kilometres from the northern frontier, with special arrangements to safeguard Israel's border areas.

If the Christian militias were prepared to battle on their own for the control of West Beirut, Israel would do what it could to aid them – short of committing its own troops. If the Christians were not ready to do so, Israeli forces would remain at the approaches to West Beirut and exercise military pressure until the PLO terrorist organizations were evacuated from the city.

To find out the measure of co-operation that could be expected from the Christians, Sharon decided to meet with the leaders of the Free Lebanon Front. On 12 January 1982, at nightfall, he flew by helicopter to the Christian coastal resort of Junieh, a few miles north of Beirut. The large party of army officers and security guards that accompanied him included Deputy Chief of Staff Moshe Levy, Yehoshua Saguy and myself.

That night we had talks with Bashir Gemayel and his close associates; we then drove to Christian East Beirut, where we visited the command headquarters of the Free Lebanon Front and cruised along the line separating East Beirut from Moslem West Beirut. In a more comprehensive tour early next morning, we were taken to observation posts overlooking the Moslem quarter of the city; to the Christian-held ridges that dominated Beirut from the east; to the commanding snow-covered height of Mount Sanin to survey the stretch of the Damascus–Beirut highway that traverses the Shouf Mountains; and to the northern part of the area controlled by Gemayel's Christian Phalange up to the road-block they had erected on the coastal highway to Tripoli.

We returned to East Beirut for lunch and discussion with the two veteran Christian leaders, Camille Chamoun and Pierre Gemayel. This took place in the spacious Gemayel home in the affluent suburb of Bekfaya. Despite their ages – Chamoun was over eighty, Gemayel was in his early seventies – they showed no dimming of intellect and gave us their thoughts, and above all their requests, with the utmost clarity. After the preliminary greetings, we sat in the living-room in deep armchairs, with side-tables bearing varied sweatmeats and drinks brought by Bashir's attractive wife. In this relaxed atmosphere we started our four-hour talks, which went on through a luncheon of the finest delicacies Franco–Lebanese cooking has to offer.

Israel's proposed action, they told us, presented them for the first and perhaps the last time with the historic opportunity of determining the fate of Lebanon. They were, therefore, most anxious to hear from Sharon how far the Israeli army would advance. Would it again go only as far as some line in Southern Lebanon with the sole aim of clearing that area of PLO bases? Or would the Israeli force this time, as they hoped, advance further north, link up with the Christian forces in the Junieh–East Beirut sector and liberate West Beirut, the Shouf Mountains and the Beka'a Valley?

Bashir Gemayel had already spoken of this to Sharon during the morning tour. He had said that if Israel intended to move beyond Southern Lebanon, he would be able to use his force to liberate those Christian areas that were under Syrian control in the north, between Beirut and Tripoli. However, if the capture of West Beirut was not included in the Israeli plan, his men would be unable on their own to clear it of the leftist Moslem–Druze Front, the PLO and the Syrians, who together numbered some 10,000 men. If he tried, it could be assumed that Syrian units from the Tripoli area would attack his Christian forces in the north, and Syrian troops in the Beka'a Valley would do the same to his forces in the east, with the object of putting an end to independent Christian-held territory. It was essential, he said, to reserve the main part of his military strength in order to prevent this. Some of his units in the Christian villages in the Shouf Mountains could aid Israeli troops advancing up the winding paths by scouting the area ahead and serving as guides.

Camille Chamoun and Pierre Gemayel asked Sharon to transmit their heartfelt gratitude to Prime Minister Begin for what Israel had done to help the Christians in Lebanon. They would never forget it, and when the fateful moment arrived with the liberation of their country, Israel would find a true friend in the Lebanese nation. However, Israel had to know that it was Syria who prevented Lebanon's existence as an independent sovereign state, who endangered the physical existence of its Christian population and who protected the PLO that carried out terrorist and sabotage operations against Israel from Lebanese soil.

Sharon asked what the Christians would do if West Beirut were liberated. They said they would set up a transitional government, in co-operation with President Sarkis, in which Bashir Gemayel would serve as Minister of Defence. This government would then conduct the struggle to eject the remaining Syrian and PLO forces from the country. With this accomplished, a new President would be elected and a strong and stable government established for the whole of Lebanon. 'But,' said Bashir, 'until Lebanon is completely free of the Syrian and PLO presence, the Israeli army must remain in Lebanon to defend us.'

In his reply, Sharon made it absolutely clear to his hosts that if and when Israel were to take action in Lebanon, its objective would be solely to destroy the terrorist bases in Southern Lebanon and create conditions for the total departure of the PLO from the country. Israeli forces might, therefore, halt at the approaches of Beirut. The Israeli army would not be used to remove the Syrian army from Lebanon, nor to liberate territory in which Syrian units were deployed. There would be battle with the Syrians only if they tried to prevent Israeli forces from pursuing their objective.

Sharon added in no uncertain terms that the Israeli army would not enter West Beirut. This was the capital of Lebanon, and a city of mixed communities. The city constituted a challenge to the Christians to gain the fulfilment of their political ambitions. Israel would help them with air and artillery support; it would be prepared to maintain a reserve force in the Christian zone which could be used in the event of a Syrian attack from the north or east; it would also be prepared to cut the Damascus–Beirut highway to stop Syrian reinforcements from reaching Beirut. In his reconnaissance that morning, said Sharon, he had looked for a suitable spot from which this could be effected. But, he repeated once more, the Israeli army would not enter Beirut and would not fight the Syrians as long as they refrained from attacking Israeli troops and as long as they did not endanger the Christians' very existence.

At the end of our meeting, Sharon told the Christian leaders that if we decided to take military action (which would be any day), its scale would be such as to offer them the historic opportunity – perhaps the last, as they themselves had said – to clear their capital, and after that the whole country, of the murderous occupying forces who were sapping the vitality of their nation. It would be an opportunity to establish a regime which would govern a sovereign, stable and secure Lebanon, and which would live at peace with Israel. We would help them as much as we could, but we could not fight their wars. The representatives of the Israeli General Staff would work together with Bashir's staff and prepare what was necessary to make ours a fruitful co-operation.

Later, in a more intimate talk with Bashir, Sharon told him that if he could not use his forces to clear West Beirut, it was important at least to secure control of the strategic high ground of the suburb of Ba'abda in East Beirut, where the Presidential Palace and the Ministry of Defence were situated. To this Bashir replied: 'What use would be my control of Ba'abda when it is dominated from the east by the heights of Aley, where the Syrians are sitting with tanks and artillery?'

On the following night, we returned to Israel by helicopter, again flying without lights over the sea, beyond the range of shoulder missiles known to be in the possession of the PLO. Sharon had his face glued to the windscreen of the aircraft, picking out from the clusters of lights familiar places along the Lebanese coast – Sidon, Tyre and the estuaries of the Rivers Awali, Zaharani and Litani. At one point, as I stood at his side, he gave voice to some of his thoughts on the matters we had discussed with the Christian leaders. The problem, he said, was indeed complex where PLO bases and Syrian troops were in the same area or linked in some way. This was true of Beirut, if we sought to enter it, and true of the Damascus–Beirut highway, along which Syrian troops were deployed. It would also be the case if we were to neutralize PLO artillery in the

Southern Beka'a Valley held by the Syrians. It would therefore be best, perhaps, to take advance measures that would enable us to prevent the Syrian army from intervening and to defeat them if they did.

I could understand his reflections. He considered it essential that the PLO be driven out of Beirut and, after that, out of all Lebanon. We could then enjoy greater security and peace not only from Lebanon but also in a Greater Israel which included the West Bank, the Gaza Strip and the Golan Heights. The conquest of Beirut required control of that stretch of the Damascus–Beirut highway which ran through the Shouf Mountains, as that would isolate the Syrian troops in the Beirut area and stop reinforcements reaching them from the main body of the Syrian forces in the Beka'a Valley. Gaining control of that section of the highway would mean battling against an expanded Syrian brigade which was dug in along it. Two questions arose: who would do the fighting to wrest West Beirut from the armed forces that held it? And how would we cut the Shouf Mountains section of the Damascus–Beirut highway?

I returned to my seat in the helicopter, but despite fatigue was unable to doze off. The reason was not so much the noise of the rotors but the disturbing thoughts going round in my head. At home I set them down before going to bed. Here are some of the points I noted that night:

- How do the Christians propose to gain control over all Lebanon when they cannot eject the Syrians by military force and Israel is not prepared to do so?
- Israel will not use its army for this purpose. It neither has nor should have such an objective. On no account should it interfere in the internal problems of Lebanon, nor should it be diverted from its main aim, which is to strive for peace with its neighbours – including Syria.
- Syrian forces in Lebanon do not endanger the national security of Israel – as long as Syria does not breach the 'red line' set by the policy of Rabin's Labour Alignment Government and that of Begin's first Likud Government.
- True, Syria's deployment of SA missiles in Lebanon is contrary to the 'red line' and has created a problem that should be solved by political means.
- It is inconceivable that the US will take on the military task of getting the Syrians out of Lebanon, either directly or through an international force. Similarly, no Arab country or Arab bloc will do so.
- This being the case, the evacuation of foreign forces from Lebanon so that it can be an independent country can only be achieved by political means. Such a political solution is possible only if it is

based on agreement by the two major camps that divide Lebanon, the Christians and the Moslem–Druze, to establish a stable coalition government for all of Lebanon. This must not be a government in which one camp dominates the other. It must be remembered that the Lebanese civil war broke out because of the refusal of the Moslem–Druze camp to be reconciled to the hegemony of the Christians, particularly as the Christians no longer constitute the majority of the population, as was the case when the 1943 Constitution was drawn up.

The second step should then be the departure of the PLO terrorist organizations and the Syrian army from Lebanon, following a request by the new government, representing all factions in the country, and also following an Arab League decision that a Syrian deterrent force in Lebanon was no longer required. Syria should be given the necessary guarantees regarding its security concerns in Lebanon as well as its special political and economic ties with Lebanon.

If, as I believe, this is the only way to solve the problem of Lebanon, it follows that Lebanon is unlikely to sign a separate peace treaty with Israel for years to come. Whoever holds out for a Christian Lebanese state must know that it can only exist in part of the country. It was my definite impression from our talks with the Christian leaders that they preferred an undivided country under a Christian–Moslem coalition government (in spite of the concessions required from them to form such a government) to a wholly Christian administration in only part of the country, which would need the protection of the Israeli army from internal and external dangers.

Following the meeting in Beirut, there was feverish activity to put the Israeli army in a state of preparedness for action in Lebanon – completing operational plans, readying the formation that would be engaged and finalizing arrangements for co-ordination with the Christians.

Encouraged by Chief of Staff Eitan, Sharon now made a fundamental change in the original plan of attack. That plan, it will be recalled, provided only for a thrust in the western (coastal) sector, up to the approaches of Beirut. Sharon now decided to widen the geographic scope of the operation to encompass the whole breadth of Lebanon, from the Mediterranean coast to the Syrian border. This more ambitious concept had been germinating in his mind since his visit to Beirut in January and his talks with the Christian leaders.

The revised plan was dubbed Operation Pines. It called for a triple thrust: the advance in the western sector towards Beirut; another in the

123

central sector to get astride the Damascus–Beirut highway in the Shouf Mountains area; and a third in the eastern sector, in the Beka'a Valley, to deter the Syrians from intervening elsewhere, and to put pressure on them to get rid of the PLO groups operating their artillery from within the Syrian lines at the southern edge of the Beka'a Valley.

Operation Pines aroused strong reservations within the General Staff. Its most vocal opponent was the head of the Intelligence Branch, General Saguy. He had no confidence in the Christian Lebanese and warned against relying on co-operation with their militias. He did not believe in the need for Israel to help the Christians gain control of Lebanon. Furthermore, the plan would inevitably lead to military conflict with the Syrian forces in Lebanon. If these were brought to the brink of defeat, it could mean an all-out war with Syria, with the Golan Heights as well as Lebanon as the battlefield. Israel should not risk such a war in order to get the Syrian army out of Lebanon. With his superiors pressing for action, Saguy was overruled, but courageously continued to maintain his dissident views.

Operation Pines was not approved by the Israeli Government, even though it was favoured by the Prime Minister, the Minister of Defence and the Chief of Staff. Most of the ministers withheld their support because they feared it might plunge us into war with Syria and involve us in the complex internal problems of Lebanon.

The General Staff was directed to prepare a more modest plan of action, with the limited objective of destroying the PLO bases in a belt of Southern Lebanon, to put Israel's northern settlements beyond the range of PLO artillery.

Such a plan was prepared, based on the same three-pronged advance as in Operation Pines, but with a sharp curtailment in the depth of the advance. In the western sector, instead of reaching Beirut, the Israeli troops were to go only as far as, and including, the port city of Sidon. In the central sector, instead of advancing to the Damascus–Beirut highway, they were to stop at the River Awali in the Jezzin region. The plan in the eastern sector was left unchanged.

However, even the limited advances prescribed for the more modest plan failed to remove the possibility of battle with the Syrian forces. In the central sector, a Syrian battalion was stationed in the Jezzin region. And with the unchanged advance in the eastern sector, the prospect of a serious clash could not be discounted.

In the latter half of May 1982, Sharon was due to visit the United States on a fund-raising mission and was invited to Washington for talks with Defence Secretary Caspar Weinberger and Secretary of State Haig. The obvious purpose of the invitation was to work on the 'Strong Man' of the Israeli Government and persuade him that the Government should not embark on military action in Lebanon. I accompanied Sharon to the United States and was present at his talks with the American leaders. The meeting with Haig lasted over two hours. Philip Habib also took part.

Sharon told Haig that we were in a serious dilemma over the problem of Lebanon. We could not allow terrorist activity to continue from there and Premier Begin had written to this effect to President Reagan. It was Israel's purpose to rid Lebanon of the PLO's military and political base and to relieve Israel of terrorist attacks. It was not our aim to bring about the restoration of an independent Lebanon or to secure the evacuation of the Syrian forces, though these might be the indirect effects of our action. The question was, would the Syrians understand that ours would be a limited action not directed against them but against the PLO?

Sharon mentioned that he had given Weinberger data on terrorism in Europe. Almost all the terrorist movements in Europe were linked to the PLO and the Soviet Union supported international terrorism. Sharon said that we did not want war, and certainly not with Syria, but there was no other course open to us but to go into Lebanon and clear it of the PLO. He could not say when we would take action, but it could be at any time. He was telling this to Haig because he did not want the US Administration to be taken by surprise.

Haig said that he understood our problem and that there had been long discussions about it with Premier Begin. He could not tell us, as America's ally, not to defend our interests. But we should not lose our sense of proportion. For the Israelis, a single victim of terrorism justified action. But in this case, once the action was launched it became a different ball-game. He hoped, too, that we would be sensitive to the international aspect; it should be recognized that there had been clear provocation.

Haig added that a way had to be found to solve the Lebanese problem and create new conditions in that country. The United States wished to see the Syrians out of Lebanon perhaps more than we did. They also wanted a PLO retreat and the setting up of a strong Lebanese government which was friendly to Israel.

Habib said that he would soon be coming to the Middle East and would discuss with us what could be done to improve the situation. Together, we should try to find a way to do so without military action.

Sharon reacted to Haig's remarks about a sense of proportion and a clear provocation. He asked: 'How many Jews must be killed before these requirements are met? Our dilemma is grave and so far we have acted with great restraint.'

In earlier discussions with Premier Begin, said Haig, he had gathered that if Israel took action it would be a 'substantial move'. He had now gained the impression that what we had in mind was a 'major retaliation'. Would Sharon like to clarify what the scale of the contemplated action would be? Sharon avoided the question. He replied: 'We understand your concern. We have a democratic government and it will decide. I don't think the operation will be on too large a scale. We want to avoid war. We shall try to gain our objective by means as limited as possible but also as effective as possible.'

Haig commented that the Israeli Government had the right to take independent decisions; but it was in our mutual interests to consult with each other and to speak openly with each other. Military action would create difficult political problems. He added that he had been much disturbed by the passage of the Knesset bill extending Israeli law to the Golan Heights. This obstructed the peace process, and the negative reaction to it was only to be expected.

Before the meeting ended, Sharon pointed to two recent developments. First, we had completed our withdrawal from Sinai exactly on time in spite of all the difficulties. And second, since 24 July 1981 (i.e. in the previous ten months) our casualties from terrorist action had been twenty-five killed and 250 injured, and there had been 170 breaches of the ceasefire agreement by the PLO – yet we had shown maximum restraint. We had now reached a situation where we were compelled to react.

Sharon carried away from the meeting the impression that the United States was not really opposed to Israeli military action in Lebanon and reported to the Government accordingly. Apparently, the White House became concerned lest Haig had left such an impression. On 28 May, Begin received a letter from Haig clarifying the American position. It urged the need for 'absolute restraint', expressed the fear that military action would have unforeseeable consequences and stated that Philip Habib was being sent back to the region to deal with the Lebanese problem. But the tone of the letter was too lacking in pressure to avert the war preparations which were already in their final stage.

In my judgment, the assumption that the US had given us the green light for military action was unwarranted. Habib was sent to the region in a last-minute effort to secure the separation of forces between Israel and the PLO. Haig had earlier suggested to Begin that a joint Israeli–American committee be formed to co-ordinate policy in Lebanon. However, Begin would only agree to such a committee if its purpose was limited to co-ordinating Israeli and American aid to the Lebanese Christians. If an Israeli offensive against the PLO could not be avoided, the American concern was to limit its scope as far as possible.

A few days after Sharon's return to Israel from Washington, he left for a brief working visit to one of the East European countries; again I accompanied him. Apart from the formal business sessions, our hosts had laid on a trip into the mountains. We were entertained by performances in the villages given by local folk dancers and singers, and visited the castle of a noted count whom I had always seen presented in films as a vampire but who was regarded as a national hero in that country. It was while we were there that I turned on the small radio I had taken with me so that we could listen to Israeli broadcasts and heard the news, on 3 June 1982, that Israel's Ambassador to London, Shlomo Argov, had been critically wounded in an assassination attempt.

We got a call through to Jerusalem, and Chief of Staff Eitan informed Sharon of the Government's approval to send in the air force to bomb the PLO bases in Lebanon, including those in the Beirut area. As expected, PLO artillery retaliated by shelling Israel's northern settlements. On Saturday 5 June, Sharon was summoned back for an emergency Cabinet meeting, which was to be held that night in the Prime Minister's residence. An air-force plane flew us back to Israel.

On that Saturday night, the Cabinet took a four-point decision:

1   The IDF was to ensure that all the Galilee settlements would be outside the range of fire from the terrorists concentrated with their headquarters and bases in Lebanon.
2   The operation would be called Peace for Galilee.
3   In carrying out this decision, the Syrian army was not to be attacked unless it attacked our forces.
4   The State of Israel continued to aspire to the signing of a peace treaty with an independent Lebanon, with respect for its territorial integrity.

On Sunday 6 June, at 1100 hours, Israeli forces crossed the frontier into Lebanon. Nobody in Israel could imagine at that moment that the IDF would withdraw only three years later after what was meant to be a swift forty-eight-hour operation.

10

OPERATION PEACE FOR GALILEE

As Sharon and Eitan would subsequently stress, the Cabinet decision did not expressly limit the advance of the IDF to a depth of forty kilometres. But the record indicated that that was what the Cabinet understood, with the added proviso that the action was expected to last only a couple of days. In official statements to the Knesset, the public and the press, it was made clear that forty kilometres was the distance which would put the northern border areas out of artillery range. This was also explained by Begin to President Reagan in reply to an urgent message brought to the Prime Minister by the American Ambassador early that Sunday morning. And that was what the US passed on to President Assad in Damascus after the operation had started.

On Tuesday (the third day of the war), Begin told the Knesset that if we reached a line forty kilometres from our northern border, our job would be done. He added: 'We are not interested in a war with Syria. From this rostrum, I call upon President Assad to order the Syrian army not to harm Israeli soldiers, and no harm will befall them in return.' By that Tuesday, our forces had already gone beyond the forty-kilometre line along most of the front.

But the fighting did not stop. What was unfolding on the ground was not the brief limited action which the Cabinet had considered at its Saturday night meeting, but Operation Pines, the far more ambitious plan which was meant not only to solve Israel's immediate security problem but also to change the basic situation in Lebanon. The size of the Israeli forces engaged, and the nature of the three-pronged advance in the western, central and eastern sectors, were suited to the far-reaching objectives that had remained in the minds of Sharon and Eitan and had been discussed with the Christian Lebanese leaders as far back as January.

It is not surprising that the Government, the public and even commanders in the field became confused about the actual aims of the campaign. As it developed, the army was plunged more and more deeply into the Lebanese morass. How did Sharon gain the power to plan, launch and personally direct the war in Lebanon? This was not due just to his tough and forceful personality. Part of the explanation lies in the change that came over Begin at this time, and in the kind of people who could influence him.

During the Likud's first term of office (1977–81), Begin had been the strongest Prime Minister the nation had known since Ben-Gurion. But in the second Likud Government (1981–4), Begin's authority waned. He appeared ill and had spells when he was listless and withdrawn. With Yadin, Dayan and Weizman no longer in the Government, politicians with more extreme views came into key positions and their impact on policy increased. Responsibility for the security of the state had passed into the hands of two men – Defence Minister Sharon and Chief of Staff Eitan – who believed in the use of military power to solve Israel's strategic problems. Government control over these two men was inadequate. They succeeded in getting Begin's support for their concept of the Lebanese war. Their design to set up a new order in Lebanon would turn out to be a costly exercise in self-delusion.

Why, indeed, did Begin follow the lead of Sharon and Eitan? Was it because his state of health had dulled his political instincts and powers of decision? Or was it because of the exaggerated esteem he had for Israel's generals as the heroes of our independence? The hardship and sufferings that the Jewish people had undergone through the centuries, culminating in the Nazi Holocaust, were deeply engraved on Begin's consciousness. He was determined, through the use of armed strength, to safeguard the Jewish state that had arisen out of the ashes of the gas chambers. His military advisers knew this and could play on it to gain his backing.

Already on Sunday, the first day of Operation Peace for Galilee, its campaign objectives were altered in a way that extended it far beyond the forty-kilometre line and set the army on a collision course with the Syrian forces in Lebanon. That day, while Begin was visiting Northern Command Headquarters, Sharon proposed to him that the advance in the central sector should be continued to the Damascus–Beirut highway; it should then turn east to secure the strategic Dahr el-Baida pass through which the highway crosses the Shouf Mountains. By that means, the Syrian units in Beirut and to the east of it would be cut off; we would be able to link up with the Christian militias; and the main Syrian force in the Beka'a Valley would be outflanked and threatened from the rear. A situation would be created in which the Syrian army could be compelled to withdraw from Lebanon.

Begin, it seems, was excited by the prospect of such a bold stroke and the bloodless victory it could produce. He asked Sharon to return to Jerusalem in order to get Cabinet approval for the proposal. In the Cabinet meeting, Sharon claimed that the Syrians had attacked our troops by shelling them. That left us with two options – either a frontal assault on the Syrian army, or the outflanking movement to the Damascus–Beirut highway. The latter course was recommended by the Prime Minister, by Sharon as Minister of Defence and by the General Staff. The Cabinet gave its approval, though with some hesitation.

The following day (Monday), Sharon briefed the army command on the proposed thrust in the central sector and its objectives. He also directed that the air force should be prepared for a strike against the Syrian SA missile batteries in the Beka'a Valley.

On the evening of the next day, Bashir Gemayel was flown in an Israeli helicopter to the Northern Command Headquarters for a meeting with Chief of Staff Eitan, at which I was present. Gemayel was informed of the plan to cut the Damascus–Beirut highway and link up with his forces. Eitan told him that he should be ready to go into action in order to seize control of West Beirut. A government should then be formed which would renew Lebanon's independence and sovereignty.

Gemayel evaded making any commitment to take action. There were other ideas in his mind, which would become apparent as the war developed. He wanted to keep his own forces intact and leave the fighting to the Israeli army. Moreover, he had political ambitions, and the previous November had announced his candidature in the presidential elections due to take place in the summer of 1982. If elected, he would need to come to terms with the Lebanese Moslem leadership and to seek an accommodation with Syria.

The air strike against the missiles took place on Wednesday, after Cabinet approval. For the first time, the Israeli air force employed highly sophisticated electronic devices, which Israeli scientists had been working on secretly for nine years. The operation was a spectacular success. Seventeen out of nineteen missile batteries were destroyed or damaged, and in the battle twenty-nine Syrian fighter planes were shot down. All the Israeli planes returned safely to base. The result was to give Israel control of Lebanese air-space. (This extraordinary feat with its technological implications came as a shock to Syria's Soviet patron and as a welcome surprise to NATO.)

On the other hand, the advance on the ground was running into greater obstacles than had been anticipated. Our forces had to move through difficult terrain along narrow winding roads. Unlike Operation Litani four years earlier, the estimated 6,000 Palestinian armed irregulars in Southern Lebanon put up a stubborn resistance. In the western sector, the Israeli force advancing up the coastal plain took two days to capture Sidon and a week to reach the approaches to Beirut. Groups of Palestinian fighters in the densely populated refugee camps were a particularly awkward problem, and it took bitter fighting to subdue them.

In the central sector, the advance towards the Damascus–Beirut highway reached the Christian mountain town of Jezzin, where it was held up by a Syrian garrison of battalion strength. In the eastern sector, orders were given on Wednesday to attack and roll back the Syrian forces in the Beka'a Valley, but in the three days of fighting that followed, the Israeli troops made little headway.

By now Washington had become alarmed at the turn of events and the risk of an all-out Israeli–Syrian war. On Thursday (the fifth day of the war), Begin received a message from President Reagan urging the Israeli Government to accept an immediate ceasefire with Syria. It was arranged through Habib and came into effect at noon on Friday 11 June.

The day before the ceasefire, Sharon reviewed the situation with the army command and set a number of targets for the next stage.

In the western sector, the push to Beirut would continue. Part of our forces would turn north-east to the hills and halt when it reached the Christian hill suburb of Ba'abda on the eastern edge of the city.

On the assumption that the ceasefire with the Syrians would not hold, the attempt in the central sector to break through to the Damascus–Beirut highway would proceed slowly and carefully to minimize casualties. In the eastern sector, the Syrian forces in the Beka'a Valley were to be pushed back to forty kilometres from Israeli territory. The air force was to destroy the remaining Syrian missiles and the new ones the Syrians had brought up.

By Sunday 13 June, the Israeli advance in the coastal sector had reached the southern outskirts of Beirut and Ba'abda, where contact was made with commanders of the Christian forces. The Israeli siege of the city had begun, giving a completely new dimension to the war.

On the day of the link-up with the Christian forces, I drove with Eitan on a tour of the front-line positions we had reached. We travelled by jeep in the wake of the paratroopers, who had battled their way in bloody hand-to-hand fighting through rugged territory held by the Syrian forces. Scattered along the route were Syrian tanks knocked out by our troops, some still smoking. Dead enemy bodies were still strewn around, some already attracting swarms of flies. Along the side of the road were our own tanks and armoured troop carriers. The sooty faces of their crews wore the exhausted after-battle look. Most of them lay stretched out; some read newspapers that had reached them from Israel, while others stared at the range after range of mountains that surrounded them. They waved and shouted 'Shalom' when they spotted the Chief of Staff, who was a popular hero with the soldiers in the field – a sturdy, veteran paratrooper who had risen from the ranks to the top command of the armed forces.

After several hours of driving along tortuous roads, weaving in and out of convoys, we got back on time to the meeting-point in East Beirut which had been arranged with Bashir Gemayel, only to find that he had not yet arrived. He eventually turned up with his party looking very troubled. As he told me in a talk we had later that night, he now faced the problem of closest, personal concern to him: how to become President and unite Lebanon under his leadership.

Months before, when the political future of the Christians had depended on Israeli military action, Gemayel had made far-reaching promises including the signing of a peace treaty with Israel. Now that Israel had halted at the Damascus–Beirut highway without having taken West Beirut or driven the Syrians from the Beka'a Valley, he started backing away from these commitments. At this meeting, hours after the link-up between the Israeli and Christian forces, he said to Eitan: 'If I am elected President of Lebanon, I will in due course come to Jerusalem and make peace with Israel. But I must do this in my own way and I require time to do so. I beg you to show understanding and patience. I need time to convince the moderate Arab states, particularly Saudi Arabia, that I am doing the right thing. I also have to build an army strong enough to neutralize internal opposition to the course I want to take. I would like the Israeli army to remain in Lebanon until our own army is able to handle internal problems.' He added that he would explain to the United States that it was vital for Lebanon that the Israeli forces should remain for a further period: 'I propose to follow a pro-American policy. I must depend on the United States for massive military and economic aid; and I shall co-ordinate my international policy with the United States.'

This reliance on the American connection represented a key change in his outlook. One of his closest associates put it to me this way: 'You have done fifty per cent of the job. But the other fifty per cent – securing a united Lebanon under Bashir as President – we can achieve only through the United States.'

At this time, Philip Habib was promoting Gemayel's election as President. He explained to the veteran Sunni Moslem leader, Sa'ib Salam, that the political alternatives now facing Lebanon were a broad-based coalition government committed to a united Lebanon under Gemayel as President, or a narrow government under Gemayel that would plunge the country once again into civil war. The inference for us was that Lebanese unity was to be achieved at the expense of Israeli–Lebanese ties.

The Syrian army was still strongly entrenched to the east of Beirut, on the dominating high ground of Aley and the mountain resort of Behamdoun. By 24 June, the Syrian positions had been attacked and taken by Israeli forces, giving them control of twenty kilometres of the highway up to Beirut. Soon after, the ceasefire was renewed.

One problem Begin and Sharon now faced in the conduct of the war was the difficulty of obtaining Cabinet endorsement for further military action. Most of the ministers felt that the Government had been drawn step by step into a major conflict it had not expected or wanted. The Israeli public was becoming agitated over the course of the war and could not understand its direction. Casualties were mounting, and for the first time in Israel's troubled history, soldiers were asking themselves, 'What are we doing here anyway?' Israel was increasingly isolated in world public opinion.

On 12 July, Begin met with Sharon, Eitan and other army commanders for a debate on the Beirut problem. One option was to maintain the siege, sit tight and wait for Philip Habib's efforts to bear fruit. (From the beginning of July, Habib had been striving to negotiate an agreement whereby the PLO and the Syrian troops would be evacuated from West Beirut, Israel would withdraw five kilometres from the city and a transitional Lebanese government would be formed with the consent of the major communities.) At the meeting, Begin expressed a total lack of confidence in Habib who, he said, was being misled and was misleading others. The PLO kept putting forward new conditions and demands, which were simply stratagems for them to remain in Beirut. We had already been waiting before the gates of Beirut for a month. He would give Habib another few days before proposing to the Cabinet that we attack. It would have to be a Cabinet decision.

Begin added in an emotional tone: 'It may be brutal to suffer and inflict casualties, but we shall ourselves be brutalized if the situation continues as it is. This war in Lebanon is the worst we have ever experienced. Nor will our public stand for it. If there is a true ceasefire, with no more of our men killed or wounded, our people can wait a few weeks for Habib. They will understand that we are doing all we can to drive out the terrorists. But if we suffer thirty casualties a day as we suffered yesterday – two killed and twenty-eight wounded – this we cannot tolerate. . . . I believe that our army is not built for such a role. Either one goes into battle or one goes home. Doing nothing but wait and sit around in dug-outs or tanks and being fired on from time to time makes no sense to our troops, and we have to take account of that. It's part of our national character.'

Eitan stressed that we had to step up the military pressure. He wanted concentrated air strikes against selected PLO targets in Beirut – artillery and rockets, armoured vehicles, command posts and fortified positions. There had already been several instances, he maintained, where the terrorists had been on the brink of collapse as a result of our air strikes, and the local residents amongst whom the PLO operated had wanted the Israeli troops to come in and take over. But the various ceasefires had allowed the PLO to recover and reorganize. Eitan also proposed that we move forward in South Beirut and occupy the international airport buildings and the suburbs where the PLO were no longer present. This local advance would increase the pressure and would serve as a springboard for a further drive into Beirut if so decided. He did not think the Shi'ites living in the poor quarters of South Beirut would resist us.

To Begin's question as to the exact purpose of the bombing, Eitan replied that it would sap the enemy's military strength; and it would pave the way for our ground forces to assault and capture West Beirut if the Government took that decision.

In Sharon's opinion such a decision was a hard one, but had to be taken under the circumstances. The indirect and tangled negotiations we had been conducting with the PLO through Habib would get nowhere. He thought that the Cabinet should first take a decision authorizing a softening-up process by air and artillery bombardment, and then decide on the final assault by the ground forces. Begin disagreed. In the existing atmosphere, any action we took would arouse strong protest. It was better to get a single Government decision for one decisive overall job in Beirut.

During the discussion, Begin pointed out two factors that would have to be taken into account. One was the estimated number of our casualties. He knew that there could be no battle without casualties, but were they likely to be light or heavy? 'I will not approve an action where the initial casualty estimate is that scores of our men will be killed. That I cannot do.'

Then there was the factor of casualties to Lebanese civilians among whom the terrorists were based. Some casualties were unavoidable and that should not deter us: 'And let no one moralize to us about this, neither those who dropped the atom bomb nor others. When terrorists operate from the midst of a civilian community, civilians are bound to get hurt.' But here again, he could not countenance an operation that might result in hundreds of civilian casualties. However, we would have to be reconciled to minimal civilian casualties. There was no other way.

Whatever course we followed, said Begin, he would like frank and specific answers on these two factors – what could we expect in the way of casualties among our own troops and among civilians?

Turning to the political aspect, the Prime Minister referred to a 'verbal note' he had received from President Reagan concerning Beirut. The significant sentence in it was a warning that if the Israeli army forced its way into West Beirut, it would have grave consequences for the bilateral relations between the US and Israel. We certainly had to give our most earnest consideration to such a warning from such a source. But, Begin declared, if he reached the conclusion that there was no alternative but to seize West Beirut, he would want to go ahead. What would the US do to us? An arms embargo? We had had one in Kissinger's day and a freeze on arms delivery during Reagan's presidency. An arms embargo was not eternal; it would pass. A suspension of American aid? In a similar situation, Yigal Allon had once reacted by saying '*Am Yisrael chai*' (the people of Israel lives); Begin would always remember Allon for that. While we had to take the American position very seriously, we could not accept orders from anyone. If a confrontation with the United States became unavoidable, our people had to be prepared to live on bread and margarine.

Begin had in mind to call a Cabinet meeting shortly. He would do his best to persuade the Cabinet, with the help of the military arguments that Sharon and Eitan would present. Opinion in the Cabinet would be divided, but he thought he could get a majority for taking action. If not, our planned attack would not take place.

Begin's assessment was correct. Cabinet approval was obtained in principle for an attack on West Beirut. But the decision was taken by a slim majority, with no less than nine ministers opposed to it, including two senior members of Begin's own Herut Party. With the survival of the coalition government at risk, anti-war sentiment rising in the country and strong American pressure, the plan to send the army into West Beirut was no longer politically feasible. Instead, the bombing and shelling was intensified. The water and electricity supplies to West Beirut had already been cut. Despite the efforts to pinpoint PLO concentration and weaponry, the civilian population in Beirut suffered as did Israel's image in the free world.

In the meantime, Philip Habib doggedly pursued what most observers regarded as a 'mission impossible'. He occupied a residence in the Ba'abda suburb of East Beirut. From here he carried on his manifold efforts. He shuttled between Beirut and several Arab states to induce them to receive PLO units which would be evacuated from the city. Through prominent Sunni Moslem Lebanese, principally Prime Minister Shafik el-Wazzan and former Prime Minister Sa'ib Salam, he negotiated with Arafat's henchmen about the terms on the basis of which the PLO would be prepared to leave. He arranged conciliation talks between the leaders of Lebanon's conflicting factions in order to bring about the establishment of a transitional coalition government, which would extricate the country from its state of anarchy. He made arrangements for a multinational force (MNF) of US marines, with French and Italian contingents, to be deployed in Beirut and supervise the evacuation of the PLO and the Syrian troops, overland and by sea. And he sought the agreement and co-operation of the Israeli Government in solving the immediate problem of Beirut as an essential first phase in solving the problem of Lebanon as a whole.

Sharon had several meetings with Habib at the latter's Beirut residence. Accompanying Sharon at these talks were David Kimche, the Director-General of the Foreign Ministry, General Saguy, head of Army Intelligence, a senior representative of the Mossad (Israel's CIA) and myself as National Security Adviser of the Ministry of Defence. Sharon rejected Habib's proposal that the Israeli army withdraw to a distance of five kilometres from Beirut, for what Habib called a 'separation of forces'. Nor did Sharon agree to several other proposals by Habib. He did not believe Habib's assurances that he would free Beirut of the PLO and the Syrians. In Sharon's opinion, Arafat's intention was to concentrate the terrorists in the Palestinian refugee camps in Beirut under the protection of the MNF, and Arafat was manipulating Habib to this end.

On occasion, Israeli artillery would open fire at the time when we were sitting with Habib on the terrace of his house. From that vantage-point, we could hear the explosions and see the flashes of fire and the clouds of smoke and dust that leapt up over West Beirut, while crowds of refugees pressed towards the army road-blocks around the city.

Few believed that Habib would manage to decrease the gaps between Israel and the PLO. The following were the main points of divergence with Habib's mediating proposals:

The Withdrawal Procedure

Israel demanded that the principal PLO organizations be evacuated from Beirut before the MNF was brought into the city. Sharon sought to prevent a situation in which the PLO could remain in Beirut under an MNF umbrella. The PLO demanded that the first step should be the deployment of the MNF to protect the Palestine refugee camps in the Beirut area. Thereafter, the PLO units would be assembled in these camps and evacuated from them under the supervision of the MNF. Habib's compromise proposal called for the evacuation by sea of part of the PLO a few days before the deployment of the MNF. After that, the remainder of the PLO and the Syrian troops in Beirut would be evacuated from Lebanon under MNF supervision.

The Places to Which the PLO Evacuees Were to Be Sent

Israel wanted them sent directly outside the borders of Lebanon. The PLO wanted to be moved to the Syrian-controlled Beka'a Valley, as a transit station before their final dispersion. Habib accepted the Israeli view.

Israeli Withdrawal from the Beirut Area

Habib at first supported the PLO demand that Israeli troops withdraw to a distance of five kilometres from Beirut when the evacuation started, thus ensuring a 'separation of forces'. Israel flatly rejected this and Habib did not press it.

PLO Arms

The PLO wanted to take all their weapons with them. Israel was willing to let them take personal weapons, but their heavy arms were to be destroyed by the MNF. Habib's compromise proposal, which was accepted, was that the PLO should take their small arms but the heavy arms were to be handed over to the Lebanese army.

The Timetable

Israel wanted the evacuation to be completed within fourteen days and for the MNF to leave Beirut immediately thereafter, with the Lebanese army assuming responsibility for security in the city. This was prompted by the idea that after the departure of the MNF, the Israeli army would continue to seal off Beirut and help the Christian militias clear the city of any armed terrorists that still remained as well as of the left-wing Moslem militias who were the enemies of the Christians. Habib decided that the MNF would remain in Beirut for a month – fifteen days to safeguard the evacuation of the PLO and the Syrians, and a further fifteen days to transfer to the Lebanese army responsibility for security in West Beirut.

On 18 August, the final departure plan was simultaneously presented by Habib to the Lebanese Government in Beirut and by US Ambassador Samuel Lewis to Prime Minister Begin in Jerusalem. The plan, which ran to twenty-two articles, stated that it was in accordance with the aim of the Lebanese Government that all foreign forces should be withdrawn from Lebanon as a whole. In his covering letter, Ambassador Lewis maintained that the concerns expressed to Habib by the Prime Minister and other Israeli representatives had been taken into account.

The agreed plan stipulated that the departures were to take place between 21 August and 3 September 1982. Members of the PLO leaving for Syria would go overland, using the Damascus–Beirut highway. Those going to Jordan, Iraq, Algeria, Tunisia, South Yemen and North Yemen would leave Beirut by sea. The MNF would ensure the safety of the PLO evacuees.

The final provision in the plan, Article 22, stated that, by arrangements agreed upon between the Governments of Lebanon and Syria, Syrian units would be withdrawn from Beirut with their equipment during the fifteen-day period provided for the evacuation of the PLO.

The evacuation was carried out according to plan. Two weeks after the final departure of the PLO evacuees and the Syrian troops from Beirut, and after helping the Lebanese army assume responsibility for security, the MNF was disbanded and its contingents returned to their respective countries.

After the departure of the Syrians and the PLO from West Beirut, the attitude towards Israel of its Lebanese Christian 'allies' became more evasive. This was well-illustrated by a talk Sharon had with Pierre Gemayel, who was effusive in his thanks: 'The Lord sent you to us, after he had abandoned us for seven or eight years. The Americans and the Europeans were afraid of getting their fingers burnt, so you had to do what you did. If you had not acted, our Christian community would have disappeared.'

But then he went on: 'I sense that you are not happy with the position we have taken up publicly about you. But you must understand us, for both our sakes. We have to keep the doors open to the Arab world. In the long run, the best bridge between you and the Arab world could be Lebanon, and you need such a bridge; you cannot live all the time with hand on sword. A solution must be found for you to live in peace in the region. But giving public expression to our feelings would at this stage be harmful.'

As the talk proceeded, it became clear that behind Pierre Gemayel's eloquent expressions of appreciation, friendship and common interests, he wanted from Israel the same things that his son Bashir had wanted on the day that Israel had linked up with the Christian militias in Beirut. First, that the Israeli army should remain in Lebanon until a new government under Bashir as President had consolidated its position; then the Israelis should go home. Second, that Israel should not press for a peace treaty and normal relations with Lebanon.

Sharon replied in his own blunt fashion. If the Christians wanted Israel to continue its aid, they should take a clear public stand: 'You had the opportunity two months ago to take action and liberate your capital. This did not happen. It would have been easier and less costly for us if you had, and your own situation would have been better.'

As for the Israeli army staying on to prop up a Christian regime, Sharon said: 'You must recognize that Israel is a democracy. Many of our troops have been fighting here for two months, suffering hardship as well as loss of income. Most of them are reservists, civilians who have left behind their families and their work. There is mounting pressure in Israel for our boys to come home. And, in a few days' time, there will be international pressure. We shall be told: "You wanted to get the PLO out of Beirut. Well, they have gone. Now you leave." To that we shall have no reply, neither to our own public nor to world opinion. I say this after withstanding very heavy pressure on my Government and myself personally. What would help us now is an unequivocal statement by you, saying that you are ready to sign a peace treaty with Israel, and publicly acknowledging the debt you owe Israel, whose sons have fought in this land and have suffered 2,500 casualties. Unless you are willing to make peace with us and to say so explicitly, we shall be unable to remain deployed in the Beirut area.'

At the beginning of September 1982, Bashir Gemayel was elected President of Lebanon. A week later, he had a secret meeting with Begin near the coastal resort of Nahariya in Northern Israel. I was present at the meeting. After warm words of congratulation on Gemayel's election, Begin presented him with the bill: peace.

It was a depressing encounter. Facing each other across a table sat men who for years had nurtured a special relationship between Israel and the Lebanese Christians. It had involved massive Israeli aid running into hundreds of millions of dollars to help organize and equip the Christian forces, including tanks, artillery, transport and light naval vessels for reconnaissance. I could not help recalling secret meetings in the dead of night during the previous seven years, when Gemayel and his aides would be waiting for us at a helicopter pad in Lebanon, drive us to a small deserted bay and ply us with food before getting down to business. Gemayel had a tremendous admiration for the IDF and tried his best to mould his Phalangists on the Israeli pattern. He was a charismatic figure; when he drove through the streets of Christian East Beirut or Junieh, people would greet him with adulation.

He was now President Elect of his country, a goal he had dreamed of. And here he was in Israel, sitting with the Prime Minister who had pledged his Government to safeguard the existence of the Lebanese Christians and had directed Israel's armed forces accordingly. The Prime Minister was now asking Gemayel to settle this obligation with a peace treaty, and Gemayel was turning him down. His priorities now were elsewhere: Christian–Moslem conciliation in Lebanon and ties with the Arab world. Relations with Israel had to be subordinated to these needs. A deeply disappointed Begin had some hard things to say, but they did not alter Gemayel's views of the realities he faced. He did, however, accept that the withdrawal of the Israeli army from Lebanon had to be followed by a system of security and normalization arrangements, falling short of peace. It was agreed that a joint commission would be set up to draft proposals in these areas and submit them to the two leaders.

When we were dispersing after the Nahariya meeting, I was buttonholed by Joseph Abu-Halil, Gemayel's senior aide. He tried to explain why Lebanon could not conclude a peace treaty with us. 'With whom do you wish to sign such a peace treaty, with Bashir or with Lebanon? You must understand that we have a grave problem with the Moslems. They want the President to be President of all Lebanon and not just of the Christians, and they are opposed to a separate peace with Israel. Bashir Gemayel can't be like Major Sa'ad Haddad, controlling a strip of Southern Lebanon through Israel's support. To sign a peace treaty the President must have the backing of his state. . . .'

Shortly after the Nahariya meeting, events took a dramatic turn. On 14 September, before Gemayel's inauguration as President, he was murdered on the instructions of Syrian intelligence. With Begin's approval, Sharon immediately sent the Israeli army into West Beirut to keep order. Two columns of troops advanced into the city from the south and the north, seized key positions and road junctions, and sealed off the Palestinian refugee camps in South Beirut. The Christian Phalange was given the task of clearing out the pockets of PLO terrorists remaining in the camps. For this purpose, the IDF allowed Phalange units to enter the Sabra and Shatilla camps. The Phalange men proceeded to carry out a brutal massacre of the camp inhabitants in revenge for the death of their leader. The number killed was later estimated at seven or eight hundred, including women and children. The atrocities sent a shock-wave throughout the world. In Israel, there was an uproar. A mass protest rally in Tel Aviv was attended by 400,000 people. The Begin Government yielded to public pressure and appointed a State Commission of Enquiry headed by Chief Justice Yitzhak Kahan. (The Commission's report, four months later, would base itself on the stern Judaic tradition of indirect responsibility. One result would be the ousting of Sharon from the post of Minister of Defence.)

11

THE STILLBORN TREATY

With the death of Bashir Gemayel in September 1982, and the election of his brother Amin as the new President, hopes of an Israeli–Lebanese peace evaporated. Amin had not been a party to the Lebanese Christian relationship with Israel over the years and he felt no obligation to Israel. In any case, Amin was as much a prisoner of the facts of life in Lebanon as Bashir had been. Southern Lebanon and Beirut had been cleared of PLO and Syrian forces, but the Syrian army still remained in control of roughly half the country. There were still Palestinian terrorist groups in Syrian-occupied territory. There was the pro-Syrian and anti-Gemayel faction of the Christian community led by ex-President Suleiman Frangieh. There was the leftist Moslem–Druze Front headed by Walid Jumblatt. These elements were all dependent in one degree or another on Syrian patronage; they were opposed to an independent Lebanese regime in the hands of the Gemayel family; and they were against reliance on Israel. The seven-year-old civil war still simmered and could burst out again at any time.

The Israeli Government had to adjust to these facts, and to the war-weariness in Israel which had intensified after the Sabra and Shatilla refugee camps affair. The Government was now more willing than before to co-operate with the United States in removing from Lebanon all the 'foreign forces' (Syrian, PLO and Israeli) and to negotiate with the Lebanese regime conditions for withdrawal that would give Israel the security on its northern border which had been the initial aim of Operation Peace for Galilee.

At the end of September, Sharon initiated General Staff consultations on the terms to be negotiated with Lebanon. The discussions focused on two proposals – one by Deputy Chief of Staff Moshe Levy and the other by myself.

General Levy proposed that the withdrawal security arrangements should be based on the permanent presence of Israeli forces together with those of Major Haddad in a security belt extending to a depth of forty-five kilometres from the border. This made good military sense but raised political problems. Syria would not pull out its forces as long as the Israeli army remained in Southern Lebanon. The result would be a *de facto* division of the country between Israel and Syria. In any case, the Lebanese Government was not likely to accept such an arrangement. The United States would not look kindly upon an Israel that was acting as an obstacle to the basic objective: the departure of all foreign forces and the restoration of a sovereign and stable Lebanon.

My proposal accepted the principle that all foreign forces including our own should be withdrawn from Lebanon. Our withdrawal would be subject to an agreement with Lebanon on security and normalization arrangements. The IDF would not move from its existing position until all remaining PLO terrorist groups had been evacuated from the country. The Lebanese Government would negotiate parallel agreements with Syria and Israel for the simultaneous withdrawal of their forces in designated stages. Israel's withdrawal would be conditional on Syria complying with its own agreement with Lebanon. Only if the PLO and the Syrians failed to withdraw would there be a continued military presence in Southern Lebanon, which the Lebanese Government and the United States would be asked to accept.

After the withdrawal had been completed, the Israeli–Lebanese agreement on security and normalization arrangements would come into effect. The general provisions in the agreement I proposed called for the termination of the state of war and a prohibition of the use of one party's territory for hostile acts against the other.

In Southern Lebanon there would be a security zone to a depth of forty-five to fifty kilometres. The sole military force in this zone would be the Lebanese army, into which Major Haddad's force would be integrated. All other militias in the zone would be disarmed. Pending a peace treaty, the zone would be kept free of artillery and missiles and no foreign armed forces would be introduced into it without Israel's consent.

The provisions in the proposal for normalization of relations called for open borders; a joint committee to work out arrangements for trade, tourism, customs, communications and transport services by land, sea and air; and another joint committee to prepare procedures for negotiating a peace treaty at a later stage.

This plan was submitted to the Cabinet meeting on 10 October. It was unanimously approved and became government policy.

Foreign Minister Shamir had not been present at the Cabinet meeting as he had gone to Washington for talks on political arrangements in Lebanon with Secretary of State George Shultz, who had succeeded Alexander Haig. At the close of the Cabinet meeting, Sharon told me that, with the Prime Minister's consent, I was to fly immediately to

Washington to bring Shamir the approved plan so that he could present it to Shultz.

On arriving at our Washington Embassy the next day, I ran into a chilly reception from our Ambassador, Professor Moshe Arens, and then from Shamir when he returned from the State Department. (Arens, an aeronautical expert, has an urbane and persuasive manner that belies his strong right-wing views.) A frank private talk I had with Shamir cleared the air. In his view, the political handling of the Lebanese problem was the responsibility of the Foreign Minister and not of the Minister of Defence and he resented the fact that Sharon had assumed this authority with the backing of the Prime Minister.

Shamir asked me to meet that afternoon with a group of senior American officials from the State Department, the Pentagon, the National Security Council and the CIA and explain to them Israel's proposals for security arrangements in Lebanon. I spent three hours with this group.

From then on Shamir and I developed good working relations; he would include me in delegations he headed and took me along on his further visits to the United States. He was a hard-liner in Israeli politics and had, in fact, opposed the Camp David Accords and the Peace Treaty with Egypt, asserting that we had yielded too much. But I found him to be an honest person, with an agreeable manner in conversation, and a practical and persistent negotiator.

Before leaving Washington I had a talk with Robert MacFarlane, Deputy to the National Security Adviser. I had got to know him when he was assistant to Secretary of State Haig. Haig and Sharon had kept in touch through MacFarlane and myself on certain sensitive matters. This time we met primarily to discuss possible Israeli–American co-operation in some of the African countries. But inevitably we talked about Lebanon as well. At one stage I felt compelled to say that there was little point in arguing over the question whether we should or should not have launched the campaign. The fact was that the existing deployment of the Israeli army in Lebanon made it possible to achieve political results that had not been possible before. MacFarlane, a taciturn man, listened with close interest. He expressed a definite opinion on one point: that we could not reach an agreement with Lebanon which would keep a permanent Israeli military presence in the security zone.

Philip Habib, who returned to the region in November 1982, took issue with our policy on negotiations with Lebanon. He maintained that they should be confined to withdrawal and security arrangements and not be complicated by the demand for normalization of relations. President Gemayel was unable to sign the normalization agreement, just as he was unable to sign a peace treaty with Israel. If he did, Syria would not withdraw its forces and the Lebanese Moslem leaders would cease to co-operate with the President. Instead of a united and independent Lebanon, the country would remain torn between its factions. Furthermore, the Lebanese could not conduct direct face-to-face negotiations with us. They would have to follow the procedure which led to the departure of the PLO and Syrians from Beirut; that is, Habib's mediation.

President Gemayel found himself in a cleft stick. Habib's views on the nature and scope of the proposed negotiations reflected Gemayel's own wishes. But he was under pressure from the Christian Phalange, which formed the political power base he had inherited from his dead brother, Bashir. The Phalange was anxious to retain its direct association with Israel. The future was uncertain, and the Christian militias might well need Israel's military support once again.

Gemayel's way out of the difficulty was to negotiate with Israel on two levels. There would be official talks, together with the Americans, in order to reach a formal agreement. But before they took place, Gemayel would send a special emissary on a secret mission to Israel. In behind-the-scenes discussions with the Israeli authorities, a document of 'agreed principles' would be worked out. This document would then be given to the delegations to the official talks as a directive. The open negotiations would, therefore, be no more than a formality, which need not take up time and would not attract much publicity.

Accordingly, at the beginning of November, the Lebanese emissary, Sami Maroun, arrived in Israel and began secret talks with David Kimche and myself under Sharon's direction. After a number of night meetings in private homes, we reached agreement with Maroun on the text of the document. It covered three components as a single package – withdrawal of Israeli forces, security arrangements in Southern Lebanon and normalization of relations. The provisions substantially conformed with the proposals approved by the Israeli Government on 10 October with some additions and modifications. On the assumption that the document was binding on the two Governments, Sharon obtained Cabinet approval for it and let it be known in the press that he had achieved a 'breakthrough' by direct dealing with the Lebanese Government without American help. (Sharon had a strong distrust of the Americans and sought to dispense with their mediation as far as possible.)

However, Sami Maroun refused to sign the document. He claimed that, contrary to what had been agreed, its existence and the secret procedures that produced it had been leaked to the press. This had placed his President in a difficult and embarrassing position with the Moslem members of the Lebanese Government. President Gemayel would, he said, honour the 'agreed principles' even unsigned.

I was inclined to think that Gemayel was also influenced by Habib's disapproval of the secret talks which had taken place behind the Americans' backs.

Later in November, we had a tense meeting in Beirut with President Gemayel. He received us without a smile and began to speak in an angry tone. He reviewed the dealings we had had with him since he had first met Sharon and Shamir shortly after his brother's murder. He himself had said that he wanted to continue a relationship of mutual trust; but every so often we said or did things that made him doubt our motives. He then came out with a string of specific grievances, thumping the table with each point. Prime Minister Begin had spoken of him in derogatory terms. Defence Minister Sharon had ridiculed him by telling a Lebanese army group that he, President Gemayel, ruled only over his palace at Ba'abda and nowhere else. We had been critical of him in our contacts with various Christian groups. We were supporting the Druze and even supplying them with arms in their current military offensive to drive the Christians out of the Shouf Mountains. We had leaked to the media our secret contacts with him and his emissary. At each stage, when it seemed that negotiations could begin, we had raised new issues which only showed that we were not really anxious to negotiate. Israel's real intention, he asserted, was to remain permanently in Lebanon and to get rid of him: 'If you really wish to see a divided Lebanon with Israel's continued military presence in part of it, why not say so publicly? I shall then appear before the United Nations and declare that my country is under foreign occupation. Maybe I am powerless, but at least I have my pride and I shall guard that at all costs.'

After this emotional outburst, Gemayel calmed down and put to us several requests: that we halt our direct contact with the various community factions in Lebanon; that we try to stop the 'poison campaign' against him by these factions and the press; that we find a solution to the Christian–Druze strife in the Shouf Mountains and the Aley area; and that we reconsider our demand for three early-warning stations in Southern Lebanon after the withdrawal of all foreign forces from the country. As for our insistence that Major Haddad's force should continue to function within the framework of the Lebanese army, Gemayel urged that this provision in our agreement should be kept secret: 'I fear that Syria will demand a similar arrangement in the Beka'a Valley and have local forces loyal to itself merged with Lebanese army units deployed along the Lebanese–Syrian frontier.'

Gemayel said that the document of 'agreed principles' would be acceptable to him not as a final agreement but as a set of guidelines for his delegation and a basis for discussion in the official talks.

At the end of the conversation, he said that his only real friends were the

Americans and that he would encourage them to guide the negotiations and solve the problem.

In this meeting Gemayel gave us the impression that he was not a natural leader like his brother Bashir had been; that he was still very insecure in the position that had so suddenly been thrust upon him; and that he was extremely sensitive over the Israeli connection which had been part of his brother's legacy.

The start of the formal Israeli–Lebanese negotiations was delayed by disagreement over procedural questions. For obvious reasons, President Gemayel wanted the talks kept as low-key as possible. He rejected out of hand our proposal that they should be at ministerial level and should take place alternately in the two capital cities. What he wanted was that teams of military officers should meet at Rosh Hanikra, the coastal headland on the border. That was where the Mixed Armistice Commission used to meet under the 1949 Israeli–Lebanese Armistice Agreement, which, as far as Israel was concerned, had expired with the 1967 war. The Lebanese Government wished it to appear that the 1983 negotiations with Israel were within the armistice framework.

Once more, it was with the mediation of the United States through Philip Habib that a compromise was worked out. It was agreed that the delegations would be headed by senior civilian officials, while the meetings would be held alternately at the Lebanese village of Halda, close to the Beirut international airport, and at Israel's Galilee town of Kiryat Shmoneh, which had suffered more than any northern settlement from PLO shelling. After a time, the delegations also met at a more accessible place in Israel – the seaside resort town of Natanya, half-way between Tel Aviv and Haifa. David Kimche was appointed to head our delegation with myself in charge of its military committee. Ambassador Antoine Fattale was the Lebanese head. He was a seasoned diplomat who had President Gemayel's confidence. Ambassador Morris Draper, Philip Habib's deputy, headed the American team for the talks.

Draper invited the delegations to meet at his Beirut residence for an informal preliminary meeting before the talks began. Kimche opened the proceedings by declaring: 'We have a common interest in seeing an independent and strong Lebanon. Israel wants no Lebanese territory. We are anxious to leave Lebanon as soon as possible. We wish our two countries to live in peace. But,' he added, 'if Lebanon cannot yet make peace with Israel, let there at least be open relations between us.' Pointing to the example of Egypt, Kimche observed: 'Once you break through the psychological barrier, and say so publicly, there will assuredly be protests; but the Arab states will eventually accept the new situation as a fact.'

Fatalle replied that Lebanon was not Egypt. Egypt could stand up to a boycott by the rest of the Arab world, but the Lebanese economy was dependent on the Arab states. President Gemayel was faced with serious internal and external pressures. 'We Lebanese are a nation of merchants and merchants need peace; but don't rush too fast in this matter. You have the right to demand security and we shall try to ensure that you get it.' As for moving towards normalization, it should be done 'slowly and prudently', otherwise it would run into trouble.

The official talks began on 8 January 1983. Three months had already been taken up in arguments on the procedural aspect. Another five months would be taken up with meetings twice a week (or three times a week in the final stages) at the alternate venues. If the negotiations had begun sooner and been conducted continuously in a single place until agreement was reached, they need have taken no more than two months.

The waste of time would have a crucial impact on the capacity of the parties to carry out the agreement once it had been concluded, for it offered advantages to Syria which that country exploited to the full. During that period, Syria was able to rebuild its armed forces after the blows they had suffered in Lebanon. Syria absorbed the latest sophisticated weapons and equipment provided by the Soviet Union, particularly a Soviet air-defence system based on SA5 missiles manned by Russian crews. Syria also used the time to organize a Rejection Front inside Lebanon in opposition to Gemayel's regime and against any Lebanese agreement with Israel. Most of the PLO terrorist factions still in Lebanon came under Syrian control, and through them – even by fighting those PLO factions that were still faithful to Arafat – Syria aimed to thwart Arafat's intention to seek an agreement with King Hussein on a Jordanian–Palestinian confederation.

The first month of the negotiations was spent in arguments over the wording of the agenda and the order in which the different aspects of the agreement were to appear in it. One concession made by us to the Lebanese was that the word 'normalization' was dropped from the agenda and 'mutual relations' substituted for it.

When we reached the question of security arrangements in Southern Lebanon after the withdrawal, the main issues in dispute concerned the three electronic early-warning stations we wanted and the role of Major Haddad's militia.

The early-warning stations had figured in the proposals approved by the Israeli Government on 10 October 1982, and again in the document of 'agreed principles' worked out with President Gemayel's emissary. Initially, their purpose was only surveillance. During the negotiations, Begin proposed that they be called 'observation points', in the hope that this would make them more acceptable to the Lebanese. But Sharon and the General Staff wanted to give them a wider function. Israeli units would be stationed at them and be able to carry out such operational tasks in the area as patrols, ambushes and the pursuit of terrorists. When the Lebanese delegation became aware of this, they rejected the early-warning stations altogether, for fear that they would be a cover for a continued Israeli military presence. The US delegation supported the Lebanese in this.

The document of 'agreed principles' had also provided that Major Haddad's force would be integrated into the Lebanese army brigade which would be responsible for security in Southern Lebanon. Our military authorities interpreted this provision in a way that would convert Major Haddad's force itself into the Lebanese territorial brigade. The Lebanese refused to accept this and again they were supported by the Americans.

In the third month, negotiations were bogged down. As National Security Adviser and head of the military group in our delegation, I raised proposals at an internal political level that I thought could possibly break the stalemate. At a meeting called for this purpose, I pointed out that there were several major issues on which no progress had been made. I did not believe that we could reach agreement on the basis of our existing positions. 'There would appear to be three possible options,' I said. 'We can stand firm on our present policy; we can be flexible on several points in that policy in order to reach an agreement; or, we can unilaterally withdraw the army to the River Awali, the northern boundary of the proposed security zone, and remain there until circumstances arise that will enable us to achieve an agreement that satisfies Israel's needs.' I advocated the second course and put forward an alternative set of proposals, which I thought might pave the way to an agreement without prejudicing our security:

- A Lebanese army territorial brigade based on Major Haddad's force would be deployed in the southern part of the security zone between the border and the River Zaharani, which runs about twenty-five kilometres north of Metulla. A different Lebanese army brigade would be responsible for security in the northern part of the zone between the Rivers Zaharani and Awali.
- Joint supervision in the security zone under an Israeli–Lebanese committee, which would control joint patrols and operational centres for this purpose.
- Direct contact between the Israeli–Lebanese forces on their respective sides of the border, to co-ordinate action against terrorist groups.
- An agreement on normalization (now called mutual relations) would be concluded and signed before our withdrawal commenced,

and would come into operation when all foreign forces had left
Lebanon.

- Only if we could not reach agreement with the Lebanese on security
arrangements, or if they failed to sign an agreement with us on
mutual relations, would our forces withdraw unilaterally to the
River Awali and remain deployed in Southern Lebanon.

Chief of Staff Eitan advocated an immediate, unilateral and partial
withdrawal. He had become disillusioned with the Lebanese Christians
and felt that we had no further obligation to safeguard them. He argued
that the security of our northern border should be ensured by our own
forces and not rest on dubious undertakings by the Lebanese Government. Anyway, he did not believe that the Syrians or the PLO would leave
Lebanon. The withdrawal he proposed was not just to the River Awali
but further south to the River Zaharani, so as to avoid including in the
area controlled by us the seaport town of Sidon and an unduly large local
population. We should then organize for a lengthy stay on this
withdrawal line. Eitan added that while we should also demand a partial
Syrian withdrawal to the Beka'a Valley, we should not insist on this as a
condition for our own withdrawal.

I questioned the proposal by the Chief of Staff because of its grave
implications. By prematurely giving up control of the Damascus–Beirut
highway, we would be discarding a position of strength in our negotiations with the Lebanese and losing a deterrent capability against the
Syrians. Furthermore, a unilateral Israeli withdrawal was likely to be
followed by chaos and a fresh eruption of the civil war, and would
probably lead to the return of the PLO terrorists to the evacuated area. In
any case, our redeployment along the Awali or the Zaharani would be
interpreted as dividing Lebanon for an indefinite period and would be
strongly opposed not only by Lebanon but also by the United States.
Nothing was definitely decided at this meeting.

Shortly after, in March 1983, Secretary of State Shultz invited the
Foreign Ministers of Israel and Lebanon to Washington for separate talks
with him on the stalled negotiations. Begin called a special meeting of the
Cabinet to decide on the policy directives that Shamir would take with
him for these talks. Before the Cabinet met, Begin had informal
consultations with Shamir and a few other senior ministers including the
new Minister of Defence, Professor Arens. (The Kahan Commission
Report on the Sabra and Shatilla massacre, made public in February, had
sharply criticized Sharon and obliged him to resign as Minister of
Defence. Begin had kept him in the Government as a Minister without
Portfolio and brought Arens back from the Washington Embassy to take
over the Defence post.)

In the informal consultations, the policy favoured was to seek agreement with the Lebanese on the basis of the compromise proposals I had recommended. However, Shamir preferred not to raise the matter at the Cabinet meeting, where it was likely to be opposed by Sharon, Professor Yuval Ne'eman and other right-wing ministers. He decided that in Washington our point of departure would remain that laid down by the Government on 10 October 1982, but at the same time the US Administration would be sounded out on alternative arrangements. If possible, we would bring back for consideration by the Government a proposal that had been worked out with the Americans. Thus, at the Cabinet meeting the policy adopted on 10 October 1982 was simply reaffirmed.

Shamir included me in his delegation to Washington. A few days before we left, I had discussions with Draper, with General Cooley, who represented the Pentagon in the negotiations, and with General Hamdan, who headed the military group in the Lebanese delegation. I found the two Americans generally receptive to my approach, but was unable to budge them on two points: the special status we wanted for Major Haddad's force and our refusal to let UNIFIL be deployed up to our border. On the latter point, they maintained that the PLO would not leave Lebanon unless UNIFIL was able to take the Palestinian refugee camps under its protection.

In Washington we had three days of intensive discussion from 12 to 15 March. There were two plenary sessions presided over by Shultz, and smaller working groups in between. Philip Habib also took part.

In the opening session, Shamir asked me to present and explain our proposals. I started out with some general observations. We attached the utmost importance to the American efforts in Lebanon and shared their objectives. But it would take several years before the Lebanese authorities and armed forces would be able to ensure law, order and security in the country. This was certainly the case regarding the terrorist problem in the south. Lebanon was in for a period of instability, fraught with danger, until a constitution was accepted that would bring about the unity of the nation, a strong and stable central regime and genuine independence.

In these circumstances, the problem that concerned us was how to avoid a security vacuum in Southern Lebanon and prevent the situation there sliding back to what it was before Operation Peace for Galilee. This called for Israeli–Lebanese agreement on special security arrangements for a specified period, until the Lebanese authorities were in a position to assume the responsibility on their own. There was nothing in such arrangements that was incompatible with Lebanon's sovereignty.

The Lebanese said to us that if Israel was given a special status in Southern Lebanon, Syria would demand a similar status in Eastern

Lebanon. That argument was irrelevant. Israel was subjected to terrorist attacks from Lebanese soil; Syria was not. On the contrary, Syria gave protection to some of the PLO organizations based in Syrian-occupied Lebanese territory.

We were told that UNIFIL should fill the vacuum in Southern Lebanon, but UNIFIL was not designed, fit or motivated to combat terrorism nor had it a mandate to do so. Far from giving Israel security, it hampered Israel's own efforts against the terrorist organizations.

As for Major Haddad's force, there were no other Lebanese army units that could replace it and take over the important function it served.

Arrangements for the normalization of relations between the two countries, with open borders, would also have a positive effect on security.

In outlining our specific proposals, I based myself on those that had been approved by the Government on 10 October 1982, while at the same time suggesting areas of flexibility in line with our alternative proposals on certain points.

At the final meeting on 15 March, Shultz summed up the lengthy and detailed discussions we had had. It appeared that a broad range of consensus had emerged, but on a number of specific points, Shultz informed us, our positions were unacceptable to the Lebanese. Shamir requested that the US send us its own proposals for further study and consultation at home.

After our return to Israel, Shamir received a memorandum with the American proposals. We assumed that the document also reflected the Lebanese positions since President Gemayel and his Government had, in effect, left it to the United States to negotiate on their behalf.

The main points of divergence that still remained were:

Haddad's Forces

The US agreed that Haddad's unit should become the Lebanese Army Territorial Brigade responsible for security in the zone between the Israeli border and the River Zaharani. However, the Americans did not agree that Haddad himself should command the Brigade, nor that Israeli liaison officers should be attached to it. (Haddad was obviously *persona non grata* with the Lebanese Government.)

Co-operation between the IDF and the Lebanese Army

The US accepted that there should be close co-ordination, which could include regular meetings between Chiefs of Staff and local commanders, direct telephone and radio communication and concerted arrangements for the pursuit of terrorists. But they insisted that Israeli troops would not be entitled to cross the border, which we considered vital.

A UN Presence in the Security Zone

The US stipulated that two UNIFIL battalions maintain a presence in the area around the Palestinian refugee camps in Tyre and Sidon. Although responsibility for security in the camps would lie with the Lebanese forces, the refugees would feel safer if the camps were under UNIFIL observation.

Israel opposed such a UN presence inside the security zone, and especially at the refugee camps. Israel feared that UNIFIL would serve as a defensive umbrella for the organization of renewed PLO terrorism based on the camps which in the past had contained PLO strongholds.

Supervision of Security Arrangements

Israel proposed a supervision system under the control of a joint Israeli–Lebanese military committee and functioning through three joint operational headquarters and ten joint patrol teams, each containing ten men and two armoured cars from each side. This machinery for supervision should be in continuous action day and night. It would involve the stationing in Lebanon of about 200 Israeli soldiers.

The American proposal was much more limited. It provided for only one operational headquarters, only two or three patrol teams, and only four men from each side in each team using Lebanese vehicles. The Israelis were to return across the border after completion of patrols.

Observation Posts

We had originally requested three such posts and later raised the number to five. The Americans were adamant in their opposition to any such posts at all.

A Cabinet meeting was held on the negotiations, in which Shamir, David Kimche and I presented a report on our talks in Washington. We recommended yielding on the question of the observation posts and trying to find alternative arrangements. We believed that in further discussions with the US we would be able to reduce the remaining gaps in the positions to a level that would make it possible to sign an agreement. The Cabinet noted and discussed our reports, but took no decision.

During my report to the Cabinet meeting, Sharon constantly interrupted me with bitter personal attacks, blaming me for our having made too many concessions to the Americans. Begin called him to order; but when we emerged into the ante-room, where several senior officers were waiting, he again lashed out at me, saying, 'Disaster will strike us and it will be your fault.' I drew him into a side room and said to him, 'Arik, you're angry because the draft agreement does not accord with your ideas. I did not want to embarrass you by saying so in front of the Cabinet. In the negotiations, we followed present government policy, which is to seek an agreement with Lebanon whereby all foreign forces will leave that country, including our own, and the Lebanese authorities will accept responsibility for security arrangements near our border. Maybe you would rather we remained in Southern Lebanon without an agreement? If we did, we would get up to our necks in security problems by holding on to conquered territory where the majority of the population would be hostile to us.' My words had no effect and he went off in a rage. I realized that he was full of resentment at having been forced to give up his Defence post and thus no longer in a position to shape policy in Lebanon. The central aim of that policy now was to extricate Israel from the Lebanese mess into which Operation Peace for Galilee had plunged it under Sharon's leadership.

After this unpleasant episode, my mind went back to the many years Sharon and I had been friends and comrades-in-arms.

I had first met him in the winter of 1949, when we were both very young officers in a very young IDF. I was then acquainting myself with what had happened in the War of Independence while I was a prisoner of war in Jordan. One of the battles I was looking into was the unsuccessful attempt to dislodge the Jordanian Legion at Latrun, where it had cut the road from the coast to Jerusalem. In that engagement Sharon was a platoon commander whose unit was caught in enemy cross-fire and suffered heavy casualties. He himself was wounded, but extricated his men and brought them back to our lines together with all the dead and wounded. In 1949, I visited him at his parents' home in the moshav of Kfar Mallal in the coastal plain and heard his account of that battle. In 1950, we found ourselves serving together on the Staff of Central Command and developed close working and personal relations that lasted for most of our army careers.

Sharon was in his way an exceptional soldier – tough, daring and resourceful. The trouble with him was that his superiors regarded him as a problem – an impulsive and undisciplined officer who was inclined in operations to bend his orders to his own opinions. An army is, and must be, a hierarchical system, with a firm chain of command. By temperament, Sharon did not fit easily into such a body. Several Chiefs of Staff tried to get him discharged, but were prevented from doing so by political intervention. Thus, Moshe Dayan, as Chief of Staff in the 1950s, wanted to release him after he had led a large-scale reprisal raid across the border in an excessive way. But Ben-Gurion (who was Minister of Defence as well as Prime Minister) overruled Dayan because he admired Sharon as a fighting man.

In subsequent years, I more than once went to see key Cabinet ministers in order to persuade them that Sharon should be kept in the army, in spite of the friction he caused. I felt that in a country like ours, in a constant state of war, there should be room in the army for a commander like Sharon, who did not behave according to the accepted norms, but had the special talents needed for unorthodox and hazardous missions.

As an example I cited Orde Wingate. As a British army captain in Palestine during the Arab Rebellion, he had organized a number of Haganah men into what were called 'Wingate's Night Squads', to operate against Arab bands on the northern frontier. Wingate was recalled and would have been discharged but for the personal intervention of Winston Churchill. He went on to remarkable exploits in Ethiopia and then with the Chindit irregulars in Burma.

One of the reasons why Sharon left the army in 1973 and went into politics was that he was not regarded by Premier Golda Meir or Defence Minister Dayan as being qualified for the position he coveted, which was to be the next Chief of Staff. He then threw in his lot with the right-wing opposition led by Menachem Begin.

My personal relations with him had become strained after he became Minister of Defence in 1981. I was openly critical of some of his right-wing activities which I thought harmful to the state – undermining the Peace Treaty with Egypt by magnifying alleged breaches by Egypt of the security arrangements; the territorial settlement drive in the West Bank and Gaza; the hard-line treatment of the Arab inhabitants in these territories; and the destruction of Yamit to prevent it being handed over to the Egyptians.

I think military power intoxicated him, and he did not share the priority that other leaders like Dayan and Weizman gave to the search for peace.

All this came to a head over the war in Lebanon. The problem in the Government was basically the same as that in the army – how could Sharon be controlled? Begin and his Cabinet failed to meet that test, with unhappy results for our country.

In the spring of 1983, after Israel had yielded on the question of observation posts, the deadlock in the negotiations continued on other points. Secretary of State Shultz decided to visit the Middle East and try to achieve an agreement by personal diplomacy. After shuttling between

Jerusalem and Beirut, he submitted a draft agreement to the two sides. On 25 April Shamir brought the draft agreement before the Cabinet for approval. Shultz awaited the decision in his suite in the King David Hotel in Jerusalem. The outcome was not a foregone conclusion since Israel was being asked to renounce demands that for many members of the Government were basic matters of principle. Yet the Cabinet accepted the draft since it was clearly useless to prolong the negotiations any further. Shultz left immediately for Damascus to seek the co-operation, or at least the acquiescence, of President Assad. The next day he stopped at Ben-Gurion Airport on his flight back to the US and had a meeting in the terminal building with the Israeli Foreign and Defence Ministers and their aides. Disappointment showed on his face. Assad, he reported, had attacked the agreement, called it a surrender to Israel and given Shultz to understand that the Syrians were not prepared to withdraw from Lebanon in accordance with such an agreement.

On 17 May 1983, the Israeli–Lebanese Agreement was signed at Halda outside Beirut and at Kiryat Shmoneh in Northern Israel. The ceremonies were modest and few pressmen were present. Immediately after the signature, the Prime Minister's Office in Jerusalem published a statement summarizing the Agreement and stressing the advantages Israel would derive from it.

The Agreement stipulated an end to the state of war: the parties undertook to respect each other's sovereignty, political independence and territorial integrity. The existing border was accepted as the immutable international frontier. The parties were to refrain from all hostile propaganda against each other. Lebanon would, within a year, abrogate all existing laws and obligations which were in conflict with the Agreement. Israel would have the right to maintain in Beirut a permanent 'liaison office', the staff of which would enjoy quasi-diplomatic privileges and immunities. A joint committee would be set up for the development of reciprocal relations including such matters as communications and the movement of people and goods.

The Government statement asserted that these provisions created, in effect, a state of peace between the two countries. As such, it marked a continuation of the process begun with the signing of the Israeli–Egyptian Peace Treaty.

The Government statement went on to say that the main security achievement of the Agreement was the prospect it held out of a Lebanon free of the PLO terrorist organizations and of the Syrian army. Such a Lebanon would be a completely new reality.

In addition, the Agreement provided for a detailed system of security arrangements in Southern Lebanon, which conformed to the proposals we had worked out with President Gemayel's emissary and then with

Secretary of State Shultz and his aides. A security zone would be established to a depth of approximately forty-five kilometres. The Lebanese authorities would be solely responsible for security in that zone. Two Lebanese army brigades would be used for this purpose, one of which would be a territorial brigade based on Major Haddad's unit. A joint committee would supervise the arrangements in the zone, operating joint local headquarters and joint patrol teams. There would be close liaison and co-ordination between the IDF and Lebanese forces. Israel retained the right to act in self-defence where the Agreement was ineffective. To the north of the security zone, multinational forces would be deployed to assist the Lebanese Government maintain security.

The Government statement said that under this security system Israel's northern settlements would no longer be exposed to PLO artillery and rockets, and Lebanon would no longer be a base for hostile activities against Israel.

One of the benefits claimed for the Agreement was that it had been the product of a lengthy period of co-operation between the Israeli Government and the US Administration. In the process, there had been a definite improvement in Israeli–American relations and in Israel's standing in American public opinion. American support would be vital in the struggle that might lie ahead before Lebanon was freed of all foreign forces.

The statement contemplated the possibility that the Agreement might not be implemented because of Syrian refusal to withdraw its forces from Lebanon. In that case, the Israeli army would have to be redeployed in Southern Lebanon and establish a security zone based mainly on Major Haddad's brigade. But Israel's signature of the Agreement would have affirmed its willingness in principle to evacuate its forces. Israel could, therefore, expect co-operation or at least understanding from the United States and Lebanon for the security arrangements it would make unilaterally in Southern Lebanon, if the Agreement failed because of Syria.

Unfortunately, the reality in Lebanon ran counter to the expectations expressed in the Israeli Government's statement on the signing of the Agreement. The Lebanese Government, under President Gemayel, came under heavy Syrian pressure – directly, through Saudi Arabia and through those Lebanese factions taking directions from Syria. Amin Gemayel evaded carrying out the Agreement for ten months, until in March 1984 he finally abrogated it in order to save his regime from collapse. The developments in the intervening period had in any case caused the Agreement to be stillborn.

12

POST-MORTEM

When the prospect faded that the Israeli–Lebanese Agreement would be implemented, the Israeli army carried out a unilateral withdrawal from Beirut, the Damascus–Beirut highway and the Shouf Mountains, to the River Awali line. By this move, Israel relinquished the position of strength its previous military disposition had given it, in relation both to the Lebanese Government and to Syria.

The United States made no effort to ensure the deployment, in the evacuated areas, of a multinational force or units of the Lebanese army, as the Agreement had specified. In consequence, Lebanese factions under Syrian auspices gained control of these areas. This applied especially to the Druze militia under Walid Jumblatt, which extended its hold over the Shouf Mountains and part of the coastal plain between Beirut and Sidon. The pro-Syrian factions also resumed control of West Beirut. In the city, extremist groups like the Islamic Jihad (Moslem Holy War) and the Hizbollah (Party of God) inflicted heavy casualties in terrorist attacks on the American and French contingents in the multinational force. The Governments that had provided units to the MNF were compelled to withdraw them from Lebanon under pressure of public opinion in their respective countries.

The Christian Free Lebanon Front, and in particular the Phalange, were unable to impose Christian hegemony on other Lebanese factions. Furthermore, they were unwilling to make the concessions required to establish a Lebanese Government, based on a national consensus, that would seek to halt the civil war, to stabilize the country and to adopt a constitution giving a proportionate political share to each of the main communities. The internal Lebanese conflict remained unresolved – and has not been resolved to this day.

After their interim withdrawal to the River Awali, Israeli forces continued to be harassed by systematic terrorist attacks, with a mounting toll of casualties. These attacks came not so much from the PLO groups remaining in Syrian-controlled territory as from elements of the local

Shi'ite population. The most dangerous and fanatical group to emerge was the Hizbollah, supported and indoctrinated by the fundamentalist Khomeini regime in Iran. Some of their actions took the form of suicide missions using vehicles loaded with explosives.

In Israel, there was an increasing demand from the public to end its war in Lebanon. By the beginning of 1985, it was clear that there was no political or security justification for basing the protection of Northern Israel on the continued presence of the IDF in Southern Lebanon. Our forces had become the static target of a terrorist campaign, which could in due course rally behind it the bulk of the Shi'ite and Druze inhabitants in the area.

In October 1984, the National Unity Government had taken office under the premiership of Shimon Peres. In January 1985, the Government decided on a careful withdrawal in stages, spread over a number of months. In the meantime, a narrow security zone would be created along the frontier, some ten to twenty kilometres in depth. It would be occupied by the Lebanese brigade which had been commanded by Major Haddad, and had since been reinforced and converted into the South Lebanese Army (SLA). Haddad had died in January 1984, and the new commander of the SLA was a retired Lebanese Christian officer, General Antoine Lahad. The withdrawal and the establishment of the security zone were completed by July 1985.

In the years 1986–7, the Shi'ite and Palestinian organizations controlled by Syria and Iran stepped up their terrorist attacks, directed at the SLA, UNIFIL and the token Israeli military presence remaining in Lebanon to support the SLA. From time to time, long-range Katyusha rockets were fired into the Galilee from north of the security zone. As a result, the IDF had to become more active across the border in order to preserve the zone.

The security zone and the SLA have, on the whole, been able to prevent infiltration across the border and have, therefore, served as the buffer they were intended to be. Naval patrols have intercepted terrorist groups trying to circumvent the zone and reach Israeli territory by sea. The air force has resumed precision raids on terrorist command posts and bases farther north in Lebanon.

This system of protection for the border region has been reasonably effective. The tragedy is that it did not need a three-year war to set it up. It could just as well have been organized in the first few days of the war, after the army had occupied Southern Lebanon and wiped out the PLO 'state within a state' and the military infrastructure it had developed. The Israeli Government decision of 5 June 1982, which launched Operation Peace for Galilee, would thus have been fulfilled to the letter. In fact, it would have been much easier to operate a limited security zone of this kind; the local Shi'ite population had welcomed the Israeli force with flowers as their liberators from the PLO, but subsequently had become alienated by three years of Israeli occupation.

In 1986–7, two rival Shi'ite militias were competing with each other for leadership of the Shi'ite population, of which there were 140,000 in the security zone alone. The main one, Amal, was under Syrian influence; the smaller, more extreme one, Hizbollah, was under Iranian influence. They shared the objective of terminating the Israeli security zone and ending both the SLA and the Israeli military presence in that area. Of the two Shi'ite groups, Hizbollah has been the more dangerous, and its attacks have become increasingly sophisticated and frequent. The future of the security zone depends on the ability of the SLA to withstand these attacks, and the extent to which Israel is willing to commit more forces in support of the SLA.

It would be misleading to regard the SLA simply as an auxiliary force maintained by Israel to serve Israel's security purposes. Major Haddad's force came into existence primarily to prevent the area once again becoming the battlefield between terrorist organizations and the IDF, which will fight on Lebanese soil to curb terrorist attacks. Moreover, the population of Southern Lebanon has no wish to live again under PLO domination.

It is this local interest which created common ground for mutual assistance between the IDF and the SLA. The latter is based on the Christians and Shi'ites who live in the security zone and want to protect their homes and families.

In the overall Lebanese picture, the security zone under SLA control corresponds to other areas under the control of Shi'ite, Christian, Druze or Sunni Moslem militias, or under the direct control of the Syrian army. In this chaotic situation, the security zone must of necessity fall into Israel's military sphere of influence.

The ideal solution to Israel's problem would be the emergence out of the turmoil in Lebanon of a strong, central government, capable of dismantling all local militias, procuring the withdrawal of the Syrian forces, and maintaining law and order in the whole country through an effective Lebanese army. But that prospect is still remote.

What, then, could replace the SLA? Another force would be required capable of preventing the terrorist organizations (Palestinian and Shi'ite), which operate north of the security zone, from taking control of this zone as a base for actions against Israel – as was the situation prior to Operation Peace for Galilee.

Such a force cannot be a multinational one. This idea, which constituted one of the main components of the Israeli–Lebanese Agreement of May 1983, has long faded. Nor can UNIFIL perform this task. It

159

was originally established in 1978 in the wake of Israel's Operation Litani, with a mandate to assist the Lebanese Government in asserting its authority in the area evacuated by Israeli troops. At the beginning of 1987, UNIFIL numbered 5,500 men, made up of contingents from Finland, Sweden, France, Ireland, Fiji, Nepal and Ghana.

The UN has increased the pressure on Israel to give up the security zone, disband the SLA and hand over to UNIFIL control of all the area up to the frontier. It is argued that this course would encourage moderate elements, especially Amal, to accept responsibility together with UNIFIL for the security of the area and the prevention of attacks on Israel. On the other hand (the argument continues), maintaining the security zone and the SLA would further inflame the hostility of the local population to Israel and increase terrorist attacks by the radical Hizbollah – not only against Israel and the SLA, but against UNIFIL itself.

The Israeli Government has consistently rejected this view, as UNIFIL has neither the mandate nor the capacity to curb terrorist attacks on Israel from Lebanese territory. In any case, there is no chance that the UN Security Council will change UNIFIL's mandate so as to give it 'teeth' as an anti-terrorist force and to extend its area of deployment.

This dispute has been exacerbated at times because UNIFIL's present area partly overlaps with the security zone. This has led to friction and incidents between UNIFIL and the SLA. On occasion, IDF patrols operating in the area have unintentionally clashed with UNIFIL positions, causing strain between Israel and otherwise friendly countries whose units in UNIFIL have been involved.

The only practical alternative, during the foreseeable future, for maintaining security arrangements in Southern Lebanon lies with Syria, and everything possible should be done, through the good offices of the US and other factors, to realize this option. Syrian policy should be to prevent any anti-Israeli activity from Lebanon which might lead to an unwanted war with Israel; while Israeli policy should be directed towards reaching a 'red line' agreement with Syria. This line should run along the River Awali, to the south of which no Syrian forces should be deployed.

If and when an understanding with Syria is reached concerning 'red line' arrangements, which will prevent the execution of terrorist activities in Lebanon directed against the security zone and Israel, then it will be possible to place the security and stability of the whole area south of the Awali (including the security zone) in the hands of joint Amal, Shi'ite and South Lebanese forces, in conjunction with UNIFIL which would then be deployed as far as the international border.

At the end of February 1987, Syrian forces took control of West Beirut and, subsequently, of the Beirut–Sidon road. This dramatic step brought the Syrians back to the same positions they had occupied prior to

Operation Peace for Galilee. At that time, apart from holding positions in the Lebanese Beka'a Valley (bordering Syria), they had also been deployed along the Damascus–Beirut highway, in West Beirut and along the coast road from Beirut to the River Awali.

In 1976, the Syrians had taken control of these areas in order to prevent the PLO, the Druze and the extreme Sunni Moslems from destroying the Christian forces and disrupting the local balance required by Syria to control Lebanon in as indirect a way as possible. This time, the Syrians again took these positions in order to prevent any disruption of the balance on which its control over Lebanon depended, following the renewed strengthening of the PLO in West Beirut and the Sidon area and, as a result, of the risks created to Syrian interests in Lebanon by the Iran-supported Hizbollah organization.

The Syrian deployment in February 1987 may create serious risks for Israel if Syria aims to liquidate the security zone by deploying Syrian forces up to the Israeli border and by providing assistance to anti-Israeli terrorist operations from within this zone. On the other hand, the Syrian deployment can create stability in Southern Lebanon and also facilitate Israeli–Syrian 'red line' arrangements (as described above), if Syria aims to keep Lebanon under its umbrella without risking war with Israel.

In the above situation, Israel must keep the door open for any positive moves, while at the same time maintaining the guidelines it has laid down for its policy in Lebanon – the maintenance of the security zone and the prevention of the following Syrian actions: crossing the Awali line; deployment of ground missile batteries in Lebanon; and active support for terrorist organizations operating against Israel.

Meanwhile, the internal struggle in Lebanon continues unabated, with bewildering shifts of alliance between the warring factions. What follows describes the chaotic picture at the beginning of 1987. The PLO was attempting to stage a comeback in Beirut and Southern Lebanon, and to bring back fighters and weapons to the Palestinian refugee camps on the outskirts of Beirut, Sidon and Tyre. The Shi'ite Amal militia's determination to prevent this PLO revival brought about the 'War of the Camps', which raged in 1986–7. The Palestinian reinforcements and arms were being brought from Cyprus in small boats to the Christian port of Junieh, north of Beirut, with the co-operation of the Christian militias. The latter had been bitter foes of the PLO in the past, but were now more concerned over the rise of the Shi'ites. (In February 1987, the Israeli navy intercepted one such boat and captured fifty trained Fatah fighters on board.) Amal was at the same time fighting a bloody battle with a Druze–Communist Front for control of West Beirut.

Syria maintained direct military control of the Beka'a Valley in Eastern Lebanon and the Tripoli region in Northern Lebanon. The objectives of this deployment were twofold: to secure Syria's Lebanese flank against a possible Israeli offensive from that quarter; and to prevent internal developments that could undermine Syrian influence and its political–strategic interests in Lebanon. In Lebanon's factional strife, Syria gave substantial military support to Amal, for several reasons: to thwart the PLO attempt to regain its former positions of strength; to neutralize the Hizbollah as the vehicle of Iranian intrusion into Lebanese affairs; and to use both Shi'ite militias as proxies to eliminate the Israeli security zone. In the Gulf War, Syria, like Libya, was supporting Iran against Iraq, another Arab state. Yet the Syrian leadership was aware that the Khomeini regime aspired to spread its fundamentalist Islamic revolution to other Middle East countries. Syria had become nervous at the thought that Iran might gain the allegiance of the Lebanese Shi'ite community and use it as an instrument for turning Lebanon into an Islamic state within Iran's sphere of influence.

At the end of February 1987, Syria reluctantly moved 7,000 troops into Moslem West Beirut to restore order and halt the battles between the Lebanese militias in which Amal, Syria's protégé, was faring badly. Later, Syrian troops moved southwards along the coastal road as far as the River Awali. Israel kept a wary eye on this deployment, in order to fathom ultimate Syrian intentions.

In retrospect, the military situation created by Operation Peace for Galilee, with Israeli forces in control of Beirut, the Damascus–Beirut highway and the Shouf Mountains, could have been exploited to further two political objectives: first, to reach a renewed understanding with Syria; secondly, to move towards a solution of the Palestinian Arab problem, as I have already explained (see Chapter 8). However, these possibilities were not explored because those who were directing the war were the prisoners of the illusory war aims they had set themselves: to drive the Syrian army out of Lebanon and isolate Syria from any role in political negotiations; to expel the PLO from the whole of Lebanon and destroy it as a political factor; and to assist the Christian Lebanese to establish a regime which would make peace with Israel.

Some time before the start of the Lebanese war, we had had a tacit 'red line' understanding with Syria, reached through American mediation. It derived from the recognition by each that the other had vital interests in Lebanon and that these interests need not conflict. As a result, Israel was left free to operate against the PLO in Southern Lebanon without Syrian intervention. That understanding had collapsed before the Lebanese war. A new 'red line' understanding with Syria might have been worked out through the US at the time when the Israeli forces were astride the Damascus–Beirut highway and posing a direct threat to the Syrian forces in the Beka'a Valley. This understanding could have included a Syrian undertaking to co-operate in curbing terrorist activities in Southern Lebanon. That would not have been an undue price for Syria to pay for an Israeli withdrawal.

Syria could at the same time have been associated through the US with the negotiations which produced the Israeli–Lebanese Agreement. The Agreement would have had to be modified in certain respects to take account of Syrian positions. For instance, Syrian withdrawal of the bulk of its forces could have taken place, for face-saving reasons, after an Israeli withdrawal instead of simultaneously with it. Again, special arrangements in the Beka'a Valley could have been devised to safeguard Syrian security interests there.

As it was, the attempt to force the Syrian army out of Lebanon and to come to terms with Beirut while ignoring Damascus turned out to be a failure. Syria not only rejected the Israeli–Lebanese Agreement, but succeeded in sabotaging it, and it remained a scrap of paper. A Syrian army of 25,000 men has remained on Lebanese soil, and Syria has become the dominant force in Lebanese affairs. Moreover, Syria has been left free to support terrorist activities in Southern Lebanon, with the object of undermining Israeli security arrangements by proxy, without the risk of direct military confrontation.

Obviously, there can be no certainty that President Assad would have responded at all if overtures along the above lines had been made to him through the US. However, no attempt was made to get his co-operation.

It may be said that to dwell on the might-have-beens of the past is a futile academic exercise. But those concerned with national security cannot think that way. When a war is over, it must be subjected to intensive scrutiny, in order to note its mistakes and to learn its lessons for the future. In this instance, the cruel verdict of history must be that the prolongation of the war after its initial few days was a major blunder, based on illusory expectations. Nothing was achieved thereby that could justify the expenditure of blood, resources, reputation and national cohesion which the war entailed.

The record speaks for itself. No peace with Lebanon was attained, and the Agreement that *was* attained did not survive. Israel still has to cope with the problem of Peace for Galilee. In the West Bank and Gaza, no indigenous leadership has emerged (or is likely to emerge) that will willingly accept permanent Israeli rule. Syrian troops remain deployed in Lebanon. Syria is a stronger military power and a more formidable force than it was in 1982 when the Lebanese war started. Lebanon is still a fragmented country with a weak Government unable to rule it effectively, a weak army unable to keep order in it, and bouts of in-fighting among its factional militias. As Syrian soldiers try to enforce brittle truces, they discover that 'a policeman's lot is not a happy one'.

The people of Israel feel nothing but relief that its army is no longer bogged down in Lebanon. There is little likelihood that Israel will plunge again into that morass in the years to come.

PART THREE
ELEMENTS OF ISRAEL'S
NATIONAL SECURITY

13

BORDERS FOR PEACE OR WAR?

No country in modern times has had borders that have shifted as often as Israel has had. They have shifted not only in location but also in status: ceasefire lines, truce lines, armistice demarcation lines, disengagement-of-forces lines or interim agreement lines, drawn in the wake of successive Israeli–Arab wars. Only after the 1979 Peace Treaty with Egypt did Israel's southern border become its first permanent and recognized international frontier.

In assessing these borders as a defence perimeter, worrying questions confront those responsible for national security. Are the borders defensible? Do they provide strategic depth? If not, is the inference that in wartime the battle must be carried quickly into enemy territory? If Israel is faced with imminent attack, should it risk a pre-emptive strike?

A more acute dilemma arises when Israel is called upon to pull back from existing borders, in the course of negotiations for peace, or for interim arrangements falling short of peace. In the domestic debate, the sceptics argue that Israel may be giving up vital strategic assets in exchange for dubious political gains. In time of war, the whole country becomes the frontier. That is why Israel is so reluctant to shrink back upon itself and to reduce still further the relatively small distance between its Arab neighbours and its main centres of population. The only time any border felt far enough away was between our occupation of Sinai in 1967 and its return to Egypt under the Peace Treaty of 1979.

As I tried to explain to President Carter at Camp David, for Israel to give up military control of the Jordan Valley would put it in an even more vulnerable position than before 1967, because of the much greater striking power of Arab armies today.

The border problem is compounded by the fact that most of our people and economic life are crowded into the narrow coastal plain. Cultivable land was more easily available there; water sources more abundant; and there was a natural tendency for population and industry to cluster round the seaports – Haifa, Ashdod and, in Mandatory times, also Tel Aviv–

Jaffa. In 1948, independence opened the gates to a huge influx of immigrants, and it was quicker and more economical to absorb them in the already developed coastal plain, which greatly increased its population density.

This strip now holds seventy per cent of Israel's population; seventy-five per cent of industry; over ninety per cent of its electricity-generating capacity; its ports and main airports; and its oil refineries and reserve oil stocks. Furthermore, a substantial part of our military installations are concentrated in this area.

To those concerned with national security, this situation has serious implications. The concentration of population and of economic and military facilities into relatively small areas creates vital strategic targets for enemy attack, which in future may not be confined to conventional means. Sound national security planning on a long-range basis must include serious effort at population dispersal. This process can be aided by the Defence establishment through locating military facilities where they can provide employment and homes away from the main urban areas.

The Israeli border story started before the birth of the state. On 29 November 1947, the United Nations adopted a partition plan for what was Western Palestine under the British Mandate. The plan cut the small country into a jigsaw puzzle of seven pieces: three of them to form a Jewish state, three of them an Arab state, and a Jerusalem enclave under an international regime. Access from one part of the Jewish state to another, or from one part of the Arab state to another, was to be through two common 'kissing points'.

Critics of the plan rightly pointed out that the borders of such a Jewish state would be wholly indefensible. The only answer to that objection was the hope that the Arab side to the conflict would come round to accepting the proposed compromise solution, as the Jewish side had done, and that the two peoples would settle down to peaceful coexistence.

That hope was soon shattered. The Arab states not only rejected partition, but went to war to destroy the infant State of Israel. As a result, the UN partition plan remained on paper.

The borders that actually emerged from the 1948–9 War of Independence were the demarcation lines laid down by the armistice agreements Israel signed in 1949 with its four Arab neighbours: Egypt, Jordan, Lebanon and Syria. The Palestinian Arab state contemplated by the UN partition plan did not come into existence. Most of the territory allotted to it was annexed to Jordan and became the so-called West Bank. The Gaza Strip remained under Egyptian military control. The international regime for Jerusalem failed to materialize, and the armistice demarcation line between Israel and Jordan ran through the heart of the city, dividing it into two.

By their own terms, the armistice agreements were to serve as a termination of a state of war and a transitional stage to an early peace. Endorsement of the armistice regime by a unanimous decision of the UN Security Council gave the demarcation lines the status of provisional international borders, pending peace. Israel would settle down within these borders for the next nineteen years.

The armistice lines had obvious defects as a security perimeter for Israel. The country they enclosed was very small, roughly the size of Wales or New Jersey. In shape it was long and thin – 260 miles from north to south. The border with Jordan wound round the bulge of the West Bank, leaving a waist in the middle of Israel only ten miles wide, and the Israeli half of Jerusalem at the end of a wedge-shaped corridor. There was constant terrorist infiltration. Nasser's Egypt maintained an illegal blockade at Sharm el-Sheikh at the entrance to the Gulf of Akaba, so that shipping was unable to reach the Israeli port of Eilat. From the Egyptian-held Gaza Strip, there were murderous *fedayeen* (terrorist) raids. From 1954 onwards, a flow of modern Soviet weapons reached Egypt, which was clearly preparing for a 'second round' with Israel. These ominous developments led to the Sinai Campaign of 1956. The Egyptian army was shattered and Israeli forces occupied nearly all the Sinai Peninsula.

The Israeli Government pleaded that this was an historic opportunity to promote peace talks. The plea fell on deaf ears. The UN demanded immediate and unconditional withdrawal behind the armistice line. An angry Eisenhower–Dulles Administration in Washington threatened Israel with sanctions if it did not comply. The Soviet Union, humiliated by the defeat of its Russian-armed and Russian-trained Egyptian protégé, threatened to blast Israel with missiles. Under these pressures, Israel was compelled to withdraw completely to the old armistice line, without being allowed even to negotiate peace.

The only gains were that the Straits of Tiran and the Gulf of Akaba remained open to shipping to and from Eilat, and that the Egyptian border remained quiet for the next decade, with a UN peace force (UNEF) deployed along it.

The lesson for Israel from the Sinai Campaign was that the fruits of military success could be lost if Israel found itself politically isolated, and particularly if United States support was denied.

Regarding the border situation after the Sinai Campaign, I recall a visit by UN Secretary-General Dag Hammarskjöld to Prime Minister Ben-Gurion in the winter of 1958 at Ben-Gurion's desert retreat in the Negev, Kibbutz Sde Boker. I was asked to attend the meeting since the state of the armistice regime would come up for discussion. After the Sinai

Campaign, Nasser had thought it prudent to halt the *fedayeen* raids from the Egyptian-held Gaza Strip, but there were still constant incidents along the armistice line with Jordan. Ben-Gurion asked me to give Hammarskjöld an account of our complaints on this score. I stated that Jordanian soldiers fired from the Old City walls in Jerusalem at pedestrians in the streets on the Israeli side; Jordanian border posts sniped at our farmers working in their fields; the Tel Aviv–Jerusalem railway line that ran through the Judean hills, close to the border, had been mined; Palestinian terrorists were allowed to come across from the Jordanian side; and by Article 8 of the armistice agreement, Jordan was obliged to let Jews pray at the Western Wall, but had refused to do so.

When I finished, Ben-Gurion said, 'If I had known in 1948 that we would have to face such aggressive behaviour, I would have ordered the IDF to take the West Bank and the Gaza Strip.' Hammarskjöld replied, 'You remind me of a story. My father, Hjalmar, was the Prime Minister of neutral Sweden in World War I. The German Foreign Minister said to him that if Sweden were to come in on Germany's side, it would be able to regain territories in other Scandinavian countries that had once been under Swedish rule. My father answered, "I would not want the Swedish people to live as if they had a hedgehog in their pocket." ' That was Hammarskjöld's way of stating that if we had taken the West Bank and Gaza in the 1948 war, we would have found them a very prickly possession.

While we had our problems with the armistice (which lasted from 1949 to 1967), there was a general willingness in Israel to accept an Israeli–Arab peace on the territorial basis of the armistice, with local adjustments. This attitude derived from the basic difference between borders in a state of war and the same borders in a state of peace that had removed the threat of war.

In 1966, a year before the Six Day War, I prepared and submitted a five-year plan for the development of the IDF, which was approved by the Chief of Staff, General Yitzhak Rabin. The plan was based on these strategic concepts:

1 As a general proposition, the State of Israel could progress and achieve its national goals within the territory contained by the 1949 armistice lines (the so-called 'green line').

2 If war was forced upon Israel, the IDF should carry it into enemy territory, to avoid unacceptable casualties and damage in our main population and economic centres.

3 Our war aims should be to destroy the military infrastructure for an enemy offence against Israel, and to maintain our hold on occupied territory until peace was achieved – that is, to regard captured

territory as giving us a political bargaining capacity from a position of strength.

4 In the context of a peace settlement, the international frontiers between Israel and its neighbours would, for security reasons, require adjustments of the existing armistice lines in a number of sectors – particularly the Jordanian border; the Jerusalem area (where historical and religious factors also came into play); the central coastal plain; the vicinity of Mount Gilboa; and the Syrian border.

The geography of Israel underwent a dramatic change as a result of the 1967 Six Day War. We unexpectedly found ourselves in possession of the whole area from the Suez Canal to the River Jordan and the Golan Heights. Arab spokesmen claimed that the 'Zionist state' was inherently expansionist and would not rest until it had established an empire 'from the Euphrates to the Nile'. That was a propaganda myth. The 1967 war was for Israel one of '*ein breira*' (no alternative). The issue was the survival of the state, not its expansion.

The hostilities with Egypt began in the early morning of Monday, 5 June 1967. That same morning Prime Minister Levi Eshkol sent a message to King Hussein of Jordan through UN and American channels. He urged the King to keep out of the war and assured him that if he did so, no harm would come to Jordan. If Jordan attacked us, however, we would respond, and the King would be responsible for the consequences. The Jordanian reply was a heavy artillery bombardment of Jewish Jerusalem, the seizure of the UN headquarters in Government House, and an opening of fire on Israel's towns and villages along the armistice line. Israeli reinforcements were rushed up to Jerusalem. By Wednesday afternoon, the Old City had been captured and the whole of the West Bank was in our hands.

In a book he published later, King Hussein explained that he had made a commitment to Nasser to join in the war and his honour as an Arab ruler was at stake. He also admitted that he had been misled that morning by Egyptian reports of fictitious successes on the battlefront. Whatever the reasons, his rash decision that Monday morning was a fateful one for both Jordan and Israel. If he had heeded the Israeli Government's plea, East Jerusalem and the West Bank would have remained under Jordanian occupation to this day.

Shortly after the end of the war, the Israeli Government made a peace proposal to Egypt and Syria through the good offices of the United States. Israel offered to sign peace treaties with them based on the pre-1967 borders (except for Jerusalem) with some local modifications for security reasons and the demilitarization of the evacuated areas. The offer was

171

rejected. In August, a collective Arab position was adopted at the Arab Summit Conference in Khartoum, capital of Sudan. It consisted of three 'noes': no peace with Israel, no negotiations with Israel and no recognition of Israel. Nasser declared that 'what was taken by force will be regained by force'. This totally negative attitude was reinforced by the Soviet Union through a vast air-lift of planes, tanks and other war material, accompanied by thousands of Russian advisers and experts to rebuild the shattered Egyptian and Syrian armies. By this investment the Soviet Union underlined the dependence of these two Arab countries on their Russian 'Big Brother'. At the same time, the wealthy Arab oil states – Saudi Arabia, Kuwait and Libya – provided Egypt with substantial funds for its military build-up and undertook to finance the revived Palestine Liberation Organization, to which a number of terrorist groups were affiliated. The proclaimed aim of the PLO was the destruction of the 'Zionist entity' (i.e. the State of Israel) and the establishment of a Palestinian state over the whole country. After Khartoum, the peace offer of the Israeli Government lapsed.

At the Security Council meetings after the Six Day War, the American attitude was the reverse of that adopted by the Eisenhower Administration in 1956. This time the US backed the Israeli position that the defeat of the Arab armies, and the occupation of territories which resulted from it, should be exploited to move towards peace. The unanimous Security Council Resolution 242 of 22 November 1967 called for a 'just and lasting peace', which would include the application of two principles:

1 Withdrawal of Israeli armed forces from territories occupied in the recent conflict.
2 Termination of all claims or states of belligerency and respect for and acknowledgment of the sovereignty, territorial integrity and political independence of every state in the area and their right to live in peace with secure and recognized boundaries free from threats or acts of force.

The Resolution was deliberately noncommittal about the extent of the withdrawal. Proposals by the Soviet and Arab delegations to have the text read 'all the territories occupied . . .' were rejected by the Council. What was clear was that the first of the above two principles (withdrawal) was tied to the second one (peace and security).

In spite of the Arab attitude, the belief persisted until about 1969 that a settlement would be reached by trading most of the occupied territories for peace. That was the period when Dr Gunnar Jarring, an experienced Swedish diplomat, was shuttling between Jerusalem and the Arab capitals as a UN mediator to promote the implementation of Resolution 242. On the assumption that our occupation would be temporary, the IDF had destroyed military installations captured in the territories, so that they should not again be available to enemy forces after our departure. When it became evident that no peace was in sight, we had to rebuild the fortifications, camps and other installations at great cost, so as to develop a military basis for an indefinite stay.

The policy that crystallized in the Labour Alignment Government was that the frontiers to be sought in future peace negotiations should be 'security borders' based on territorial compromise. This policy involved substantial withdrawal from the ceasefire lines that emerged from the Six Day War, but it ruled out a return to the pre-1967 armistice lines (the 'green line'). The contemplated security borders would run as follows:

In Sinai

A line would stretch from El Arish on the Mediterranean coast to Ras Muhammad, the southern tip of the Sinai Peninsula. This line would have several advantages. It would retain a measure of strategic depth on Israel's southern flank. The western shore of the Gulf of Akaba, including Sharm el-Sheikh, would remain in Israeli hands, thus ensuring that freedom of navigation through the Straits of Tiran and the Gulf could be safeguarded.

As Minister of Defence, Dayan worked to create facts that would turn the proposed border into a reality on the ground. These efforts concentrated on military and civilian projects in the zone of Eastern Sinai which lay between the El Arish–Ras Muhammad line and the international border during the Mandatory period. The town of Yamit arose on the Mediterranean coast, surrounded by new agricultural settlements. Another new town, Ophira, was developed near Sharm el-Sheikh, also a naval base. Three sophisticated modern air bases were constructed in Sinai: Eytan, near Rafiah in the north; Etzion, near Eilat in the centre; and Ophira, near Sharm el-Sheikh in the south. Early-warning stations came into being.

As has been shown, in the end, the Peace Treaty with Egypt made the El Arish–Ras Muhammad line only a first-stage withdrawal line, with the Mandatory international frontier as the final Israeli–Egyptian border. The whole of the Israeli presence in Eastern Sinai, with all its military and civilian development, had to be abandoned as part of the price of peace.

In the West Bank

The Allon plan, drawn up by Deputy Premier Yigal Allon after the Six Day War, was accepted as a guideline. By this plan, the territory would be

173

divided between Israel and Jordan. Israel would keep the western side of the Jordan Valley, to a depth of about nine miles; the western shore of the Dead Sea and the adjacent area of the Judean Desert; some of the hills overlooking the coastal plain and an enlargement of the Jerusalem corridor. The more thickly populated areas in the West Bank (about two-thirds of the total country) would be handed to Jordan, demilitarized and linked to Jordan by a corridor in the Jericho area.

The rationale behind the Allon plan was to give Israel a security border along the River Jordan and control of localities on the West Bank important to its defence, with a minimum increase of the Arab minority in the state.

On the Golan Heights

The security border would be a line that included the dominant heights of Mount Hermon and the edge of the plateau overlooking the Upper River Jordan and the Sea of Galilee.

In 1975, before the Interim Agreement with Egypt was signed, I was instructed by Defence Minister Peres to draw up detailed maps, based on the Government's policy regarding security borders. In submitting the maps, I expressed scepticism as to whether the proposed security borders in Sinai and on the Golan Heights would be acceptable to Egypt, Syria or the United States as final peace borders. I therefore recommended that we think of peace frontiers based on adjustments in the pre-1967 borders with these two neighbouring countries, rather than attempting to divide with them the territories that we had occupied. Needless to say, I was accused of being defeatist.

I also explained why I could not see in the Allon plan a possible basis for an agreement regarding the West Bank and the Gaza Strip. In 1975, while the negotiations for the Interim Agreement with Egypt were in process, I had gone with Yigal Allon on a tour in Sinai that included the Mitla and Gidi Passes. On the way I had asked whether he really believed peace with Jordan was possible on the basis of the territorial compromise set out in his plan. 'I cannot imagine', I had said, 'that Jordan will be willing or able to sign a treaty giving up Arab claims to East Jerusalem and a substantial part of the West Bank. In any case, Jordan cannot negotiate with us on the future of these territories without the backing of at least one of the two important Arab states involved in the conflict, Egypt and Syria.' I went on, 'In our secret contacts with King Hussein, he has always flatly rejected the Allon plan.' Allon answered, 'Abrasha, the borders in my plan are meant to serve as security borders until we have obtained a real peace with our neighbours. Only then will we be able to finalize the permanent international borders.'

I cannot say that this flexible concept was shared by Allon's Cabinet colleagues or by the General Staff. They regarded the proposed security borders as the irreducible final frontier.

I have already dealt (in Chapter 8) with the peace proposals I submitted to Defence Minister Peres in 1976. The Peace Treaty of 1979 established a permanent international frontier between Israel and Egypt. As far as the borders with Syria and Jordan are concerned, my views have remained unchanged since the 1976 peace plan. The main points are:

- The frontiers between Israel and those two neighbouring Arab states can be finalized only in the context of a comprehensive and stable peace that has removed the threat to Israel's national security. Until then, Israel cannot withdraw from the existing ceasefire lines.
- In the case of Jordan, the border question is bound up with the future of the West Bank and the Gaza Strip. My 1976 plan envisaged the final border as one between Israel and a Jordanian–Palestinian federal state; after a transitional period of a functional nature, under a joint Israeli–Jordanian–Palestinian administration.

14

THE TERRITORIAL DILEMMA

The future of the West Bank and the Gaza Strip is in dispute not just between Israel and the Arab world, but within Israel itself.

Israel's 1967 victory created favourable conditions for a political settlement on the basis of the 1949 borders, with adjustments for security reasons. That opportunity was lost mainly because of three developments. First, there was the negative Arab response at the Khartoum Summit Conference. Second, the Arab states launched the War of Attrition against Israel with the help of the Soviet Union. Third, there grew up in time a segment of Israel's political spectrum that aspired to push out the borders of the state by annexing the West Bank and the Gaza Strip, as well as the Golan Heights and substantial areas of Sinai.

The prolonged occupation of the West Bank and the Gaza Strip has left Israel facing a territorial dilemma. It involves issues fundamental to the future: national security; the final borders of the state; its demographic make-up; the democratic nature of its government and society; and the prospect of a peaceful solution to the Israeli–Arab conflict.

Facing each other are political parties willing to give parts of these territories for peace (the territorial compromise school) and parties unwilling to give up any part of them even for peace (the Greater Israel school).

This difference in the ultimate objective is reflected in a difference in the policy of Jewish settlement in the territories.

As explained in the previous chapter, the policy of the Labour Alignment Governments from 1967 to 1977 was the 'Jordanian option' – a territorial compromise based in a general way on the Allon plan. Consequently, Jewish settlement in the territories focused on those localities which would remain in Israel according to that plan. When the Likud Government came into power in 1977, its policy aimed at the eventual incorporation of these territories into Israel and, accordingly, there was a radical shift in Jewish settlement policy across the 'green line'. In a drive spearheaded by the nationalist–religious group Gush Emunim, new settlements were planted in the most populated Arab areas of the West Bank, with the avowed purpose of paving the way for annexation.

The National Unity Government set up in 1984 was a temporary partnership between the two main political parties, Labour and the Likud. Its main concern was to deal with two pressing problems: the state of the economy and withdrawal from Lebanon. The division of opinion between them on the territories was not an urgent matter and could, in effect, be put on the back-burner for the duration of the Government. However, should peace negotiations actually get under way, the nation would have to face up to this divisive issue, and it is improbable that the National Unity Government could survive the test.

The Greater Israel school calls for an undivided state that extends from the Mediterranean to the River Jordan – that is, the area which was Western Palestine under the British Mandate. The arguments in support of this claim are partly strategic and partly religious–historical.

On the strategic level, it is maintained that control of the West Bank is the key to Israel's defence. If it was under Arab rule, the military infrastructure could be developed for a devastating surprise attack by the Jordanian army, together with other Arab forces on the eastern front. From this nearby hill terrain, every household in Central Israel and in Jerusalem would be within artillery and rocket range; while ground-to-air missile batteries would effectively cover Israel's air bases. Moreover, the West Bank and also the Gaza Strip would serve as bases for terrorist attacks, as they have done in the past. Only by holding these territories could Israel secure the minimum depth for its defence.

A Greater Israel would bring into the state over a million more Arab inhabitants in the territories, in addition to the half-million who are Israeli citizens. The problem they would create, it is argued, could be met by autonomy for the Arabs in the territories, or an Arab canton within an Israeli federal system.

The national aspiration of the Palestinian people, it is asserted, could be satisfied in a Jordanian homeland. The majority of the citizens of Jordan are Palestinian Arabs; moreover, the territory of Jordan was part of Palestine under the British Mandate. In 1922, shortly after the Mandate began, the Middle East was in ferment. Winston Churchill, then the British Colonial Secretary, flew to Cairo to deal with the crisis on the spot. As part of the settlement he arranged, Transjordan (five-sevenths of the total Mandatory area) was handed over to the Emir Abdullah, marching up from Saudi Arabia with a force of Bedouin tribesmen. The Jewish National Home provisions of the Mandate were then confined to Western Palestine, and Transjordan was closed to Jewish immigration and settlement. In due course, Transjordan became the Hashemite Kingdom of Jordan, a purely Arab state without a single Jewish resident. Why, it is asked, should Western Palestine not now become the Jewish state, with the River Jordan as the frontier between the two? That would be giving belated effect to the original 1922 partition.

The proponents of a Greater Israel are sceptical of the axiom that peace would be the best security. Israel exists in an unstable region. Whatever Israeli–Arab agreements are signed, much of the Arab world will continue to pursue the hope that the Jewish state could be eliminated. From its birth, the state has been locked in a bitter struggle for survival, and paid a heavy price in human lives and economic burdens. Facing an uncertain future, it is Israel's right and duty to retain the vital strategic terrain it now possesses.

The Greater Israel school points to precedents in Europe for a stable status quo based on unresolved territorial questions. For instance, the reunification of West and East Germany is frozen in the adversary relationship between the superpowers, as are the permanent borders for some East European countries. The European nations live with such interim arrangements and accept that they should be changed only by peaceful means. On that analogy, Israel has the military and political capacity to maintain and defend the existing borders until such time as the international community recognizes them as permanent frontiers.

The strategic and political arguments for the Greater Israel concept are reinforced by historical and religious sentiment. The aim of Zionism was to revive the national identity of the Jewish people in its ancient homeland. In biblical times the hill-country of Judea and Samaria was the Jewish heartland. It would fly in the face of history, religion and the Zionist vision, it is maintained, to relinquish any part of the Land of Israel to foreign sovereignty. The settlement drive in Judea and Samaria after 1967 was, therefore, propelled by a heady mixture of nationalist and religious zeal.

Those are the arguments for a Greater Israel. Yet the Labour Alignment, and all opponents of the Greater Israel concept, put forward formidable reasons for rejecting it. Israel would lose its Jewish character and Zionist vocation, and turn into a binational Jewish–Arab state torn from within by two contending national entities, as was the case in Mandatory Palestine. If the Arab population was denied full and equal rights of citizenship, and given a separate and inferior status, that would mean abandoning the democratic principles of Israel and instituting a form of racial 'apartheid'. A swollen Arab minority, forced into the state against their will and feeling no allegiance to it, would form a huge 'fifth column' in wartime. Annexation would slam the door on any hope of future peace negotiations with Jordan.

At the heart of this clash of opinion is the demographic factor. Population statistics projected to the year 2000 AD show that the number of Palestinian Arabs in the areas that came under the Palestine Mandate after World War I will by the end of the century be as follows:

In Israel (pre-1967)	1,260,000 (22 per cent of total population)
Judea and Samaria	1,220,000
Gaza Strip	850,000
Israel + Judea, Samaria + Gaza Strip	3,330,000 (43 per cent of total in Greater Israel)
Jordan*	1,440,000 (38 per cent of total in Jordan)
Jordan* + Judea, Samaria + Gaza Strip	3,810,000 (60 per cent of total in these areas)

These projections show that the incorporation in Israel of these territories would produce an Arab population constituting forty-three per cent of the total in 2000 AD. Since the rate of actual increase of this Arab population is higher than that of Israeli Jews, a Greater Israel is likely to have an Arab majority within a generation from now, or a little more. The Greater Israel school tends to shut its eyes to this demographic prospect, with all its manifold implications. There are small, insignificant right-wing elements in Israel who believe that the bulk of these Arab inhabitants can be induced by financial incentives or by pressure to go somewhere else, but that is wishful thinking.

Should the territories of the West Bank and the Gaza Strip become an independent Palestinian Arab state? To many people, there is a superficial attraction in this option, as a means of satisfying the national aspirations of the Palestinian Arabs and so solving the conflict. But this proposal is firmly rejected by both major parties in Israel, and their negative attitude is shared by Jordan, Egypt and the United States. They all agree that to create such a mini-state sandwiched between Israel and Jordan would create fresh problems instead of solving existing ones. Such a state could not be economically viable, and politically it would be a subversive factor in the region, serving only Soviet interests. Looking again at the statistics above for the year 2000, such an independent state, with its two million inhabitants, would aspire to gain the allegiance of the Palestinian Arab communities in the two neighbouring states – the one-and-a-half million in Jordan and the one-and-a-quarter million in Israel. It would be against all political and security logic to spread the Palestinian Arab population in this area over three national states instead of two.

*These numbers refer to Palestinian Arabs who migrated into Jordan from what was Western Palestine, from 1948 onwards. Actually, all Jordanians are Palestinian Arabs, since Transjordan (now the Hashemite Kingdom of Jordan) was an integral part of Mandatory Palestine.

The 'territorial compromise' proposed by the Labour Alignment makes sense, since it seeks to provide for Israel's minimum security needs without upsetting the existing ration of Jews and Arabs in the state. Yet it does not appear to be a realistic political basis for Israeli–Jordanian negotiations. It would arouse fierce opposition inside Israel, while King Hussein is unlikely to sign away Arab claims to East Jerusalem and parts of the West Bank.

The solution favoured by Jordan, Egypt and the United States (the Reagan plan) is to bring about in these territories a Palestinian Arab national entity linked to Jordan in a single federal state. This solution would be welcomed by many, if not most, inhabitants of the territories, as a means of ending Israeli rule and bringing them under Arab sovereignty.

In February 1985, all those supporting this approach were much encouraged when King Hussein and Yasser Arafat signed an agreement in Amman that accepted in principle a future Jordanian–Palestinian framework and provided for a joint Jordanian–Palestinian delegation to be formed for negotiations. But by 1986, it had become clear that Arafat's signature meant little, as he had failed to bring the PLO into line with the agreement. In February 1986, the disillusioned King broke off co-operation with him, closed down Fatah offices in Jordan and expelled some of Arafat's lieutenants.

Even without that default on the Arab side, the proposed Jordanian–Palestinian solution would have run into trouble on the Israeli side. The Begin Government rejected the Reagan plan outright, since it was in total conflict with the Greater Israel concept. The Labour Alignment, then in opposition, expressed a cautious willingness to discuss it; but it too was not prepared to return to the 1967 borders.

My conclusion is that there does not appear to be any prospect of an Israeli–Jordanian peace based on any one of these three solutions for the territories:

1 Their absorption into Israel
2 Handing them over as a whole to Jordan
3 Turning them into a separate Palestinian Arab state

A decade ago, when I submitted peace proposals to the Minister of Defence on behalf of the Joint Planning Branch, we expressed the view that the future of these territories could best be settled in the framework of a confederation between Israel and a Jordanian–Palestinian federal state.

I continue to believe that that is the only context in which the complexities and contradictions of demography, security and national aspirations might be resolved. Such a confederation would also facilitate joint economic projects, such as the development of water resources, tourism and Dead Sea minerals, and the integration of posts, airports and transportation systems.

I have already stated my opinion that as an interim or transitional stage, the most feasible arrangement would be a joint administration (condominium) system. I would add that a *de facto* basis for such a system already exists. In twenty years of Israeli military government, the Arab inhabitants of Judea and Samaria have retained Jordanian citizenship, and Jordanian law and institutions have remained intact. Jordan pays salaries to West Bank teachers and lawyers, and subsidies to municipalities. Under the 'Open Bridges' policy instituted from 1967 by Moshe Dayan, as Minister of Defence, the inhabitants of Judea and Samaria cross and send their produce freely over the River Jordan. Every day some 100,000 Arabs from the territories come to work in Israel – that is, within the 'green line'. Informal contacts between Israel and Jordan have recently yielded positive results in such matters as the appointment of mayors in the main West Bank towns, and the opening of an Arab bank branch in Nablus, for the first time since 1967. After King Hussein broke off talks with Arafat, the Jordanian Government announced a five-year development plan for the West Bank, with the intention of reasserting Jordanian influence.

Occupation is an unnatural regime, resented by the occupied and unpalatable for the occupier. Israel has no choice but to maintain it until the political future of these territories is settled. Meanwhile, it is worth recording that a pattern of day-to-day coexistence and co-operation has grown up which could, if wisely nurtured, evolve into a permanent solution acceptable to Israel, Jordan and the Palestinian people.

Moreover, such an outcome would be in substantial conformity with UN Resolution 242, the Camp David Framework Accord and the Reagan plan. It should, therefore, have the endorsement and backing of the United States, Egypt, Jordan and the Palestinian people, and of all other countries interested in a peaceful end to the Israeli–Arab conflict.

181

15

THE MOULDING OF THE ARMY

In British Mandatory Palestine, the *Yishuv* (Jewish community) became a 'state-in-the-making', the forerunner of the sovereign State of Israel. As one facet of this process, the self-defence organization of the *Yishuv*, the Haganah (a Hebrew word meaning 'defence'), was the predecessor of the Israel Defence Forces, the official army of the state.

The Haganah was not in itself an army. It was an informal, volunteer militia, without uniforms or ranks. Its primary purpose was to protect Jewish settlements against Arab attack – a role that became vital during the Arab rebellion in Palestine (1936–8). To finance the Haganah, the *Yishuv* imposed on itself a defence tax that nobody was legally obliged to pay and everyone paid without demur. In time, the Haganah developed a counter-attacking capacity through the Palmach, elite assault units based on the kibbutzim.

In the eyes of the British authorities the Haganah was illegal, and any of its members caught in possession of a weapon was jailed. Hence it trained in isolated places in the hills and kept its arms in hidden caches in the settlements.

The men who would later mould the Israeli army and serve as its top commanders – such as Moshe Dayan, Yigael Yadin, Yigal Allon and Yitzhak Rabin – all emerged from the pre-state Haganah. Like most of my generation, I became a Haganah member while still a teenager.

Israel's War of Independence in effect began before the state. The adoption by the United Nations of the Palestine partition plan on 29 November 1947 was followed by armed violence throughout the country. Arab irregular forces, reinforced from beyond the borders, attacked Jewish settlements, urban quarters and Jewish traffic on the roads. In Jerusalem, 80,000 Jews were isolated and under siege.

By April 1948, a month before independence, the Haganah was able to go on to the offensive. It held the Jerusalem highway open for a massive food convoy to be rushed through to the city's starving Jews. It gained control of Haifa and at Mishmar Haemek in the Galilee repulsed an attack by the so-called Arab Liberation Army. The tide had turned.

But a far more formidable test lay ahead. The British Government had declared that it would terminate the Mandate on 14 May 1948: the Palestine Administration would be dismantled and British forces withdrawn from the country. The day set for the proclamation of Israel's independence was, therefore, 14 May. It was also D-day for the combined regular armies of the Arab states to cross the borders, for the avowed purpose of 'throwing the Jews into the sea', occupying Palestine and turning it into an independent Arab state. The odds were heavily against the survival of the infant State of Israel, with a Jewish population of 650,000 and an 'army' improvised out of a civilian militia, without planes, tanks or field artillery. There were not even enough light weapons to give each man a rifle of his own.

What the Jewish defenders did possess in abundance was that intangible secret weapon – motivation. Our soldiers were fighting for the physical survival of their families and themselves; for Jewish statehood renewed after 2,000 years; for the Holocaust survivors and the Jews in danger in Arab countries, waiting outside to 'come home'. They fought with a revolutionary *élan* reminiscent of the American colonists in their own War of Independence.

The conversion of the Haganah into an organized army for nationwide defence took place under the stress of battle. The IDF was formally established by law on 26 May 1948, two weeks after independence. Two small breakaway groups, which had been in the underground resistance movement during the Mandate, were disbanded and their members drawn into the army. One was the Irgun Zvai Leumi (the Irgun, or Etzel, for short) led by Menachem Begin; the other was the Stern Gang, also known as Lehi, with Yitzhak Shamir as one of its commanders. The first Prime Minister, David Ben-Gurion, kept in his own hands the post of Minister of Defence. More than anyone else, he was the architect of the IDF.

Fortunately, the army could at the outset draw on a pool of veterans of World War II. One source was the Jewish Brigade, which had served in Europe in 1944–5. Another source of trained manpower lay in the Jewish ex-servicemen of Western countries who had fought in the Allied armies during the war and now came to join as volunteers in Israel's fight. The value of these *machal* (foreign volunteers) lay not so much in their numbers – about 5,000 – as in their experience and skills in specialized fields, notably with the fledgling air force and other professional military services.

In the first few weeks of the fighting, Israel was in mortal danger. The Arab strategy was to attack simultaneously on all fronts, carve up the state into isolated segments and overcome them piecemeal.

In the south, the Egyptian army captured Beersheba, cut off the Jewish settlements in the Negev and developed a two-pronged advance that reached the outskirts of Jerusalem and in the coastal plain came within twenty miles of Tel Aviv.

The Jordanian Arab Legion overran the Gush Etzion group of settlements, occupied what later became known as the West Bank, captured the Old City of Jerusalem, bombarded the Jewish Quarter of West Jerusalem, and cut the Jerusalem–Tel Aviv highway at Latrun.

In the centre, an Iraqi expeditionary force thrust from Jordan across the hills of Samaria, with the intention of cutting the Sharon coastal plain in the vicinity of Netanya and reaching the Mediterranean coast.

The Syrian forces in the north-east aimed at occupying the Huleh Valley panhandle, the Upper Jordan Valley and the Sea of Galilee area, and then pushing into the Galilee highlands.

Palestinian irregular forces based in Lebanon continued to operate in the Western and Central Galilee.

In the first three weeks of fighting, the Arab advance was brought to a halt on each front. In the month's truce that followed under UN auspices, the IDF used the breathing-space for intensive redeployment, training and planning. A General Staff was set up, with separate commands for each of the major fronts. Arms and equipment were acquired from World War II surplus and brought in clandestinely, because of the UN truce restrictions and the arms embargo imposed by the US and other Western powers. One essential acquisition concerned some old German Messerschmidt fighter planes smuggled in from Czechoslovakia in parts and secretly assembled in Israel.

In the ten days of fighting that followed the first truce, before it was renewed, the IDF went on to the attack everywhere. In October the Galilee was cleared, and a counter-offensive in the south broke through the Egyptian lines, took Beersheba and linked up with the Negev settlements. A later offensive in January 1949 completely routed the Egyptian forces and pursued them across the frontier.

By the 1949 armistice agreements with the four neighbouring Arab states, the war ended with the IDF holding a contiguous territory 8,000 square miles in extent, stretching from Metulla in the north to Eilat in the south, with a corridor to West Jerusalem declared the capital of the state.

The time had come to assess the lessons of the War of Independence and to put the IDF on a systematic footing. In September 1949, the Knesset adopted the Defence Service Law. It was based on the realistic premise that the nation had to be ready at all times to fight another war against the combined Arab states, yet could not afford to keep a large standing army.

The solution was compulsory military training for men and women for two years from the age of eighteen. After that, there was part-time service in reserve units, with annual training periods. Liability for military service extended to the age of fifty-five for men and thirty-eight for unmarried women. The standing army at any given time thus consisted of the conscripts doing their military service, with a nucleus of permanent force officers and NCOs for staff duties, instruction and specialist jobs. In time of war, there would be a call-up of the reserve units. In a surprise attack or sudden emergency, the standing army had to bear the brunt of defence until mobilization of the reserve units could be effected.

Because of Israel's small size, long borders and lack of strategic depth, call-up procedures were designed for maximum speed. Israel is the only country where within twenty-four hours civilians can leave their homes and jobs and become soldiers serving with their units in the field.

The IDF thus became in a real sense a 'people's army', somewhat in the spirit of the Haganah. In the early, formative years of the state, it served as a major instrument for integrating the mass of immigrants from seventy different countries into a cohesive Israeli nation.

In the years between the War of Independence and the 1956 Sinai Campaign, the IDF developed rapidly into an effective fighting machine. The country was divided into three regional command areas, the North, the Centre and the South. The air force and the navy were organized not as independent services but as branches of the IDF, under a single Chief of Staff and General Staff. Special ordnance, supplies, engineering, communications and medical corps were set up. For lack of sources from which to acquire new armaments, the IDF had to buy out-of-date tanks and heavy equipment discarded by other countries and renovate them in Israel. That was the beginning of a local arms industry.

Much thought and discussion was devoted in those early years to evolving war doctrines, battle tactics and training methods adapted to the special problems of Israel's defence. Emphasis was placed on integrated land, sea and air operations, on speed and mobility, and on the personal initiative of officers and NCOs at all levels. Lack of depth, meagre resources and reliance on mobilized reserves required that a prolonged, static and defensive war had to be avoided at all costs. The battle had to be carried quickly into enemy territory, and the opposing forces had to be kept confused and off-balance by rapid advance, outflanking movements and deep penetration into their rear areas. With all the risks involved, the central objectives should be to destroy the enemy's arms, occupy enemy territory and shorten the war as much as possible. Victory and conquest were not conceived as ends in themselves but as means to a political end – namely, to convince the Arab states that their conflict with Israel could not be settled by military force but only by negotiations. These guiding principles of the IDF have remained constant through all the changes it has undergone down the years.

The first major test for the new army came with the Sinai Campaign. In military terms it was an outstanding success, even taking into account that Egypt had also to face the abortive Anglo–French expedition at Port Said. The Egyptian forces in Sinai were routed, its fortified positions overrun and thousands of its soldiers taken prisoner. The IDF halted near the Suez Canal, while one column made its way along the eastern shore of the Gulf of Akaba and captured Sharm el-Sheikh, thereby breaking the Egyptian blockade of the Gulf. The whole campaign lasted a hundred hours.

The decade between the Sinai Campaign and the Six Day War saw a continued rapid development in all areas – armour, air force, navy, airborne and seaborne assault troops and the local production of weapons and equipment. A thorough study was made of the Soviet military doctrines on which the Syrian and Egyptian armies were based. Theoretical answers were worked out and tested in training exercises, simulating Soviet models.

This was the period when France was Israel's closest ally and major supplier of military equipment. (The 'French honeymoon' would cease abruptly in 1967, when de Gaulle had disengaged France from the war in Algeria and had thereby ended its own conflict with the Arab world.)

The advance in Israel's military capacity after 1957 was demonstrated in the Six Day War of 1967. From Monday to Saturday of the same week, the armies of Egypt, Syria and Jordan were defeated and the Israeli forces occupied Sinai, the West Bank, the Gaza Strip and the Golan Heights.

The great disappointment of the war was that Israel's resounding victory did not create openings for a political settlement of the conflict. The Arab states continued to war by other means. This was so especially with Egypt. Under the guidance of its Russian advisers, it devised and launched a totally different kind of war, with which the IDF was unfamiliar. It became known as the War of Attrition, a term the dictionary defines as 'a wearing or grinding down'. Its objectives were to make the IDF positions along the Suez Canal untenable and to weaken Israel through casualties, continued mobilization and economic strains, without Egypt incurring the risks of a pitched battle.

The offensive opened in September 1968 with a sudden concentrated artillery barrage on the Israeli forces deployed along the Suez Canal, inflicting heavy casualties. Israel responded by constructing fortifications, by commando raids, by air attacks on the Egyptian artillery batteries, and by retaliatory shelling of the towns in the Canal zone.

To neutralize Israel's air superiority, the Soviet Union established behind the Canal a screen of SA3 ground-to-air missiles, the first of their kind to appear in the Middle East. Israel gained the upper hand when its planes succeeded in overcoming these missile bases. In the summer of

1970, the Egyptian Government agreed to renew the ceasefire that Nasser had renounced in launching his War of Attrition.

In the War of Attrition the IDF had had to meet new challenges, such as the construction of dug-in fortified positions able to withstand pounding by massed Soviet artillery – and coping with an air-defence system based on Soviet ground-to-air SAM missiles and fighter-interceptor planes.

Of the men who built up Israel's armed strength in the 1960s, four merit special mention. As Deputy Minister of Defence (1959–65), Shimon Peres laid the foundations for the research, development and production of the highly sophisticated weapons systems the IDF possesses. He was also the person most responsible for the close co-operation with France in the defence field from the Sinai Campaign to the Six Day War.

General Yitzhak Rabin, as Chief of Staff (1964–8), guided the overall development of the IDF along the lines that proved themselves in so spectacular a fashion in the Six Day War.

General Ezer Weizman, as Commander of the Air Force (1958–66), shaped it into a superb instrument, capable of gaining air supremacy in war within twenty-four hours, to defend the state against air attack and to ensure a rapid outcome in battle by combined operations with the land and sea forces.

General Israel ('Talik') Tal built up and commanded the armoured corps as the backbone of the ground forces. He formulated the IDF doctrine of mobile warfare and was responsible for the development of the 'Merkava' as the world's most advanced battle-tank.

All these men shared a common belief, that Israel's central war aim should be not only to secure its survival, but also to create the conditions for peace with its neighbours. In later years, Peres, Weizman and Rabin would each play a prominent role in the peace process.

In the years after 1967, the IDF had to adjust itself to the new reality that resulted from the Six Day War. The territory to be defended and the length of the defence perimeter had dramatically expanded. A corresponding (and very costly) expansion had to take place both in the standing army and in the military infrastructure – fortifications, roads, airfields, camps, maintenance depots, electricity grids and a naval base at Sharm el-Sheikh.

The period of compulsory military service for men was extended to three years, since additional manpower was needed to cope with new needs: the War of Attrition on the Suez Canal accompanied by stepped-up terrorist activities across the Jordanian, Syrian and Lebanese borders; the longer defence lines; control of the occupied territories and their administration by a military government; and additional tank and mechanized brigades.

Among the military factors to which special emphasis was given at this time were mobile artillery (one of the main lessons from the War of Attrition), air defence, the transport of assault troops by helicopters and landing-craft, and the crossing of water obstacles.

The domestic armaments industry developed rapidly. This productive capacity complemented the advanced types of aircraft, missiles and other equipment Israel was now acquiring from the United States, in what had become a closer strategic partnership.

The strides made in the fighting capacity of the IDF after 1967, and the defensive depth that resulted from the Six Day War, enabled Israel to withstand the massive surprise attack that launched the Yom Kippur War in October 1973. The combined Egyptian–Syrian assault was halted in the first few days. After that, the Israeli forces went on to the offensive. At the end, they were in a position to advance to the gates of Cairo and Damascus, but for the intervention of the superpowers.

Yet the shock of the war, and the lessons it taught, brought about revolutionary changes in Israel's defence strategy.

In every long-term development plan for the IDF, there are basic factors that remain constant. One of these is the numerical imbalance between Israeli forces and those of the Arab confrontation states. The size of the forces has been heavily in favour of the Arab side, and the rates of main weapons systems – such as fighter planes, missiles, artillery, naval craft or assault helicopters – vary from 4:1 to 7:1 to Israel's disadvantage. This disparity is compounded by the fact that while the Arab states maintain standing armies, the IDF has in wartime to rely mainly on reserve units. Israel may, therefore, be exposed to the danger of a sudden surprise attack, as happened in the Yom Kippur War.

Another problem facing Israel's defence planners is that its manpower and financial resources are strained to the utmost to maintain the minimum of national security. The Arab confrontation states do not lack the men or the money needed to increase their armed forces. Nor are they limited in arms supplies – from the two superpowers for political motives and from countries like Britain and France for commercial profit.

Another constant factor is geographical – Israel's lack of size and strategic depth. This factor has grown in importance with the years. Up to the Yom Kippur War, the armies of the Arab states relied mainly on infantry. Today, their land forces are based on armoured and mechanized forces, supplemented in a mobile attack by helicopter gunships and airborne, seaborne and commando formations. Their air forces and missiles have the capacity to strike at strategic targets inside Israel; while the missile carriers, submarines and sea-to-sea missiles in their navies could threaten Israel's navigation routes and coastal targets. Israel must

188

also safeguard against the possibility that nuclear or chemical weapons may be used against it in the future.

To maintain its deterrent strength, Israel has to compensate in other ways for the quantitative imbalance between itself and Arab confrontation states and its geographical limitations. The IDF depends on qualitative superiority in the training and motivation of its soldiers; the qualities imbued in the commanders at all levels; very sophisticated weapons systems; maintenance of sufficient standing forces to withstand surprise attack, without imposing an undue economic burden; techniques for swift mobilization; early-warning systems; and the harnessing of the best scientific and technological skills in the country to the task of national security.

Even after the Peace Treaty with Egypt, Israel continues to exist in a dangerously unstable and hostile region. What is crucial is the psychological balance denoted by the word 'deterrence': the growing awareness in the Arab mind that the IDF has the capacity not only to defend the state (as it has done for almost forty years), but also to deliver devastating counter-blows at any attacker.

16

LESSONS OF THE YOM KIPPUR WAR

The way the Yom Kippur War began was the most shattering experience in the history of Israel. Our political and military leadership was sanguine that the Arab states would not start another war in 1973; and, if they did, that our defence lines could contain the offensive until the reserves were brought into action. That is what should have happened; what actually happened was quite different. Egypt and Syria did launch a war; the IDF was taken by surprise and unprepared; and the enemy forces swept through our defence lines on the Suez Canal and the Golan Heights before the reserve units could be deployed. Within a few days the tide had turned, but the initial shock remained.

After the war, an august State Commission of Enquiry was appointed to examine what had gone wrong, who was to blame and what could be recommended to avoid such a situation in the future. The Commission was headed by Chief Justice Shimon Agranat and included Supreme Court Justice Moshe Landau, State Comptroller Yitzhak Nebenzahl, and two former IDF Chiefs of Staff, Yigael Yadin and Haim Laskov.

For each of us Israelis, those fateful days remain an intense personal memory. My own experience at that time can serve to introduce some general comments on the lessons of the Yom Kippur War.

The Egyptian–Syrian offensive opened at precisely 1400 hours (2 p.m.) on the day of Yom Kippur (the Day of Atonement, the holiest day of the Jewish Year) on 6 October 1973. A few hours later, I walked into the underground General Staff Command HQ, which was crowded. Other senior staff officers who had not been summoned were milling around seeking information and disturbing those at work. Nobody knew what to expect. The Chief of Staff, General David ('Dado') Elazar, was in the War Room, giving instructions over the communications network. His face was gloomy and his eyes puffy from lack of sleep. I could feel the burden on him in this grim hour. (For years, Dado had aspired to be Chief of Staff, while other candidates had been preferred by Defence Minister Dayan. He was finally appointed with the support of the retiring Chief of

Staff, Chaim Bar-Lev, and of Deputy Premier and Foreign Minister Yigal Allon, who had been Dado's commander in the Palmach before the state. He would be forced to resign after the war as a result of criticism by the Agranat Commission.)

In the next room sat General Israel Tal, head of the General Staff Branch, who was absorbing a stream of confused reports from the fronts. The atmosphere was tense. I decided that as head of the Planning Branch, I was not needed here, and there was nothing better for me to do than to join the soldiers in the field. I immediately left for Beersheba, where the reserve division under Arik Sharon was hurriedly being assembled before moving off to the Suez Canal front.

Until a few months earlier, Sharon had been GOC Southern Command, which included Sinai. He had been released from the permanent army as he wanted to run in the Knesset elections due in October. He had then been assigned to the command of this division as his posting in the reserves. My own posting in an emergency was as Chief Assistant to Sharon, the Divisional Commander.

In Beersheba, I found him at his command post in a camp where the reserves were being equipped as they reported in. He was issuing orders to the brigade commanders on their deployment at the Canal front. According to the freshly marked intelligence map hanging in the room, two entire Egyptian armies, comprising five divisions with 70,000 men, had already forded the Canal along its whole length. Our fortified positions strung out along the east bank of the Canal had been evacuated or were cut off. Two armoured brigade groups under General Avraham Mendler were fighting a fierce battle along a 100-mile front to stem the Egyptian advances deeper into Sinai. Mendler's men would have to continue this non-stop holding action for at least twenty-four hours more, although sustaining severe losses, until two reserve divisions could be mobilized and transported across the Sinai Desert. Sharon's division would then take over the central sector of the front, and the division commanded by General ('Bren') Adan would be deployed in the northern sector, with responsibility also for the coastal highway. Mendler's battered force would then remain in charge of the southern sector, which included the vital Mitla and Gidi Passes through a range of hills.

That first night of the war, after Sharon had issued all the necessary commands in the Beersheba assembly camp, the division started out on its 200-mile trek to the Suez Canal front. The men knew there would be no rest when they arrived, for they would be flung at once into the battle. I set out with Sharon in a Land-Rover. Next afternoon we reached Mendler's headquarters in the Refidim base and worked out with him the arrangements for taking over the central sector of the front later that day. Mendler was tired but unruffled, and confident that the enemy forces would be halted before gaining any significant objectives in Sinai. I thought, not for the first time, how calm the commanders were in action, and how panic and anxiety grew the further away one was from the front lines.

Mendler briefed us on the immediate situation, which was still unclear. One of his two armoured brigades was fighting against the whole Egyptian Second Army, which had crossed in the sector between the Bitter Lakes and the Mediterranean coast. The other armoured brigade was engaged with the whole Egyptian Third Army, which had attacked in the sector between the Bitter Lakes and the Gulf of Suez. The Egyptians had succeeded in advancing about three to five miles east of the Canal; behind them, some of the fortified Israeli positions on the Canal were still holding out, though surrounded.

We left Mendler and drove on towards the Canal. At the edge of the hills traversed by the Mitla and Gidi Passes, we stopped at a point from which we could see to the west. The Canal sector was covered in a blue-grey mist. The desert silence was intermittently broken by gunfire. Here and there columns of smoke rose into the sky – whether ours or theirs, we could not tell. Sharon turned round and saw me leaning against the jeep. 'Why are you looking so dejected?' he asked. I did not answer. What I had been thinking was that when this war was over, there would be much heart-searching over the reasons why we had unexpectedly found ourselves in such a tough situation. Our basic defence concepts would have to be thought out afresh.

I shall now comment on some of the grave issues raised by the war.

Regulars and Reserves

It is a stark fact that the numbers and types of Israeli regular forces in Sinai and on the Golan Heights failed to prevent the Egyptian and Syrian armies from breaking through our forward positions and advancing into territory held by us. I have described what happened on the Suez Canal front. On the Golan Heights, the Syrian vanguard reached almost to the River Jordan. For the first twenty-four hours a single formation commanded by General Rafael Eitan fought heroically to slow down the enemy advance until the reserve units could be deployed. Only then could a counter-attack be launched and a start made to drive the Syrians back.

A crucial factor was the strategic depth afforded by the Sinai Desert and the Golan Heights. If the IDF had still been standing on the pre-1967 borders, the Arab attack would have driven straight into Israel's populated areas, and they would have become the battlefield.

The central lesson of the war was that fortified lines, even with strategic depth behind them, were not enough in themselves for Israel's defence. In conditions of modern warfare, the regular forces had to be capable of withstanding a massive surprise attack on all fronts, repulsing it, launching a counter-attack and transferring the war into enemy territory – all, in the initial phases, independently of the arrival of reserve units. This objective required a fundamental reorganization of the IDF. It involved not just strengthening the ground forces, but determining the optimum balance between its different components – armour, mechanized infantry and field artillery. While there is close co-operation between the various branches, each formation and each weapons system must be capable of operating with great flexibility in both offensive and defensive roles. The IDF of the 1980s is an essentially different army from that of the 1970s.

Surprise

It is generally believed that the Egyptian and Syrian attack could not have been foreseen. This is not so. After the Six Day War, a mood of complacency developed in the country. It was felt that the military superiority Israel had so strikingly demonstrated in that war would deter the Arab states from attacking again, and that a situation of 'no-war, no-peace' could be maintained indefinitely until our Arab neighbours were prepared to make peace with us. Not all of us in the military establishment shared that comfortable belief. As the General Staff officer responsible for strategic planning, I made an assessment as early as 1971 that deterrence alone would not guarantee the indefinite continuation of the status quo, and that war might break out 'in the summer of 1973' if practical negotiations were not opened by then, at least with Egypt. This prediction was derived from an analysis carried out by my staff of the Soviet build-up of Egyptian and Syrian forces, and the time when their offensive capability would reach its peak.

In 1971, I also prepared and conducted a 'war game' predicated on a combined Egyptian–Syrian surprise attack on Israel. (Ezer Weizman, then head of the GHQ General Staff Branch, played the role of an Arab commanding general.) The scope of the enemy attack, its objectives, its achievements and the reactions of the IDF, as reflected in this 'war game', would bear a startling resemblance to what actually took place in the Yom Kippur War two years later.

As often happens, these predictions were dismissed as one of the exercises which every General Staff carried out to meet all theoretical contingencies. They did not have any impact on the prevailing preconception that we would not have to fight again. A false sense of security accounted for the fact that the enemy troop concentrations were misinterpreted by our military intelligence as merely large-scale manœuvres – an impression deliberately fostered by Egypt and Syria.

Another reason why we were taken off-guard was our confidence in the capacity of our defence lines to withstand attack. This applied especially to the Suez Canal front. The Canal was regarded as a formidable water barrier which would be almost impossible for the Egyptian forces to ford in any strength under fire from fortified Israeli positions and mobile armed forces on the opposite bank. The War of Attrition had shown that these positions were vulnerable to concentrated artillery bombardment. As a result, a line of specially designed concrete bunkers was constructed at a huge cost, which became known as the Bar-Lev Line, after the Chief of Staff at the time. In General Staff discussions, some of us expressed reservations about this Maginot-Line approach and suggested alternative strategies, more in keeping with the IDF's reliance on mobile warfare. The most outspoken critic of the Bar-Lev Line was Sharon, who offended Bar-Lev by an unbridled attack on the concept.

The moment of truth came on the day of Yom Kippur 1973. The massive Egyptian assault swept through the Bar-Lev Line in hours, having forded the Canal with the use of advanced bridging equipment developed by the Soviet Union to cross the European river systems. This deep-rooted Israeli attitude of dismissing a threat of Arab attack persisted almost to the twelfth hour, the Thursday night before Yom Kippur (which began on Friday evening). I was summoned to a General Staff meeting to consider the latest intelligence reports of Egyptian and Syrian troop movements. Defence Minister Dayan and Chief of Staff Elazar took part in the discussion. The general feeling was that these movements did not mean war – though certain precautionary measures had been taken, such as putting some air-force and armoured units on alert, and sending forward some reinforcements. I expressed my own forebodings, but I had for long been regarded as an alarmist in this matter, so my opinion was disregarded.

The next day, Friday, Prime Minister Golda Meir remained very disturbed by the reports reaching her. She singled out as particularly ominous one report that the families of Russian advisers in Syria were being evacuated. She called an urgent meeting at her home, attended by Dayan, Elazar and Bar-Lev, who was then Minister of Commerce and Industry. They assured her that war was not imminent. At 4 a.m. that night she was told by telephone that, according to definite information just received, Egypt and Syria would launch a simultaneous attack in force later that same day. For the rest of her life, Golda did not forgive herself for not having acted on her own instincts and ordered a general mobilization.

Golda's feelings of guilt bear out one important point. Where there has been a miscalculation about enemy intentions, there is a tendency to make a scapegoat of the Intelligence branch. That is often unwarranted. Intelligence has two aspects: one is collecting information; the other is making assessments and recommendations on the basis of that inform-ation. Whether to accept the assessments and act on the recommend-ations is the responsibility of those who have to make decisions – either the military command or, at a higher level, the political echelon. Golda did not query that. A leader who never shirked responsibility, she accepted the simple Harry Truman axiom that 'the buck stops here'.

The basic Intelligence error in this case was that it focused not on actual troop *movements* (which were accurately observed and reported) but on mistaken assumptions regarding enemy *intentions*. That is a fragile basis for security decisions. Such assessments may be subject to human error, or coloured by preconceived ideas, which happened in this case. Moreover, the enemy will take measures to conceal its real intentions and mislead its opponent, which is what Egypt and Syria did in the six months of secret preparations for their offensive. (For instance, the previous May they staged a false alarm, which led to a partial Israeli mobilization. The psychological result was that Israel was reluctant to repeat the experience in October, before the real assault took place.)

In order to make a sound assessment of enemy intentions, one has to grasp what options are open to the enemy. The failure to do so before the Yom Kippur War was a direct cause of the surprise. When the prospect was dismissed that the Arabs would launch another war on Israel, our Intelligence service and policy-makers had in mind a full-scale war – that is, one aimed at the defeat of the Israeli army and the invasion and occupation of the country. The War of Independence and the Six Day War were full-scale wars in this sense. The Yom Kippur War was not. In launching their attack, Egypt and Syria had limited objectives, which were political and psychological as much as they were military.

The military objective for Syria was to regain the whole Golan Heights. The military objective for Egypt was to break the Israeli hold on the eastern bank of the Suez Canal and regain Western Sinai, at least as far as the Mitla and Gidi Passes. It was assumed by them that the superpowers would promptly intervene and impose a ceasefire before the Israeli forces could rally and mount a counter-offensive to regain lost ground.

These limited aims were quite realistic, taking into account the advantages of surprise and initiative, and the tremendous force of the simultaneous thrust that had been prepared with Soviet help. To illustrate the unprecedented scale of the attack, Syria threw 1,400 tanks against a narrow front of the Golan Heights. Israel had 180 tanks on that front at that time.

In planning their attack, the Egyptian and Syrian leaders calculated that even limited military successes would have a devastating effect on Israeli morale, while wiping out the psychosis of defeat on the Arab side. On the political front, the international community, and the two superpowers in particular, would be alarmed out of their inertia and exert intense pressure on Israel to give up the territories occupied in 1967.

As invariably happens in war, this one failed to go according to plan. There were initial successes, but by the time the United States and the Soviet Union jointly imposed a ceasefire, eighteen days after the start of the war, the tables had been turned on the battlefield. The Egyptian army was in a desperate position, with the IDF deployed across the Canal. On the Golan Heights, the Syrians had been pushed back beyond their starting-line and the IDF was within striking distance of Damascus.

Yet, while Israel had won the military showdown, the psychological and political objectives for starting it were to some extent realized. The war left Israel in a sober mood, with a loss of confidence in the nation's leadership. On the international level, the dormant peace process was actively revived.

Pre-emptive Strikes

On Yom Kippur day, a matter of hours before the war started, Chief of Staff Elazar requested permission to launch an immediate attack by the air force on enemy concentrations and vital targets. In her autobiography, Golda Meir quoted her reply: 'Dado,' she said, 'I know all the arguments in favour of a pre-emptive strike, but I am against it. There is always the possibility that we may need help, and if we strike first, we will get nothing from anyone. I would like to say yes because I know what it would mean, but with a heavy heart I am going to say no.'

At a crucial stage of the war, when an American air-lift started bringing in urgently needed military equipment and supplies, Golda felt that her instinctive decision had been right.

In a situation of imminent danger, it makes military sense to forestall an attack, on the Josh Billings' principle that,

> Thrice is he armed that hath his quarrel just,
> But four times he who gets his blow in fust.

Yet the political price may be exorbitant. The international community always clings to the hope that a crisis may still be defused and hostilities averted at the last moment. (The Cuban missile crisis is the classic example in our time.) Hence, whichever side fires the first shot is liable to be branded as the aggressor, unless it is obviously acting in self-defence.

196

That was the case with the Six Day War. It actually started with an Israeli air strike, which virtually destroyed the Egyptian air force on the ground. That was the decisive action of the war. But during the agonizing weeks that preceded it, the outside world had watched impotently while the noose tightened round Israel, until its very survival was at stake. Nobody in the West, except de Gaulle, accused Israel of starting the war.

A small country like Israel, lacking in strategic depth and surrounded by enemies, can never forego the possibility of a pre-emptive strike against an imminent threat. As the Yom Kippur War showed, Israel's neighbours have acquired the capacity to attack it with tremendous force and speed. But the decision to strike first is always a difficult and risky one, involving a delicate balance between military and political factors.

A Testing-Ground for Weapons

As with every armed conflict, the Yom Kippur War was a testing-ground for new types of weapons and for existing battlefield concepts. As such, it was closely studied by General Staffs and military experts everywhere, including those of NATO and the Warsaw Pact. What gave the war importance from this point of view was that it was an encounter between the Soviet arms supplied to Egypt and Syria, and Israeli–American weaponry.

It was the first time in history that missile battles took place at sea. The daring tactics evolved by the Israeli naval craft, equipped with Israeli-made missiles, were completely successful and gained control of both the Mediterranean coast and the Red Sea. On the other hand, the disturbing rate of Israeli plane losses was due almost entirely to the effectiveness of Soviet ground-to-air missiles. This raised serious questions about air support for ground forces. In the years to come, Israeli scientific research would develop answers to this problem, as was demonstrated in the Lebanese war.

The main focus of international interest concerned the role of the tank in modern warfare. An unpleasant surprise for the IDF was the Soviet anti-tank weapon (the Yagger) distributed in great numbers to the Egyptian and Syrian troops. The IDF had to improvise means to cope with it. In general, the tank losses of both sides in the battles in Sinai and the Golan Heights were unprecedented. Israel destroyed approximately 1,100 Syrian and 1,000 Egyptian tanks, some of them of the latest Soviet models. The tank had been master of the battlefield since the 1920s. After the Yom Kippur War, the general verdict was that its day was over. But that conclusion was premature; and one is reminded of Mark Twain's cable to the Associated Press that 'the report of my death is an exaggeration'.

197

Withdrawal

In terms of Security Council Resolution 242 of 1967, Israel was not obliged to withdraw from any of the territory occupied in the Six Day War, except in the context of 'a just and lasting peace'. Yet after the Yom Kippur War, the Israeli Government was willing to consider partial withdrawals in exchange for partial agreements that fell short of peace. This shift in Israel's position led to the Disengagement-of-Forces Agreements with Egypt and Syria in 1974, and the Interim Agreement with Egypt in 1975.

The rationale of the Rabin Government for this changed attitude was twofold. In military terms, the loss of strategic territory would be compensated by the creation of buffer zones containing elaborate systems of safeguards against surprise attack. Moreover, it would be accompanied by an augmented supply by the United States of sophisticated military hardware. In political terms, partial agreements might pave the way for eventual peace treaties. There were risks involved in this, but it did in the end lead to the Peace Treaty with Egypt.

Superpower Intervention

The two superpowers played a major part in the Yom Kippur War. Their intervention went through three phases. The first concerned military supplies to the combatants. From the beginning of hostilities, the Russians supplied the Egyptian and Syrian armies through a massive air-lift, followed by sea transports. It was soon evident that Israel too was losing planes and tanks and expending ammunition at a rate that made their replacement essential. By the second day of the war, the Israeli Government had turned to Washington to provide the needed supplies and to bring them in by air-lift. The request ran into political and bureaucratic obstacles in Washington, and the air-lift finally started on 14 October, the ninth day of the war, on the personal orders of President Nixon. The air-lift was not only crucial to the military balance; it served notice on the Arab Governments concerned and their Soviet backers that the United States would stand by Israel.

The next phase concerned the ceasefire. When the IDF had gone on to the offensive, and the Egyptian and Syrian armies faced complete defeat, the Soviet Union approached Washington about a ceasefire. Secretary of State Kissinger flew to Moscow and returned with a signed text that was pushed through the Security Council as Resolution 338.

The ceasefire was to come into effect on 22 October. But, in fact, fighting went on for another five days. The 20,000-strong Egyptian Third Army on the eastern side of the Canal was completely cut off from supplies, and would have been forced to surrender in a matter of days. This precipitated the third, climactic phase of superpower intervention. The Soviet Union demanded that the two superpowers together relieve the Egyptian Third Army, otherwise the Soviet Union would do so alone. Reports reached Washington that four Russian airborne divisions were in readiness. President Nixon responded by ordering a global 'red alert' of all American strategic forces, including nuclear ones. At the same time, the United States put heavy pressure on the Israeli Government to let non-military supplies through to the Egyptian troops. The immediate motive was to avert a US–USSR conflict. Furthermore, Kissinger maintained that an Egyptian military débâcle would shut the door on any chance of negotiations after the war. Israel had to give way and forego the decisive victory that was within its grasp. The international media were treated to a strange spectacle: crates and sacks of food being transported through the Israeli lines to the water's edge, ferried across the Canal on boats, and carried away from the opposite bank on the backs of Egyptian soldiers.

The way the war ended sharply reminded Israel of the external constraints on its freedom of military action that could be imposed by one or other superpower, or both together. Their rivalry in the Middle East appeared to be governed by certain unwritten rules of the game. In a local war, they could use military supplies to influence the outcome. But a threat of direct military intervention by the Russians would provoke an American reaction. And the two superpowers would act together to stop the war when the danger arose that it might bring them into direct confrontation with each other.

Consequently, in any war the Israeli Government has to calculate carefully how much freedom of action it has, and for how long. In the Sinai Campaign, the IDF routed the Egyptian army but had to withdraw again in the face of American pressure and Russian threats. In the Six Day War, the IDF had twenty-four hours to break through the Syrian fortifications and take the Golan Heights, in order to beat a Security Council ceasefire supported by both superpowers. In the Yom Kippur War, it was very doubtful whether the Russians would actually have intervened. But they may well have done so if the IDF had marched on Cairo or Damascus, as it could have done. As it was, the Russian threat was enough to bring American pressure down on Israel.

Arms Supply

After the initial shock and confusion, the most anxious time for Israel in the Yom Kippur War was the delay in the American air-lift of military supplies. (At one point, Golda Meir considered flying incognito to Washington to see President Nixon about it.) This episode underlined Israel's unhappiness at having to depend on uncertain foreign sources for the weapons it needed to defend itself.

From the War of Independence onwards, Israel has encountered recurrent arms embargoes imposed by the United States and other friendly Western countries. The reasons have been political – reluctance to be involved in Israeli–Arab wars, fear of damaging interests in the Arab world, or displeasure at actions taken by Israel. On a number of occasions, military equipment already purchased by Israel has not been allowed to leave the exporting country when hostilities have broken out. For instance, for a decade after the Sinai Campaign, France was Israel's main supplier of weapons. But with the outbreak of the Six Day War, President de Gaulle abruptly broke off that relationship and imposed an embargo. With the American air-lift in the Yom Kippur War, Britain and Western European countries refused to allow the planes even to land on their soil for refuelling.

After the war, Israel found during the negotiations with Egypt over the Interim Agreement, and again over the Peace Treaty, that the United States could use the supply or withholding of weapons as leverage to extract political concessions.

It is not surprising that from the beginning Israel should have set itself the task of building up a domestic arms industry to reduce its dependence on imports. In the War of Independence, Israel's fledgling army was gravely handicapped by a shortage of weapons due to the embargoes imposed by all Western countries, including the United States. Israel started to produce small arms and mortars in primitive workshops. It also became adept at overhauling old tanks and aircraft acquired from World War II surplus. The arms industry developed rapidly using the nation's advanced scientific institutions, technological skills and native ingenuity. The main enterprises were state-owned: the Israel Military Industries, the Israel Aircraft Industries, the Rafael Armament Development Authority and the Haifa Shipyards. In addition, hundreds of private plants receive orders from the Ministry of Defence.

After the Yom Kippur War, there was a striking advance in the field of electronic warfare, in co-operation with the United States. The air force and the navy are today in the front rank of the world's armed forces in this respect.

Israel produces a fighter plane, the Kfir; a battle-tank, the Merkava; missile boats for the navy; and a wide range of missiles and artillery. It also began developing the Lavi, an advanced and versatile fighter plane for the 1990s – the most ambitious and costly technological project in the country's history.

In order to maintain its arms industry, Israel has had to do what all other arms-producing countries do, that is, to seek export markets for its products. It ranks among the ten leading arms exporters in the world.

American arms, know-how and military grants are of the greatest importance if Israel is to maintain a qualitative edge over Arab armies. At the same time, Israel has made, and will continue to make, Herculean efforts to be able to defend itself even if it is cut off from all outside sources of supply. (Incidentally, the Israeli–American relationship in this field is a two-way street. The American armaments industry gains much from Israel's battlefield experience, its encounters with Soviet weaponry and its technical innovations.)

Border Settlements

In the period between the Six Day War and the Yom Kippur War, insufficient attention was given to the integration of civilian border settlements into a broad defence system. In the British Mandatory period before the state, the defence of the *Yishuv* in outlying areas was based on the self-defence of the settlements. Their role was symbolized in the 'stockade-and-tower' new settlements, which could be erected in a single night during the Arab disturbances of 1936–8 and were ready to withstand attack by dawn. The network of settlements played a key part in the War of Independence and the six months of fighting that preceded the proclamation of the state.

The Six Day War produced new, extended borders on the Suez Canal, the River Jordan and the Golan Heights – all far removed from existing settlements that had been close to the pre-1967 lines. The only borders that remained unchanged were those with Lebanon in the north and with Jordan in the Wadi Araba, between the Dead Sea and the Gulf of Akaba. Settlement activity by the Labour Alignment Governments after 1967 was concentrated in those areas which Israel hoped to retain in a peace settlement – the Eastern Sinai between the old international border and the El Arish–Ras Muhammad line; the Golan Heights; and certain parts of the West Bank. The motive was to draw the future political map, while the defence aspect of settlement was neglected. This derived from the belief (which turned out to be fallacious) that the IDF deployment in the occupied territories provided the necessary strength and depth to deal with any dangers that might arise along the borders. No attempt was made to introduce civilian settlement in Sinai west of the El Arish–Ras Muhammad line. On the Golan Heights, some of the settlements established after 1967 had to be hurriedly evacuated in the Yom Kippur War as the Syrians advanced.

201

After the war, the concept revived that settlements in exposed border areas had to be given their place in an integrated defence system, provided with air-raid shelter and minefields, and equipped with arms appropriate to their potential task, including anti-tank weapons and artillery.

Mobilization and the Economy

Any prolonged mobilization of the reserves and of civilian transport causes severe disruption to Israel's economy. The Six Day War was preceded by a whole month of crisis, during which most of the reserves were deployed along the fronts, though the war itself was short and decisive. On the other hand, in the Yom Kippur War, there was no period of mobilization beforehand, but the war itself continued longer than had been estimated in the 'war models' on which the integration of the state's resources with IDF manpower and equipment needs had been based. Moreover, after the Yom Kippur War, it was still necessary to maintain a large number of reserves along the various fronts. Consequently, it was decided to develop a system whereby the national economy could continue to function as well as possible in wartime or during emergencies that required substantial mobilization. In addition, changes were introduced into the 'war model' that constituted a basis for economic planning.

17

DOES DETERRENCE WORK?

After the unexpected Egyptian–Syrian assault in the Yom Kippur War, the question was asked whether Israel had in fact succeeded since its establishment in avoiding war by means of deterrence – a word the dictionary defines simply as 'prevention by fear'. The succession of Israeli–Arab wars suggests a negative reply. However, this pessimistic view does not stand up to examination. A more accurate analysis shows that deterrence is a cumulative process that has already had a marked impact on the conflict, and hopefully will continue to do so.

In the Yom Kippur War, Egypt and Syria set their armies limited objectives because they recognized the overall capability of the IDF. That is to say, Israel's military strength deterred them from planning and launching a full-scale war – a comprehensive offensive intended to break through to Israel's vital areas. They also refrained from bombing Israel's centres of population, for fear that their planes would not return and that the Israeli air force would respond in kind.

Jordan sent an armoured unit to reinforce the Syrians on the Golan Heights, but did not participate directly in this war. It was deterred by the disastrous consequences of its joining in the Six Day War, when it lost the West Bank and East Jerusalem. Similarly, in the Yom Kippur War, Iraq and Saudi Arabia limited themselves to token participation.

What have been the developments since the 1973 war?

After a state of war lasting for thirty years, Egypt, the largest and most important of the Arab states, decided in 1977 to move towards a state of peace with Israel. The cost of previous wars, and its estimate of Israel's strength, had led it to the conclusion that its objectives should be sought by political, not military, means. Thus, the deterrence factor was the real background to the Israeli–Egyptian Peace Treaty of 1979.

Other Arab states regarded as moderate – Jordan, Saudi Arabia, Morocco, Tunisia, the Sudan and the Persian Gulf Emirates – continue, in principle, to maintain a state of war with Israel, but have also moved towards acceptance of the (for them) unpalatable fact that Israel is here to

203

stay and that the Arab quarrel with it cannot be resolved by force of arms. This shift in attitude, derived from past wars, was dramatized in October 1986 when Prime Minister Shimon Peres was invited to visit Morocco, and was openly and publicly received by King Hassan II, who happened at the time to be the current Chairman of the Arab League. The two leaders failed to agree on a solution to the conflict, and nobody expected them to do so. But the meeting in itself was a further step in the process of Arab adjustment to Israel's existence on the Middle East map.

In May 1983, the Governments of Lebanon and Israel concluded a treaty to end the state of war between them, to remove the PLO and other foreign forces from Lebanese territory, and to establish in Southern Lebanon a system of security arrangements. The treaty was abortive, as the regime of President Amin Gemayel yielded to internal and external pressures and repudiated it. But the fact that such a document was signed at all was of psychological importance.

Even in Syria one can discern signs of awareness that the military option will not destroy Israel or force surrender terms on it; and that the conflict can be resolved only by political means.

The deterrence factor has also had an impact on Arab attitudes to the terrorist weapon. For many years now Egypt, Jordan and Syria (on the Golan Heights) have not allowed Palestinian terrorist organizations to operate from their territory across their borders with Israel. The main reason for this ban is that such terrorist attacks invite Israeli counter-blows, and may drag the Arab host country into conflict with Israel. At present, Lebanon and Syria remain the main bases for terrorism, but they are not on a par. The problem in Lebanon is that an impotent government is not in control of its own territory. The only regime that overtly supports terrorism is that of Colonel Gaddafi in Libya.

Within the Palestinian Arab fold, there is a growing acceptance that the 'armed struggle' against Israel is futile, and that their problem can only be solved by a negotiated agreement, preferably within a Jordanian–Palestinian context. The PLO itself has been deeply split on this issue.

In recent years, there has been a marked shift in the international approach to terrorism. It is recognized that PLO terrorism is at the core of an international terrorist network, which has become a serious menace to the free world. Western countries are now willing to combat this menace by all available means and to co-ordinate anti-terrorist measures. Israel is no longer isolated in this respect.

While there have been encouraging results to deterrence, Israel cannot relax. It lives in a region that is unstable and still largely hostile, and cannot foresee what fresh dangers may arise. It must, therefore, continue to maintain and develop its deterrent strength, and with it the Arab perception that renewed hostilities against Israel would be too hazardous to attempt.

This deterrent policy requires Israel to maintain an overall qualitative superiority of land, sea and air forces, and to make Arab leaders aware of it. (For example, there is a noticeable Arab reluctance to confront the Israeli air force in aerial combat.) In the light of what occurred in the Yom Kippur War, Israel must be able to carry out a rapid deployment of forces to prevent the enemy from making limited territorial gains and retaining them by means of a Soviet 'umbrella'. Furthermore, Israel must openly and explicitly draw 'red lines', i.e. state which development would invite a military reprisal from it. Such deterrent warnings should refer, amongst others, to these contingencies:

- A serious violation of the security arrangements in Sinai set up by the Peace Treaty; or of those on the Golan Heights set up by the Israeli–Syrian Disengagement-of-Forces Agreement of 1974.
- A massing of forces near the borders that could be construed as a threat of attack on Israel (the situation to which we failed to react in time before the Yom Kippur War).
- The deployment of significant Iraqi forces in Jordan or in Southern Syria.

The above analysis concerns dangers to Israel from conventional weapons. Nuclear war demands completely different rules, because it creates the possibility of destroying a country in one surprise blow, or at least causing it heavy damage, without crossing any border or spending the relatively long space of time it takes to deploy conventional forces.

A political nuclear threat to Israel cannot be dismissed any longer as a purely hypothetical possibility. In the beginning only the United States had the bomb. Then the Soviet Union broke that monopoly. The US shared atomic secrets with Britain, and France under de Gaulle developed its own *force de frappe*. Attempts to limit the nuclear club to the four powers, and to prevent proliferation, have not succeeded. A growing list of countries are regarded as possessing what is termed 'nuclear capability'.

For many years the fate of the world has depended on the doctrine of Mutual Assured Destruction (what Winston Churchill called 'a balance of terror') between the two superpowers. That kind of reciprocal deterrence implies rational calculation on both sides. But a nightmare prospect for the international community is that nuclear weapons may come into the hands of 'crazy states' that could use them irresponsibly, or of terrorist organizations that would use them to blackmail governments. Israel has every reason to share that fear.

Libya's Colonel Gaddafi openly calls for the production of an 'Arab bomb', and diverts some of his oil revenues to Iraq and Pakistan for this purpose. In 1981, Israel took the daring and risky step of an air-strike against a nuclear reactor being constructed with French help in Baghdad. The message was that Israel would go to extreme lengths to deter the production and deployment of nuclear weapons in Arab states. In theory, Israel should have the capacity to nullify a nuclear threat through a local version of Mutual Assured Destruction – that is, a credible balance of deterrence that can imbue the Arab regimes concerned with the belief that an attempt on their part to destroy Israel by nuclear weapons will expose their own countries to destruction.

Israel will have to take into account that superpower sensitivities will be greater in a Middle East armed with nuclear weapons than in a Middle East armed only with conventional weapons. Washington and Moscow may, separately or jointly, develop their own ways of controlling such a situation, out of concern lest the use of nuclear weapons in a regional conflict may escalate into a full-scale nuclear confrontation.

A potential nuclear risk to Israel, and the need that would arise to deter it, raises questions far too complex to be probed here. But no discussion of the deterrence aspect of the Israeli–Arab conflict can fail to mention a possible nuclear dimension to the subject.

There is another kind of non-conventional weapon that has already appeared in the region: chemical warfare. Both Iraq and Syria have constructed large, secret installations for the production of poison gas, acquiring the materials and the technical know-how from industrial firms in Western countries. Iraq has already used mustard gas against Iranian troops in the Gulf War, in blatant defiance of the ban on this form of warfare imposed by international conventions. The Syrian armoury contains Soviet ground-to-ground missiles that have a range of 1,000 kilometres and are, therefore, capable of carrying war-heads with toxic chemical materials deep into Israeli territory. Here, too, the policy of deterrence must extend to persuading the Syrian leadership that there would be a devastating response from Israel.

One form of deterrence in the region that operates against Israel is the threat of Soviet military intervention on behalf of its client-states. Such deterrence would serve to prevent the collapse of a Soviet-sponsored regime, or provide it with a protective umbrella against air or sea attack, or involve Soviet participation in the general defence of the country concerned.

The states in the Middle East–Red Sea region under Soviet strategic control, in which active intervention of the above kind could be expected, include Syria, Libya, South Yemen and Ethiopia. In greater or lesser degree, the facilities for intervention already exist in these countries – Soviet air and naval bases, stocks of Soviet heavy weapons and joint defence treaties. In Ethiopia (as in Angola), the Soviet Union exercises control and deterrence through the introduction of Cuban troops.

For Israel, the main significance of Soviet deterrence relates to a possible Syrian attack. The threat of Russian intervention might neutralize Israel's ability to retaliate; and where a surprise attack has achieved territorial gains, Israel might be prevented from regaining lost ground.

The only factor that can deter the USSR from active military intervention in an Israeli–Arab war is the United States. Depending on the circumstances, the US might react in several ways, all of them dramatically illustrated in the 1973 Yom Kippur War. When the Soviet Union sought to tip the scales of battle against Israel by pouring fresh arms and supplies by sea and air into Egypt and Syria, the United States redressed the balance by an air-lift to Israel. When the Soviet Union threatened direct intervention with its airborne troops, the US warned it off by ordering a global alert of American strategic forces. But to avert the danger of a direct superpower confrontation, the United States and the Soviet Union acted together to impose a UN ceasefire. (Similarly, the 1967 Six Day War was halted by a UN ceasefire backed by both superpowers.)

Past experience has taught Israel two lessons. First, when it achieves the upper hand in a war, it has a limited time to make significant gains before the superpowers blow the final whistle. Second, it needs a strategic understanding with the United States to deter Soviet intervention on the Arab side.

18

THE AMERICAN CONNECTION

Everyone agrees that there is a special relationship between the United States and Israel, even if they are 7,000 miles apart; but it is not easy to explain.

In February 1987, the Reagan Administration accorded to Israel the status of a 'non-NATO ally' – a distinction shared with Egypt in the Near East and Japan, Australia and South Korea in the Far East. But that gesture did not so much create a new relationship as set a formal seal on one of long standing.

Arab propaganda attributes American support for Israel to the political clout of the large and important American Jewish community. This community matters a great deal to the Jewish state, both for its direct aid and its influence on American policy towards Israel. But pro-Israeli sentiment in American public opinion extends far beyond the Jewish community. Among Israel's staunchest supporters in Washington have been presidents, cabinet ministers, senators and congressmen who did not need the Jewish vote. Moreover, support for Israel has been bipartisan, cutting across the dividing lines between Republican and Democrat, Conservative and Liberal.

Clearly, there are deeper roots to this relationship than electoral expediency. The early American colonists were profoundly influenced by the Scriptures, and the Declaration of Independence is infused with Judaic traditions. There are segments of the American people for whom the modern return of the Jews to their ancient homeland is the fulfilment of biblical prophecy. On the contemporary scene, Israel is an integral part of the Free World, of which the United States is the leader. The two republics, one so immense and one so small, share the same attributes of democratic government, open societies, freedom of expression, concern for human rights, informal ways and the integration of immigrant communities.

Today, these intangible ties are reinforced by 'realpolitik' – an acceptance in the United States that Israel is its only stable and reliable ally in a strategically important but volatile region, which is exposed to Soviet penetration.

For us in Israel this special relationship cannot be taken for granted. It has gone through periods of strain – for instance, over the Sinai Campaign, the 1975 Interim Agreement with Egypt, the bombing of the Iraqi nuclear reactor and Israel's invasion of Lebanon. In 1986–7, the relationship was shaken by two 'affairs' – one that came to be called 'Irangate', and the other the Pollard spy case.

'Irangate' concerned the secret supply to Iran, in co-operation with Israel, of a limited amount of American arms, and the subsequent diversion of part of the proceeds to the Contra rebel forces in Nicaragua. These disclosures caused the gravest political crisis in the United States since Watergate and seriously weakened the Reagan presidency. The Israeli Government declared that it had acted in the matter at the instance of the United States; that it had no knowledge of the transfer of funds to the Contras; and that it would co-operate with US investigations.

I would only add the comment that the United States and Israel share a genuine strategic interest in seeking contacts with moderate Iranian circles (especially in the armed forces), in the hope that they might bring about a change in the regime in the post-Khomeini era. That interest has existed ever since the downfall of the Shah. In April 1982, when I accompanied Sharon, then Minister of Defence, to talks in Washington with Secretary of State Alexander Haig and his advisers, one point that came up concerned the Gulf War between Iran and Iraq. 'It is a mistake', Sharon commented, 'to support Iraq. It is better that the outcome be inconclusive, that the Iranians do not enter Baghdad and the Iraqis not be the victors. The Iraqi threat in the Persian Gulf is bigger than Iran's. Iraq is a medieval nation that is not going to change. We view very negatively the aid policy adopted by Jordan, Saudi Arabia and Egypt, who sell to Iraq hundreds of American tanks and other equipment. Such action will let the Soviets into Iran and then we will find the USSR planted on the Gulf shore. That is the real threat.'

Haig said that we were mistaken regarding US policy. They did not want a victor in the Gulf War and they had not assisted either side. Maybe Israel had. They had no interest in pushing Iran towards the USSR or in it receiving Soviet aid through Syria. But the anxiety in the Arab Gulf states was very real. The United States had to be careful lest conditions were created in that area that would be opposed to both American and Israeli interests. Personally, he did not believe that Iran was lost to the West in the long run. But, meanwhile, Arab fears had to be taken into account.

Sharon replied that our supplies to Iran were very modest and did not include American equipment or equipment with American components: 'The army commanders that receive the equipment may have the chance in the future of being partners to negotiations. Iran is more important to the United States than Iraq.'

Incidentally, one of the people who figured as a go-between in the Iranian arms affair was an international arms merchant called Adnan Kashoggi, a Saudi Arabian, whom the press dubbed 'the world's richest man'. Whether that was true or not, he certainly maintained a life-style beyond the wildest Arabian Nights' fantasies. I met him in Cairo in the summer of 1985, and we had a few hours' talk in a luxurious private apartment, over a meal of young pigeons stuffed with rice and spices. We discussed the affairs of the Middle East and the Israeli–Arab conflict. I was dumbfounded when he proposed to me that Israel could bring peace closer by supplying arms through him to Iraq, for use against Iran. It occurred to me that arms dealers like him wanted wars to be kept going indefinitely, so that they could profit by arms sales to both sides.

'Irangate' was essentially a domestic American matter raising political, constitutional and legal issues about the way the American system of government was functioning. Israel's involvement in it was marginal. But the Pollard case was far more damaging to the ties between the two countries.

Jonathan Jay Pollard, a civilian intelligence analyst working for the US navy, was convicted of passing secret information to Israeli contacts and sentenced to life imprisonment. His wife, who had assisted him, was sent to gaol for five years. Pollard maintained that as a Jew and a Zionist, he felt a moral obligation to make available to Israel information about Arab military strength that was vital to Israel's security but was being withheld by US Intelligence. The Israeli Government stated that this was an unauthorized 'rogue' operation contrary to its policy, and it co-operated with the American authorities in the case against the Pollards. In Israel two internal enquiries were initiated – one by the Intelligence sub-committee of the Knesset Foreign Affairs and Defence Committee, the other by an independent committee appointed by the Government. Both found that no government leaders had been aware of the contacts with Pollard, but both were critical of the lack of effective political supervision of the Intelligence services.

Undoubtedly, the Pollard affair undermined at the time the mutual trust and intimacy which had developed over the years between Washington and Jerusalem. But it was a one-time episode which was unlikely to recur, and the special relationship has remained intact, as was the case with earlier periods of strain. What has particularly perturbed the Israeli public are the questions raised about the functioning of our own system of government. What is a constant factor in the Israeli–American relationship is the built-in ambivalence of American Middle East policy. It has had to straddle two aims that have often contradicted each other: a commitment to Israel's survival and welfare and, on the other hand, the need to promote US influence in the Arab countries and prevent them from being drawn into the Soviet orbit. This dualism has manifested itself in three interrelated areas that concern Israel's national security: arms supply, strategic co-operation and mediation in the peace process.

US Arms Policy

After the Yom Kippur War, the need arose for systematic consultations and co-ordination concerning US military aid to Israel. We had to prepare detailed requests for US arms supplies, based on our long-term plans for the development of the IDF, and present them for discussion in the Pentagon and the State Department. Our requests also covered the financial aspects that depended on congressional approval – the total amount, the ratio of grants to loans and the terms of the loans. The discussions thus involved a general analysis of Israel's economic situation and plans.

At the same time, close ties grew between the Intelligence services, co-operation on research and development programmes was strengthened, and a regular exchange of views took place between the bodies dealing with political–strategic planning in the American and Israeli Defence establishments. I was a regular member of the Israeli team set up for these purposes, and in 1981, when Sharon became Minister of Defence, I was appointed to head it.

After the Yom Kippur War, significant changes took place in American arms supply policy in the Middle East. The US now viewed such arms supply as an important lever in strengthening American influence in the Arab world. In addition, the US was increasingly ready to confront the USSR on this question.

From the beginning of 1978 onwards, there was a breakthrough in American arms supplies to the Arab states. It began with a 'tripartite deal' in May 1978, which for the first time made a connection between arms supplies to Israel, Egypt and Saudi Arabia. As far as America was concerned, the Israeli–Egyptian Peace Treaty of 1979 removed the final political limitations on arms sales to Egypt. This was expressed in the Administration's willingness to supply Egypt with Phantom fighters, F-16s, Hawk-eye missiles, tanks and armoured cars. Saudi Arabia received, amongst other weapons, the most advanced of American planes – F-15s and AWACS (Airborne Warning and Control System) surveillance planes.

The Reagan Administration gave significant impetus to the sale of American weapons to the Middle East. This accorded with President Reagan's general view that arms supplies were a vital tool in promoting foreign policy objectives, which required fewer moral considerations than those of President Carter.

In order to implement arms deals, the Reagan Administration maintains joint military standing committees with Jordan, Egypt, Saudi Arabia, Morocco and Tunisia. This policy is used to lay the foundation for security-based ties with Arab states which have until now been outside the American sphere of influence. Thus, at the end of February 1982, the Administration removed Iraq from the list of states supporting terrorism and thereby paved the way for arms deals with that country too. (In practice, however, the US had already been selling equipment with a military potential directly to Iraq.) At the same time, the Reagan Administration made it easier to sell civilian aircraft to Syria and the Republic of South Yemen even though these countries were still included in the list of those supporting terrorism.

The Saudis pay for the arms they purchase from the US, while those supplied to Egypt, Jordan, the Sudan and Morocco are mainly financed from the American military aid budget.

In addition to the sale of weapons, US security relations with the Arab world include the following aspects:

- A series of joint exercises which include air, sea and land forces. These are carried out in co-operation with Egypt, Somalia, the Sudan, Oman, Jordan and Morocco.
- Access services in the region for the American 'Rapid Deployment Force', which can be used in emergencies. Co-operation in this field had already begun during the Carter Administration through written agreements with Oman, Bahrein, Kenya and Somalia; it has continued with the Reagan Administration and now includes Morocco. However, the US has so far been unsuccessful in establishing an independent military presence in any Arab state.
- A ramified system for consultation, military guidance and main-tenance.

American military aid is a vital component of Israel's national security. It contributes to the balance of forces, to maintaining a qualitative edge in weapons systems, and to deterring both the direct threat of Arab attack and the indirect danger of Soviet intervention. However, this contri-bution is to a considerable extent undermined by the strengthening of some Arab armies by the United States, while the Soviet Union strengthens other Arab armies. As long as the region remains unstable and the dangers to Israel from its Arab neighbours persist, we are opposed to the supply of sophisticated American arms and equipment to Saudi Arabia, Jordan or any other country in the region not at peace with Israel. These weapons are more likely to be used against Israel (as has happened in the past) than to preserve the regimes in the countries concerned. For over thirty years Israel has faced Soviet weapons in the hands of its Arab enemies. We will continue to cope with this situation, but it is seriously aggravated when it is American arms we see across our borders.

It should be mentioned that Israel has received more aid to finance arms purchases than have the Arab countries. In this regard, one cannot neglect the following three factors:

1   The disparity between Israel's financial capacity and that of the Arab oil states.

2   Soviet arms supplies at greatly reduced cost to the states carrying the banner of confrontation with Israel – Syria, Iraq and Libya. Today, Syria's army is the largest and strongest of all the Arab armies and it is continuing to develop its military strength with the proclaimed aim of achieving strategic parity with Israel. Libya possesses Soviet arms reserves of a quality and quantity sufficient to equip several armoured divisions, and it can develop an air and sea strength capable of posing significant risks to Israeli shipping in the Mediterranean.

3   The special financial terms for military aid in return for territorial concessions by Israel have bitten deeply into its security system.

Israeli–American Strategic Co-operation

After the Israeli–Egyptian Peace Treaty was concluded in 1979, our security dialogue with the United States developed into an examination of the possibilities of strategic co-operation in the regional context. Far-reaching changes in the Middle East at that time raised new dangers both for Israel and for American and Western interests. These changes included the Soviet invasion of Afghanistan and the fall of the Shah in Iran, replaced by the extremist Khomeini regime.

In our talks with the Americans, we stressed the following points. The need for strategic co-operation between our two countries derived from a common interest in countering Soviet moves and designs in the area. The Soviet Union had already established itself in Syria, Libya and South Yemen. These countries provided facilities for the Soviet navy; centres for international terrorism as a Soviet destabilizing weapon in the West; and bases for subversive movements aimed at pro-Western regimes in the area. Potentially, they could serve as springboards for Soviet military intervention. Meanwhile, arms and supplies could be stockpiled in them for possible future use by Soviet forces. In addition, countries such as Iran and Iraq could become a corridor through which Soviet troops could pass on their way to the Persian Gulf, Saudi Arabia and the Indian Ocean – a move which would put Israel in grave jeopardy.

In all possible scenarios for USSR intervention, one had to take into account a Soviet model combining a domestic coup in a given country; rapid intervention of Soviet forces in co-ordination with the coup leaders; and the intervention of other Soviet-controlled Middle Eastern states bordering the state concerned. (Thus, a coup in Iran would trigger intervention from Afghanistan; in Saudi Arabia, from Iraq, South Yemen and possibly Iran; in Egypt, from Libya; and in Somalia, from Ethiopia and South Yemen.)

In the event of a threat of direct Soviet military intervention in the Middle East, NATO land and air forces in Europe, and NATO naval forces in the Atlantic Ocean and the Eastern Mediterranean, would presumably be put on an emergency footing. US land, air and sea forces, whose task it was to defend the Far East and the Pacific Islands, would be placed on a similar alert. But only a relatively small American force would be able to take immediate action to resist the extension of Soviet control in key areas of the Middle East. The US would not be able to guarantee the necessary air supremacy required for a large-scale and rapid concentration of air and sea forces, and the maintenance of such forces. Where the US wished to expedite forces to an infrastructure which had been prepared in advance in the Middle East and East Africa, Israel could provide an air umbrella to protect US troop movements and maintenance operations by air and sea.

Israel's own requirements for defence against the dangers posed by the Soviet Union and Soviet-aided Arab forces would necessitate augmented US military aid during the 1980s and 1990s. This was even more essential because the superpower rivalry had resulted in a steady increase, both quantitative and qualitative, of the armed strength of the Arab nations. Israel had to be in a position to defend itself with its own forces, without the intervention of American troops.

Moreover, Israel had to retain the right to act in self-defence even independently of the United States. This applied not only to direct confrontation with Arab states, but also to other situations that might necessitate action outside Israel's borders. Examples of such situations that had arisen or could arise were an Israeli invasion of Southern Lebanon to destroy PLO terrorist bases; a Syrian take-over of Lebanon or Jordan; threats to the sea or air routes to Israel; terrorist hostage-taking actions where the local government could not or would not act (e.g. the rescue mission at Entebbe in Uganda); or the need to prevent hostile Arab states from acquiring nuclear weapons that would endanger Israel's survival (e.g. the Israeli air strike against the Iraqi nuclear reactor).

Even without strategic co-operation, Israel always viewed the US, and would continue to view it in the future, as a central and positive factor in the promotion of the peace process. The US had the power gradually to stabilize the region and to encourage a comprehensive peace between

Israel and its neighbours. We had worked in co-operation with the US on all the agreements Israel had reached to date with Arab nations. We would continue to do so in order to reach a comprehensive peace based on Camp David; to wage the struggle against the USSR's destructive influence in the region; to solve the Lebanese problem; to broaden Israel's contacts with states in Asia and Africa; and to combat international terrorism.

Thus, we were ready for a political agreement on the Lebanese problem. This should have been in stages, ensuring free elections and the stipulation that Lebanon be free and independent within its own sovereign borders. The condition for implementing such a process was the withdrawal of terrorist organizations and Syrian forces from Lebanon. We would not agree to a solution perpetuating Syria's control of Lebanon or enabling terrorist organizations to continue operations against Israel from Lebanese soil. Subject to that, we could operate together with the US on the Lebanese problem.

We encouraged closer American strategic connections with Saudi Arabia, Egypt and Jordan. Such connections were preferable to letting these countries move closer to the USSR. They would also influence the creation of suitable conditions for solving conflicts and stabilizing the region, and would constitute an important stage in the gradual construction of a strategic system in the region in which Israel would also be incorporated. The aim of such a strategic system would be to deter or resist Soviet expansion in the region. But neither we nor the US wanted Israel turned into a base for rescuing Arab regimes or for intervening in inter-Arab wars. This the US would have to do through whatever facilities were available to it in Arab or Moslem countries, like Egypt, Oman or Somalia.

While there was agreement in principle on strategic co-operation, determining its scope and extent was our main problem in the talks we had in Washington. We became aware of US reservations on political grounds (how would the Arabs react?); on economic grounds (should one make a substantial investment in Israel's military infrastructure?); and on military–strategic grounds (should we co-operate with Israel in the Middle East region, or only in the Mediterranean, on the southern flank of NATO?).

We told the Americans that we sought strategic co-operation with them only in areas that were related to Israel's national security and were, at the same time, of concern to US strategy. We Jews had one small country, and our overwhelming national purpose was to defend it against hostile neighbours, whether they were aided by the Soviet Union or not. In fact, we were the only country that had fought for a generation against states under Soviet influence, with Soviet weaponry feeding their aggressive designs against us. In our defensive wars during that time, we had destroyed approximately 5,000 Russian tanks, 1,000 Russian warplanes and a great number of Russian guns and missiles.

We were prepared for strategic co-operation with the US on a broad basis, covering land, sea and air forces; production and maintenance of weapons systems; scientific research and development; intelligence; deterrence policy and medical facilities. We were not prepared to subordinate our defence policy to a narrow and restricted basis for strategic co-operation.

The whole question came under high-level discussion when Premier Begin made an official visit to Washington on 6–7 September 1981, at the invitation of President Reagan. The visit included two personal meetings between the Prime Minister and the President, meetings of working groups, meetings of the Prime Minister with Secretary of State Haig and Defence Secretary Weinberger, a state dinner at the White House and a full military reception ceremony. Begin was accompanied by Foreign Minister Shamir, Defence Minister Sharon, Interior Minister Dr Burg and advisers. The atmosphere was warm and festive, and it was felt that a new page would be opened in Israeli–American relations. The main subjects discussed by Reagan and Begin included ways of breaking the deadlock in the autonomy negotiations; the possibilities for stabilizing the situation in Lebanon; and a strengthening of the special security relations prevailing between the US and Israel.

The strategic dialogue that had been conducted for the previous two years, and the strategic ties that had been developing between the US and certain Arab states – Egypt, Saudi Arabia, Jordan and Oman – led Begin to propose the drawing up of a formal Israeli–American Memorandum of Understanding on strategic co-operation.

There were deep differences of opinion within the US Administration on how to respond to Israel's request. It was opposed by Defence Secretary Weinberger, acting on the advice of the US Joint Chiefs of Staff. They maintained that as long as the Israeli–Arab conflict persisted, the US could not afford to demonstrate strategic co-operation with Israel to the extent that American influence in moderate Arab countries would be undermined, and it would become easier for the USSR to promote coups for toppling pro-Western regimes in these countries. Specifically, they did not want to prejudice arrangements with Egypt, Somalia and Oman that would enable the US Rapid Deployment Force to be quickly activated in the Persian Gulf in an emergency.

Weinberger, therefore, argued that security relations between the US and Israel should continue with as low a profile as possible, in the form of the dialogue that had been going on since 1978. He also held that the US did not need to increase its economic and military aid to Israel unless

Israel co-operated more with the US on settling the Israeli–Arab conflict. This Israel should do by being more forthcoming in the negotiations based on Camp David; by ceasing settlement activities in the West Bank and Gaza; and by desisting from military actions likely to endanger the US position in the Arab world, such as bombing nuclear reactors or invading Lebanon.

There were pro-Arab senior officials in the State Department who supported the Pentagon position. But Secretary of State Haig held completely different views. He insisted on upholding the policy towards Israel which had been shaped by Kissinger in the wake of the Yom Kippur War, in connection with the agreements Israel had signed with Egypt and Syria in 1974 and 1975. As a senior member of the National Security Council at the time, Haig had taken part in the formulation of that policy. Its essence was that Israel could be persuaded to co-operate in the pursuit of US policy aims in the Middle East only if Israel felt assured of American understanding and support for its own security needs. There had thus been an American commitment to make military and economic aid available on a scale large enough to compensate for the territorial concessions made by Israel in those agreements, and to maintain a balance of forces with the Arab states. There was a further commitment to co-ordinate with Jerusalem political moves in the Israeli–Arab peace process.

In the spirit of this policy, Haig's recommendation was that the US should respond positively to Begin's proposal. He maintained that two strategic co-operation systems should be developed at the same time – one with Arab nations and one with Israel. This should be done in such a way that one system would not disrupt US capability to maintain the other. Thus, a clear distinction should be made between the two systems as far as strategic goals and the means of attaining them were concerned. The predominantly Arab system (including Saudi Arabia, Egypt, Jordan, Oman, Somalia and Kenya) would concentrate on the strategy for defending the oil states in the Arabian Peninsula and the Persian Gulf, and the defence of pro-Western states situated along the Red Sea coast and in East Africa.

President Reagan accepted Haig's position despite Weinberger's opposition. The President decided that strategic co-operation between the US and Israel would be broadly aimed at deterring the USSR from endangering peace in the region and would be anchored in a strategic Memorandum of Understanding. Begin was happy at this decision.

Defence Minister Sharon, however, did not then know what he discovered afterwards – that for the Americans, strategic co-operation with Israel was meant to apply to the Eastern Mediterranean, but not to the Middle East region as such. This nullified the dream of those Israelis who had expected Israel to become the bridgehead in the Middle East for the defence of the free world. These persons had hoped to achieve such a status by allowing the United States to fill Israeli stores with US equipment. Emergency stocks of heavy weapons (tanks, artillery and armoured cars) would be located in Israel and would be available to the Americans if they needed to operate in the Middle East. Such stocks were also expected to be put at Israel's disposal in emergency situations. Some in Israel had hoped the US would establish an infrastructure, such as air and naval bases, which would be of assistance to the IDF as well; or that the US would keep hundreds of American planes in the hangars of the Israel Aircraft Industries and some Sixth Fleet vessels in Israel's ports.

Such expectations were unfounded. It quickly became clear that the Americans did not intend to activate forces in the Middle East based in Israel. Their sole intention was to initiate air and sea co-operation with Israel in the Eastern Mediterranean and to establish minimal facilities (mainly medical) to this end.

The decision reached in Washington during the visit of Begin and his entourage had raised public expectations in Israel, which were dashed when the very limited scope of the proposed agreement became known. But for those, including myself, who had anticipated the nature of the agreement, it was viewed as a good one, for it created a mechanism for co-ordination and discussion on joint Israeli–American national security needs and, therefore, constituted a solid basis for increased US military and economic aid to Israel.

In November 1981, I travelled to Washington as the head of the Israeli delegation to meet with a joint delegation of the Pentagon and the State Department, led by Dr Fred Ikle, Deputy Defence Secretary for International Relations. Our task was to finalize the content of the intended strategic co-operation and to prepare a draft of the Strategic Memorandum of Understanding to be submitted for political approval by the two Governments. It was decided that, after approval, Defence Minister Sharon would come to Washington to sign the document together with Defence Secretary Weinberger.

I arrived in Washington equipped with detailed submissions for our thesis that strategic co-operation should take place in the Middle East regional context, and that it should apply in the spheres proposed by Israel, including emergency stores for the land forces, air and sea facilities, maintenance services for planes and naval vessels, joint organization, joint planning and the purchase of Israeli equipment by American forces stationed in Europe.

Among the facts I stressed to the US delegation were these. The USSR–Iran border was located 1,000 miles from the oil fields in the Persian Gulf, while the distance of the US to the Gulf was 9,000 miles. The US had no system of bases in the Middle East (like those located in Europe and the Far East) and no country in the region was prepared to provide the US with the right to set up bases on its territory. The Indian Ocean island of Diego Garcia – the only American base in the region – was too small and too far away (3,000 miles) from the oil fields to serve as an efficient forward base.

An air- and sea-lift from the US itself was not a good solution as far as deterring the USSR from attacking the Persian Gulf was concerned. It was very costly and would take too long to organize. The cheaper and less problematic solution was the advance positioning of equipment in the region, ideally at locations suitable for simultaneous action in the Persian Gulf area and from Western Europe.

The existing arrangements available to the US for the rapid deployment of forces to the region were based on the following countries:

Somalia: It was a distance of 1,580 miles from the oil fields and suffered from political instability. It demanded exorbitant financial rewards for granting the right to use its facilities. It was threatened by Soviet-dominated Ethiopia, which was able to launch an air attack on American installations without Somalia being capable of providing air cover to counter such an attack.

Kenya: It was a distance of 2,642 miles from the oil fields and was unable to supply air cover to defend American installations. It opposed co-operation between the US and Somalia.

Oman: Although only 839 miles from the oil fields, bases on its territory would constitute a target for direct Soviet attack from the Iranian border. It could not provide air cover for American installations. It was exposed to inter-Arab pressures not to allow an American military presence on its territory. It was the most distant country from the European arena if the necessity arose for dispatching troops from Europe.

Egypt: This country appeared to be an ideal Arab strategic partner for the US. It was close to the oil fields (1,086 miles) and to Europe and was able to defend installations situated on its territory. However, one had to take into account the possibility that Egypt's relationship with the US would change for the worse if it again became integrated into the Arab world. For this reason, although Egypt provided a good and convenient strategic solution, the US could not allow itself to base the defence of the Persian Gulf on Egypt alone.

Considering the problems existing in all the countries discussed, the advantages of Israel as a base for intervention in the area stood out. Israel lay 1,284 miles from the oil fields and, except for the Turkish base of

Izmir (2,074 miles from the Persian Gulf), it would be the closest base to the European arena.

These arguments did not budge the Americans from their original position, and our proposals were rejected. In the tough talks that ensued, the differences could not be bridged. I was not prepared to change the Israeli position and did not have a mandate to do so. I threatened to break off negotiations and return home with our delegation. The Americans appeared uncomfortable at this prospect for they did not wish the discussions to reach a crisis situation. Through Robert MacFarlane, later the National Security Adviser to the President, and at that time the Secretary of State's assistant on special tasks, the deadlock we had reached with the Pentagon was brought to the attention of Secretary of State Haig and of President Reagan. Eventually, a compromise was reached, based on my proposal that the Memorandum of Understanding include broad principles for strategic co-operation without stipulating exactly in which areas such co-operation would take place. In addition, joint committees would be set up to work out the details and would meet for this purpose within a month of the signing of the agreement.

On 30 November 1981, Defence Secretary Weinberger and Defence Minister Sharon signed the Memorandum of Understanding in Washington.

Its main provisions were:

- Strategic co-operation between the two parties was directed against the threat posed by the Soviet Union to the peace and security of the region, and not against any state or group of states within the region.
- The strategic co-operation would extend, subject to agreement, to military co-operation, joint exercises, joint planning and preparatory measures.
- A co-ordinating council would be set up to direct the work of joint working groups. To supervise implementation of agreed measures, it would hold periodic meetings in Israel and the United States.
- The joint working groups would deal with joint exercises, including sea and air exercises in the Eastern Mediterranean; preparatory measures, such as access to maintenance and other infrastructure facilities; research and development; military procurement; and advance stationing of forces.
- The Memorandum could be cancelled by either side on six months' notice.

In Israel, the Memorandum of Understanding aroused fierce opposition in the Knesset and the media. It was attacked on the grounds that it imposed missions on the IDF which were not connected with Israel's defence but with the defence of US interests in the Middle East; and that it thrust Israel into open conflict with the USSR.

The criticism was unjustified. Did Israel not already confront dangers originating in the USSR? Did Israel's security needs not take into account that it was for the US to deter the Soviet Union from intervening in a war on the side of the Arab confrontation states? Was not the Labour opposition, when it was in power, ready to place bases in Israel at the disposal of the US, to be used for American intervention in the region in case of an emergency? And did Israel's consent in 1970, at the request of the United States, to deter Syria from invading Jordan, have a direct connection with Israel's own security?

However, before the ink had dried on the Knesset's approval of the Memorandum, the US Administration decided to freeze it, in reaction to the application of Israeli law to the Golan Heights in December 1981. This American decision was a heavy blow to Israel, as was the temporary freeze on other security agreements – the supply of F-15 and F-16 planes; the supply of cluster bombs; $200 million worth of barter purchases between the US and Israel; and the exchange of American aid dollars into Israeli currency for the development of the Lavi fighter plane.

This was the first time in the history of Israeli–American relations that the US Administration had imposed political sanctions on Israel (the actual abrogation of a signed agreement) together with economic and military sanctions. For Defence Secretary Weinberger and the Joint Chiefs of Staff, the rescinding of the Memorandum was a cause for celebration. They had been angered by President Reagan's intervention which had led to the signing of the Memorandum. To add to their disapproval, the Memorandum failed to stipulate that co-operation would apply only to the Eastern Mediterranean. However, since the document laid down no more than a mechanism for further negotiations on the substance of strategic co-operation, the Pentagon chiefs had intended, within the joint working groups, to discuss only measures applicable to the Mediterranean area, and only for the year 1982. These included joint sea manoeuvres and the storing of medical equipment.

In April 1982, when I accompanied Sharon on a visit to the US, the Americans tried to co-ordinate positions with Israel regarding the worsening situation in Lebanon. They did not want Israel to surprise them again, as it had done over the bombing of the Iraqi nuclear reactor and the application of Israeli law to the Golan Heights.

During our meetings with Haig and Weinberger, they hinted at a willingness to renew discussion of the Memorandum of Understanding. Sharon, however, was no longer interested. He had already decided that an invasion of Southern Lebanon to destroy the PLO 'state within a state' was inevitable, and preparations for such an action were already in an advanced stage. He had come to the conclusion that the joint mechanism contemplated by the Memorandum of Understanding could be an instrument for a curtailing of Israel's freedom of action in defence matters, where such action might conflict with American policy in the region.

Since then the close ties between the two countries have been maintained on an ad hoc basis and even grown stronger in such areas as military and political consultation and intelligence. The failure of the attempt to formalize the security relationship in a written document illustrates the US dilemma. There is the desire to strengthen American influence in the region, safeguard the oil resources vital to the West and contain Soviet penetration. On the other hand, there is the sincere desire to help secure the State of Israel.

For its part, Israel must maintain an independent national security policy, and its self-defence must be based on its own military strength. However, Israel cannot give independent responses to Soviet threats, and in this respect it must rely on the United States as the leader of the free world.

US Mediation

While the US is the only outside power able to act as a mediator in the Israeli–Arab conflict, that role has not been without its problems and strains with regard to Israeli–American relations. I shall try here to define the general attitude to US mediation of the parties (Arab and Israeli) and of the US itself.

I can speak with first-hand experience on this subject. In Israel's negotiations with Egypt and Lebanon between 1973 and 1983, I was responsible for preparing all the proposals that had security implications and was actively involved in the negotiations themselves.

Israel's moderate Arab neighbours (Egypt, Jordan and Lebanon) believed that US interests in the Middle East, and its rivalry with the USSR, would lead the US to exert pressure on Israel to return the territories it had taken in the Six Day War – or, in Lebanon's case, in the 1982 Operation Peace for Galilee. These Arab regimes realized that the territories could not be recovered by military means, and that US pressure could be exercised only if and when the parties entered into negotiations. Therefore, they were willing, in principle, to negotiate with Israel. In return for that willingness, they expected to be rewarded by Israel's withdrawal from the territories, and by American military and economic aid.

On the Israeli side, three factors have influenced the decisions of the

Government. First, there has been an awareness that there was no chance of solving the Israeli–Arab conflict without American help. The US exercises a moderating influence over some Arab nations, is able to deter the Soviet Union from intervening directly in the conflict, and is committed to Israel's survival and security. Second, there is the knowledge that American and Israeli positions are at odds over the question of withdrawal. US Administrations have consistently maintained that, in return for peace, Israel would have to yield all the territories taken in the Six Day War, except for minor border adjustments. Moreover, East Jerusalem was to be regarded as occupied territory, like the West Bank. Israeli Governments have consistently rejected these views. It is true that with the Peace Treaty with Egypt Israel agreed to a total withdrawal from Sinai. But Israel does not regard that as a precedent for the West Bank and the Gaza Strip – or for the Golan Heights. Israel believes that if it stands firm on this issue, the US will in time modify its position and will influence the Arab regimes concerned to accept territorial compromises. As for Jerusalem, the whole city will, as far as Israel is concerned, remain its undivided capital for all time. Third, there has been the expectation that the US would compensate Israel for yielding strategic territory, by providing security guarantees, increased military and economic aid and strategic co-operation.

The American attitude to its own mediating role is influenced primarily by the superpower confrontation in the region. The US has aspired to achieve a position where no solution to the Israeli–Arab conflict would be possible without its good offices. Arab regimes would realize that the Soviet Union could not help them in a situation where terms could not be forced on Israel by military means. The US mediation role would thus become a vital political–strategic instrument for countering Soviet influence and drawing Arab regimes into the American orbit. At the same time, the US wants to ensure the survival and security of Israel as a democratic nation constituting part of the free world. The US, therefore, aims to solve the conflict in such a manner that Israel would get peace and the Arab side would get back the territories it had lost. But if Israel is forced to yield territory in a way that leaves it feeling vulnerable and insecure, it might resort to a pre-emptive strike when faced with danger.

In steering negotiations towards these complicated ends, and in order to gain Israel's concurrence with them, US Administrations have used 'carrot-and-stick' means. Israel has been made to feel pressure by a calculated series of threats and sanctions. At the same time, Israel has been promised US guarantees and increased military and economic aid if it makes the concessions the US requires.

Dr Kissinger was the first to employ this formula, in his 1974–5 'shuttle diplomacy' in the wake of the Yom Kippur War. In his talks with Israel's leaders, Kissinger would begin with what he called a 'strategic situation assessment'. It was based on two theories: the disaster (maybe even nuclear war) which might occur if efforts to reach an agreement failed; and his conviction that Sadat's Egypt genuinely wanted an agreement that would end hostilities and pave the way for peace. Kissinger assured Israel's leaders that they could rely on him to safeguard Israel's interests in the negotiations he was conducting. Apart from the Government's official positions, he wanted from us in confidence more flexible lines so that he could bargain on our behalf and obtain a deal acceptable to us. It invariably led to rejection by the Arab state concerned of our alternative flexible lines and the submission of Kissinger's own compromise proposals, which were acceptable to the Arab party, but not to Israel. If the Israeli Government rejected his proposals, it would be blamed for the failure of the negotiations, and the 'stick' would come into operation.

I have already described (in Chapter 1) the pressures put on Israel in 1975 when an impasse was reached over the Interim Agreement with Egypt, and the consequent tension created between Israel and the US. In the end, the Israeli Government obtained further American commitments and, in exchange, made the concessions Kissinger had urged. The Government had concluded that in the long run an agreement might prevent a slide back to war and encourage progress towards peace. In defending its decision to the Knesset and Israeli public opinion, the Rabin Government put the emphasis on the 'carrot' – the American rewards in the shape of increased aid, security assurances and a guarantee regarding oil supply.

US policy has not been consistent in seeking an exclusive 'Pax Americana' in the region. Dr Kissinger, with President Nixon's backing, successfully pursued a step-by-step approach without the Soviet Union, while paying lip-service to the Geneva Conference, which was under joint American–Russian chairmanship. But when the Carter Administration took office at the beginning of 1977, it reversed this policy. President Carter and his two chief foreign policy advisers, Secretary of State Cyrus Vance and National Security Adviser Zbigniew Brzezinski, set themselves the goal of a comprehensive Israeli–Arab peace settlement under the joint auspices of the two superpowers.

Months of discussion between Washington and Moscow produced a joint American–Soviet statement on the Middle East, issued on 1 October 1977 by Secretary of State Vance and the Soviet Minister of Foreign Affairs Andrei Gromyko. The statement called for a reconvening of the Geneva Conference by December 1977, in order to achieve a comprehensive settlement of the Israeli–Arab conflict, 'incorporating all parties concerned and all questions'. Participation in the Conference would include representatives of all the parties involved in the conflict, including those of the 'Palestinian people'. Clearly, the object was to confront the parties with a joint American–Soviet position on the peace terms. It was also intended that one of the invited parties would be the PLO, although it had been excluded from the original Geneva Conference.

The Carter Administration had totally miscalculated the domestic reaction to a policy which appeared to legitimize Soviet penetration of the Middle East and, in effect, sought to establish an American–Soviet condominium in that strategic region. The move came under strong attack in Congress and the media, and was denounced by the American Jewish leadership as a betrayal of the undertakings Kissinger had given Israel in 1975. The Administration started to back away from its policy initiative. What killed it was the reaction of the two Middle East governments most directly concerned – those of Israel and Egypt. Each had its own reasons for being wholly opposed to the prospect of a political settlement imposed by the two superpowers acting in concert. Moshe Dayan, as Foreign Minister in the then recently elected Begin Government, had already met secretly in Morocco with Sadat's representative. Further meetings paved the way for Sadat's epoch-making visit to Jerusalem on 19 November 1977, seven weeks after the American–Soviet joint statement. It was a signal to the world that Egypt and Israel were willing to settle their conflict directly, without outside intervention. With some hesitation, Washington adjusted itself to the new reality. It resumed the role of sole mediator, joining the political process that led to Camp David and the Israeli–Egyptian Peace Treaty. The Soviet Union, for its part, resumed the role of spoiler and gave its backing to the Arab Rejection Front.

The United Nations was caught in a peculiar paradox. From 1947, it had made unsuccessful efforts to promote Israeli–Arab peace. Now, at last, peace had been achieved between Israel and the leading Arab state. But, owing to the Russian veto, the UN Security Council could not endorse the Peace Treaty, or even allow a UN peace force to remain in Sinai in order to supervise the treaty arrangements.

The Reagan Administration made no attempt to revive American–Soviet collaboration in Middle East peacemaking. The Reagan plan of 1 September 1982 was a purely American initiative. And from 1986–7, the Administration has had a markedly reserved attitude to the proposal of an international conference on Israeli–Arab peace, under the sponsorship of the five permanent members of the UN Security Council.

In the years of my participation in negotiations with the Egyptians and the Lebanese, I have often asked myself how active and intrusive the Americans should be as mediators. Their role has been invaluable in helping to bring the parties together, and in offering them assurances and incentives to agree. But, in my opinion, more scope should have been given to the parties to work out their own compromises on the substance of the issues, in face-to-face dealings with each other.

As a rule, the negotiations have started on this basis, as with the Sinai security arrangements for a peace treaty with Egypt (1978), the early phase of autonomy negotiations (summer 1979) or the beginning of negotiations with Lebanon (summer 1982). But the moment it appeared that the gaps had not been bridged, the US, with the consent of the parties concerned, actually began to direct the negotiations and submit its own views. The US then became, in effect, a party to three-sided talks.

If Israel had insisted on direct negotiations without such active US participation, it is quite probable that the process would have been delayed for a time. Yet I have no doubt that the Egyptians, and later the Lebanese, would have been willing to negotiate under these circumstances, rather than to continue indefinitely in a state of deadlock. After all, their motivation to hold political talks at all with Israel derived from the belief that there was no other way of retrieving territories lost in war.

There were a number of crucial stages in the negotiations when a breakdown was averted only by open or secret contacts between the parties without the Americans. For instance, there were the direct contacts Ezer Weizman had with Sadat and his Foreign Defence Ministers, which led to understandings on such central issues as security arrangements in Sinai, Egyptian oil supplies to Israel and agreements on normalization. To quote my own first-hand experience, the detailed Military Annex to the Peace Treaty was produced in discussions between General Meguid, head of the Egyptian military delegation, and myself, without the US. Then again, the main breakthrough leading to the Israeli–Lebanese Agreement of 17 May 1983 was a result of the secret talks David Kimche and I had with President Gemayel's special envoy.

Against the background of prolonged and bitter conflict, the key to our negotiations lay not in external pressures or promises, but in the personal relations that evolved between the negotiators themselves. Each side had to discard the stereotype of the 'enemy', get to know and trust the other side on the human level, and come to understand the other side's fears and domestic restraints. This was a slow, evolutionary process that could come about only in direct, face-to-face dealings with each other.

In his address to the Knesset in Jerusalem in November 1977, Sadat eloquently called for a change in the state of mind of the parties:

> Yet, there remains another wall. This wall constitutes a psychological barrier between us; a barrier of suspicion, of rejection, of fear of deception ... of cautious and erroneous interpretation of all and every event and statement. It is this psychological barrier which I described ... as constituting seventy per cent of the whole problem ... why should we not meet with faith and sincerity so that together we might remove all suspicion of fear, betrayal and ill intentions?

226

In defending his gradualist approach to Israeli–Arab peacemaking, Dr Kissinger stressed the need for developing confidence between the parties. In an address in September 1975, after the conclusion of the Israeli–Egyptian Interim Agreement, he stated: 'The United States concluded that instead of seeking to deal with all problems at once, we should proceed step by step with the parties prepared to negotiate and on the issues where some room for manœuvre seems possible.' This method, he believed, would build mutual trust and, 'Ultimately, we expected that the step by step process would bring about, for the first time, the basic political conditions needed for the overall settlement called for by Security Council Resolutions 242 and 338.'

Whatever differences there have been between Jerusalem and Washington along the way, it is a fact that US mediation helped to conclude four Israeli–Arab agreements in the 1974–9 period. However, it may well be that the mediating role of the US has exhausted itself for some time to come.

That question is as yet hypothetical regarding Syria, which refuses to join the peace process, is a leader of the Arab Rejection Front and is under Soviet influence. But the question is relevant to the efforts that have been made, and continue to be made, to draw Jordan and the Palestinian Arabs into the peace process. The conflict here is not only between Israel and the Arab side (in this case Jordan and the Palestinian Arabs), but also potentially between Israel and the United States as long as the latter insists on a withdrawal to the pre-1967 borders.

With all the strength of the 'special relationship' between the two countries, the points of departure in their policies are not identical. I would repeat: the chief concern of the United States in the Middle East is to contain the Soviet Union; Israel's chief concern is to secure the conditions for its own survival. These two concerns may collide with each other if and when the Israeli–Arab peace process again moves into a phase of active negotiations, with the United States as mediator. Israel now holds a security border from which American aid or pressure will not move it as long as dangers to our national security persist.

I believe that the conflict between Israel, Jordan and the Palestinian Arabs, and certainly the conflict with Syria, cannot be resolved unless and until a comprehensive and stable Israeli–Arab peace becomes possible on the basis of a common strategic and economic regional system under American sponsorship.

19

ISRAEL IN AFRICA

Maybe the most important political event of the twentieth century has been the process of decolonization – the break-up of the empires of European powers and the emergence of newly independent states in Asia, Africa and the Caribbean. These regions, along with Latin America, which was liberated from Spanish and Portuguese rule in the previous century, form what is known collectively as the Third World.

As one of these new states, Israel has built up co-operative ties with most other developing nations. A network of Israeli technical assistance programmes in every field (including defence) spread to some eighty other countries. Their regimes came under intense Arab pressure, in a sustained campaign to extend a diplomatic and economic boycott of Israel throughout the Third World. These Arab efforts yielded some results in voting patterns at the United Nations and other international forums, but had little effect on bilateral relations between Israel and the other states concerned, except in Black Africa.

In the course of time, the Arabs were able to undermine the remarkable 'special relationship' Israel had developed with the Black African states. The six Arab states stretching across North Africa (including Egypt) are members of the Organization of African Unity (OAU). Pointing to African–Arab solidarity in the fight over purely African issues – South African apartheid, Rhodesia, Namibia and the Portuguese colonies – the Arabs sought Black African support in their conflict with Israel. The need of the Africans for oil and financial aid was exploited, and the Moslem communities in African lands were used as political levers. At the outbreak of the Yom Kippur War in 1973, these pressures and needs induced most of the African states to break off relations with Israel.

This setback had its implications for Israel's national security in the broad sense. It made us more isolated in the international arena, affected our external sources of raw materials, and complicated our air and sea routes.

After the signing of the Peace Treaty with Egypt in 1979, the Foreign

228

Ministry under Shamir and the Ministry of Defence under Sharon invested much effort in the renewal of ties severed by Third World countries, particularly in Africa. As National Security Adviser, I participated in the direct political–security contacts with the countries concerned. David Kimche, the talented Director-General of the Foreign Ministry, played a key role in these secret contacts. I worked with him in this area and carried out various missions to establish co-operation with some of the regimes concerned. The African states that have renewed diplomatic ties with Israel include Zaire, the Ivory Coast, Cameroon, Liberia and Togo, while others may soon follow their example.

Basically, these countries have seen that it is in their interest to adopt a national security policy that is not dependent on the goodwill of Arab nations. They have become disillusioned with unfulfilled promises of Arab economic aid. Some of them fear the expansionist aims of Libya. And they feel disappointment at the inability of the OAU to cope with the economic problems of its member-states or the political conflicts that beset the continent.

I would like to cite a conversation I had in December 1982 with the President of one African state that had sought our help, but which it would not be appropriate to name at present. This talk illustrates points that recurred in discussion with various African regimes looking for a way to resume ties with us.

The President welcomed me warmly and hoped that this would be the first of a series of visits. He said there were factors making close co-operation with Israel necessary, but also factors limiting such contacts. His country was poor and undeveloped, but potentially could have a bright economic future. Israel could help develop its agriculture, industry, natural resources and technological level. These needs were pressing, but we should take into account his difficulties concerning immediate payment. He pointed out several other limiting factors. His country was a member of the OAU, which was opposed to relations with Israel. A high percentage of his people were sympathetic to the Palestinian Arabs. There were neighbouring African states hostile to Israel that might take action against his country to prevent renewal of ties. At the top of his list of priorities was the defence problem. He wanted us to help organize his country's capacity to resist a possible armed attack in the wake of establishing relations with us again. He also urged that economic ties should be put on a firm footing before formal diplomatic ties followed.

In replying to the President, I stressed that full diplomatic relations should be established as soon as possible, to signify the seriousness of the renewed relationship. Even if diplomatic ties were not immediate, the intention to establish them, and the period of time after which this would be done, should not be kept secret, but openly stipulated in the initial agreement between our Governments. This would constitute a political basis for initiating economic programmes. Until embassies were set up in the two capitals, Israel would maintain a political representation in his country to maintain contact and to co-ordinate activities.

On the financial aspect, I pointed out that Israel's economic situation did not allow it to provide substantial aid without recompense. Part of the aid would be regarded as an Israeli grant, and part could be given on easy financial terms, or other means of payment to be decided after a survey of his country's economy and natural resources. Meanwhile, Israel would send a team of experts to determine the fields of co-operation where work could start without delay.

The President accepted my suggestions and asked his staff to have a list of his country's immediate needs prepared for me for the next day.

One of my assignments at that time was to prepare a long-term plan to meet the national security needs of Zaire, the former Belgian Congo. It was a daunting task. Of the nine countries adjacent to the borders, five (Angola, Congo Brazzaville, Tanzania, Zambia and Burundi) were in varying degrees subject to Soviet influence; while two more (the Central African Republic and Uganda) were unstable and constituted fertile ground for Soviet penetration through Libya.

In the spring of 1982, when I accompanied Defence Minister Sharon to Washington, our meeting with Secretary of State Haig and his aides was mainly concerned with the situation in Lebanon. However, Sharon also raised the question of Zaire, which was about to restore relations with Israel. 'Zaire needs help,' Sharon said to Haig. 'You offered them $4.5 million in aid. They were offended. We are supplying skills and know-how, but we need a source of funds. If you do not wish to help directly, you can do so in co-operation with us. President Mbutu is under strong Arab pressure. He has requested military aid, agricultural development aid and food. On the military aspect, we have a team of advisers there, and I believe Zaire can be put in a position to defend its own borders. But please make an effort to help them with more economic aid. A quick decision must be made.'

Haig replied: 'We are with you. Nevertheless, Mbutu is "shooting a line". We offered them $15 million. Congress wants to cut it to $4.5 million, but no decision has yet been made. Mbutu is a difficult character. You will get to know him eventually.'

During the negotiations on the Israeli–Egyptian Peace Treaty in Washington, beginning in October 1978, the US promised Israel that if the Treaty were signed the right atmosphere would be created to assist Israel in renewing ties with the Third World nations which had severed relations with it after the Six Day War. The peace was signed. The atmosphere was created. But Israel is still working almost alone to renew vital ties in Africa and Asia on the political, economic and security levels. These ties were also of importance to the United States. Here, too, Israel has felt the effects of the fact that the US suspended the Strategic Memorandum of Understanding after it had been signed.

One of my early visits to Africa brought me to Uganda, with which we had close relations at the time. The local Chief of Staff with whom I dealt was the massive Idi Amin. In discussing with him the organization of his country's armed forces, I asked the natural question: who were the enemies of Uganda in relation to whom its national security had to be planned? He looked at me in astonishment and replied, 'Enemies? The enemies are right here, inside the country!'

Not long afterwards, Idi Amin seized power and headed Africa's most brutal and bloody regime. He executed all the former Ugandan leaders he could lay his hands on, and a number of his unlucky countrymen on whom his suspicion fell were thrown to the crocodiles that swarmed in the White Nile and the beautiful lakes.

In 1976, an Air France passenger plane *en route* from Tel Aviv to Paris was hijacked by Palestinian Arab terrorists and permitted by Idi Amin to land at Entebbe Airport near Kampala in Uganda. The airport terminal where the hostages were held was guarded by Ugandan soldiers. Israeli paratroopers carried out the incredible feat of flying 2,500 miles, landing in the dark, capturing the airport and flying out again with over a hundred rescued hostages. Idi Amin's revenge was characteristic. One passenger on the plane, an elderly Jewish lady called Mrs Dora Bloch, had been taken ill and admitted to Kampala Hospital. After the Entebbe rescue, she was dragged from her bed and murdered.

My brief association with Idi Amin is not one I look back upon with pride.

20

PLANNING FOR NATIONAL SECURITY

'War is much too serious a thing
to be left to the military'
Georges Clemenceau, French Premier in World War I

During my service on the IDF General Staff, from 1958 onwards, I saw the realization slowly grow in the Defence establishment that national security planning was a much broader concept than military planning. This evolution in thinking was accompanied by successive changes in my own position.

In 1969, the Chief of Staff decided to establish within the General Staff Branch a national security planning system, and appointed me as its head. The post was designated as Assistant for Planning to the head of the General Staff Branch, at that time General David Elazar, who would later become Chief of Staff. In previous years I had been responsible in that Branch for operations and planning. The difference was that my new job concerned not just the military aspect but the overall national interest, including the political and economic aspects of security.

By this innovation the General Staff forestalled the desire of Defence Minister Dayan to establish a unit for national security planning within the civilian Ministry of Defence, to provide him, and through him the Government, with the data and assessments needed for determining defence policy and long-term planning. Dayan had in mind that it should be directed by General Israel Tal, the armoured corps commander. Tal discussed the matter with me and suggested I come into the proposed unit as his deputy.

However, the General Staff wanted to retain its time-honoured position as the sole body advising the Government on defence-related matters. There was a failure to grasp that proper national security planning involved general national needs and priorities, not only the needs of the IDF. Dayan was right in wanting to take this wider function out of the hands of the army. But, true to character, he did not want to force his view on the General Staff and gave up his own proposal.

Consequently, the responsibility for national security planning remained in the General Staff Branch.

Some time later, Dayan sent for me and wanted to know just what I was doing in this area. I explained that my section was preparing plans for the development of the IDF in the 1970s; was working out methods for ascertaining and studying wider security needs; and had commissioned research projects from experts in certain of the fields concerned. He listened without comment, except to ask questions in order to clarify some points. After our meeting he sent the following note to the Chief of Staff, from which it appears that he had not entirely given up the possibility of setting up a special body for national security planning:

To: the Chief of Staff
From: the Minister of Defence

I requested and received a definition of his tasks from the Assistant for Planning to the head of the General Staff Branch. Within this definition there is a whole world, including the assignment of research projects to various bodies both inside and outside the army. I would like to know when this programme of work will be completed – for example, which research projects he expects to receive in the near future (within a year or so). It may well be that the work carried out by him in political–strategic areas – such as anticipated changes in the Arab world and the influence of the superpowers on events in the Middle East – will cover those subjects on which, it seems to me, we lack information today. If so there may be no need to establish a special body to carry out such research. Long-term planning could be based on existing bodies for technological development, i.e. the Chief Scientist, Rafael (the Weapons Development Authority), etc; the Economic Branch; and on the political data supplied by the Intelligence Branch together with the research projects and the plans prepared by the Assistant for Planning to the head of the General Staff Branch.

This question can be discussed further only after we know what researches and political projections Abrasha can produce. I would like to know approximately when these plans and the research projects already requested will be ready so that we can ascertain their contents.

Moshe Dayan

Dayan did not really share my belief that long-range strategic planning was a key to our national survival. He was a remarkable personality, but it was not easy to work with him. He was essentially a loner. His unconventional ideas were not the result of teamwork, for which he had little patience. They crystallized in his own mind, and very few of his associates and staff were taken into his confidence. His mental processes were intuitive rather than methodical. His approach to problems was pragmatic, based on trial and error rather than on adherence to theoretical solutions. At times it was difficult for his colleagues to grasp the rationale of his proposals, or the implications for the future. That applied, among others, to these examples:

233

- There was a stage when he deemed it better to establish a border in Sinai along the El Arish–Ras Muhammad line without attaining peace, than to give up this line in return for peace.
- Another instance was his concept that in a peace treaty with Egypt, an Israeli presence under Israeli jurisdiction could be retained in Sinai while the area as a whole would be subject to Egyptian sovereignty.
- He made a similar suggestion to King Hussein regarding an Israeli presence in Judea, Samaria and Gaza. Later, he advocated *de facto* coexistence in these territories, leaving the question of sovereignty over them in abeyance for an indefinite period.
- Prior to the Yom Kippur War, he suggested a limited unilateral Israeli pull-back from the Suez Canal, as a way to bolster the no-war, no-peace situation. But this idea could not serve as a basis for negotiations, as there was no clear concept as to what should happen subsequently.

However, when some of these ideas were unacceptable to his colleagues, or reached a dead end in political negotiations, he was flexible enough to discard them. There was never any question about his basic urge, which was to create conditions for peaceful Israeli–Arab coexistence. That overriding compulsion found expression in the 'Open Bridges' policy he instituted after the Six Day War, and in his key role during the Israeli–Egyptian peace negotiations.

At the end of 1970, I placed a national security plan for the 1970s on the table of my Chief, General Elazar. This included a political–strategic outline; a military–strategic outline; a review of the risks to Israel's survival and security, and recommendations for dealing with them; a ten-year plan for the development of a national security infrastructure; a ten-year plan for the development of weapons and equipment systems; and a five-year plan for the development of the air, sea and land forces of the IDF.

The Chief of Staff convened a meeting for the discussion of these proposals, which was attended by the members of the General Staff, together with the GOCs of the three regional commands and the commanders of the air force, navy and armoured corps. Our recommendations were approved with some amendments and additions, and became the basis for the development of the IDF in the ensuing years.

As part of the political–strategic outline contained in this national security plan, we assessed possible developments in the 1970s which would affect Israel's security. This assessment derived from research and discussions carried out by 'think tanks' which included research institutes, systems analysis experts and Israeli authorities on the Arab world, the Palestinians, the Middle East, the superpowers, Third World countries, the nuclear weapons balance, the economy, demography and other subjects. This group was organized into a reserve unit known as the 'experts union' and its members could be called upon for discussions, position papers or research projects whenever these were deemed necessary.

Among the developments which we felt should be classified as 'highly probable', I shall mention two. One was the possible outbreak of another Israeli–Arab war in the summer of 1973, if the political process initiated by the United States on the basis of UN Resolution 242 became deadlocked; or if, at the very least, no interim arrangement was reached between Israel and Egypt whereby IDF forces would move back from the east bank of the Suez Canal. Another forecast we made that turned out to be correct was that there might be changes of regime in Iran and Ethiopia due to the revolutionary forces active in those countries.

Under the impact of the Yom Kippur War, national security planning in the General Staff was given a greatly enhanced status. Up to then, the General Staff had functioned through four Branches: the General Staff Branch (organization, training and operations); the Manpower Branch; the Quartermaster General (supplies and maintenance); and the Intelligence Branch.

A month after the war, it was decided to form a separate Planning Branch. As its head, I was raised to the rank of Major-General. Our Branch came under manifold pressures. We had to prepare immediate programmes for the post-war rehabilitation of the IDF and a revised master plan for the long-term development of its forces and weapons systems. Lists had to be drawn up of requests for military aid from the US. Material had to be prepared for the negotiations on the Disengagement-of-Forces Agreements in 1974 with Egypt and Syria, and the 1975 Interim Agreement with Egypt – particularly the models for security arrange-ments in the Sinai Desert and the Golan Heights.

In 1974, Yitzhak Rabin succeeded Golda Meir as Prime Minister, and Shimon Peres succeeded Moshe Dayan as Minister of Defence. Like Dayan, Peres felt that national security planning was too all-embracing a concept to remain the exclusive preserve of the General Staff – especially in the post-Yom Kippur War period, when we had entered an era of active Israeli–Arab negotiations. His solution was to set up a Joint Planning Branch of the Ministry of Defence and the General Staff, with myself as its head.

The Minister gave us the authority to plan Israel's national security needs in the following spheres: security policy, the strengthening and development of the IDF, the development of a broad security infrastructure for the State of Israel, the integration of Israel's resources to meet security needs, the development of security connections with other countries (especially the US) and political agreements with the Arab states.

This appointment, in effect, gave me the position of head of a national security staff. This body should have been responsible to a National Security Council, which would, in turn, have come directly under the authority of the Prime Minister. But this National Security Council with its own staff does not yet exist in Israel, although its need is most clearly felt here in a country which was born in war, has beaten back waves of aggression threatening its very survival and is likely to confront serious risks in the future.

In the past, there have been decisions concerning Israel's security that would have been considered and adopted in a different manner had the Government had before it the data and independent advice of its own staff, and not only the conclusions of the IDF General Staff, for whom purely military considerations are, of necessity, the dominant factor.

In October 1973, when all the factual information was available to suggest that a combined Egyptian–Syrian attack could be launched, the appraisal of army Intelligence, accepted by the military establishment, was that no such attack would take place – hence the surprise on Yom Kippur. One of the recommendations of the Agranat Commission after that war was that the Prime Minister should have his own Intelligence adviser to act as a counter-check on such appraisals.

Then, there are defence projects involving huge investments that are approved and developed on the claim that they are essential to national security. In certain cases an independent examination in depth of the data and assessments might have come to the conclusion that Israel could survive without a specific project, particularly if it was carried out at the expense of other military needs, or of other national priorities that also have a bearing on security, such as education, scientific research and population dispersal.

A recent and classic instance concerns the Lavi Project, Israel's effort to develop and produce its own advanced fighter plane. By 1987, the work on it had been in progress for seven years, had cost nearly $2 billion (funded by the United States) and employed a skilled work-force of 4,000. It then underwent an agonizing reappraisal. After three months of exhaustive debate, the Cabinet divided along party lines, and it was decided by a single vote (12–11) to abandon the project.

It is not my purpose to discuss the pros and cons of this decision, one of the most difficult any Israeli government has taken. The question remains, how did we get into this situation? In a forty-page report, the State Controller traced the history of the project and was severely critical of the decision-making process at different stages. He alleged, amongst other things, the submission of data that turned out to be faulty, and a failure to carry out proper economic feasibility studies or to examine adequately possible alternatives.

I cannot help feeling that if a National Security Council had been in existence, and had been allowed to carry out an independent scrutiny of the project before crucial decisions were taken, the outcome may have been different.

Even when the Government has determined military and political objectives in a war, it has happened that the military command has diverged from them in the field, or set itself different objectives. In such cases there has been no effective government machinery to act as a check. That is what occurred in Israel's war in Lebanon, with disastrous results.

In a memorandum I submitted to the Minister of Defence, in my capacity as head of the Joint Planning Branch, I expressed my thoughts and recommendations on this subject:

A permanent body dealing with national security at Cabinet or presidential level is a feature of every country with a regular system for consultation and decision-taking on vital security matters.

In the United States, for example, this function is carried out by a National Security Council headed by the President, and including the Vice-President, the Secretary of State and the Secretary of Defence, with the Chairman of the Joint Chiefs of Staff, and the Director of the CIA, as official advisers. The Council maintains a large permanent staff in the White House under the National Security Adviser.

In Israel's political system, the Ministerial Committee on Defence, with Prime Minister as Chairman, constitutes the regular body for this purpose. (When necessary, the whole Cabinet sits as a Ministerial Committee on Defence.) However, the Committee does not have a permanent staff to assist it at the requisite level. Such a staff should be headed by a National Security Adviser directly responsible to the Prime Minister. Its primary task would be to analyse and evaluate all the factors affecting national security policy – military, foreign, political, economic, demographic, scientific and technological. For this purpose, it must have the authority and capacity to gather and collate data from the various departments of government, Intelligence agencies and research institutes in Israel and abroad. In addition, the staff should prepare summaries of decisions taken on national security issues, for the guidance of those required to implement them, and provide the Prime Minister and the Ministerial Committee on Defence with follow-up reports on the implementation.

It is not proposed to replace existing government bodies dealing with different aspects of national security, but to establish a central co-ordinating body in the Prime Minister's Office. Representatives of the Foreign, Defence and Finance Ministries, and the IDF General Staff, will be included in the National Security Staff. The Staff should operate through two inter-ministerial groups – one for data processing and the other for assessments and recommendations. Experts on specific topics could be co-opted ad hoc, as required.

I appended to this memorandum the following diagram reflecting the organization I proposed:

NATIONAL SECURITY PLANNING
Outline of Organization and Functions

PRIME MINISTER
(Chairman of Ministerial
Committee on Defence)

NATIONAL SECURITY ADVISER

National Security Staff
(For preparing summaries,
reporting and operating
Data Centre)

Inter-Ministerial
Co-ordination

Group for Evaluation
and Recommendations

Data Processing Group
to prepare data for
Evaluation Group

As head of the Joint Planning Branch, I was in an awkward position. I was directly responsible to the Minister of Defence, and co-ordinated on his behalf all work carried out by the General Staff connected with political–strategic affairs. At the same time, I was directly responsible to the Chief of Staff, and co-ordinated on his behalf all work carried out by the General Staff connected with the planning, development and growth of the IDF. I also prepared for him proposals on the security aspects of the political negotiations with Egypt. It was impossible to prevent a clash of interests. Finally, in May 1979, following the signing of the Israeli–Egyptian Peace Treaty, the Joint Planning Branch was split into two parts: the General Staff Planning Branch and a National Security Unit headed by an Adviser on National Security responsible to the Minister of Defence.

From May 1979 until the day of my retirement from the Ministry of Defence in August 1983, I served as National Security Adviser and head of the National Security Unit under the following Ministers of Defence: Ezer Weizman (1977–80), Prime Minister and Minister of Defence Menachem Begin (1980–81), Ariel Sharon (1981–3) and Moshe Arens (1983). When the National Unity Government came into being in 1984,

238

headed by Shimon Peres, he appointed me Director-General of the Prime Minister's Office and National Security Adviser to the Prime Minister. Under the 'rotation' agreement, in October 1986 Shamir became Prime Minister and Peres Vice-Premier and Foreign Minister. Peres moved me with him to the Foreign Ministry as Director-General.

In these various positions in the Ministry of Defence, the Prime Minister's Office and the Foreign Ministry, I continued to be involved in planning and to have an active role in our negotiations with Egypt, Lebanon and the United States. That has given me some personal satisfaction, but it falls far short of the way I believe national security planning should be organized. The proposals made in my memorandum to the Minister of Defence were reinforced by the conduct of the Lebanese war. Collective Cabinet responsibility is a feature of our constitutional system; but I saw ministers share in taking decisions on vital issues of war and peace without being enabled to understand all the implications of those decisions, without being informed what alternatives there were, and without knowing that there were dissenting opinions within the Defence establishment itself.

21

LIVING WITH THE UNPREDICTABLE

We Israelis number amongst our biblical ancestors in this land the Hebrew Prophets who thundered their warnings to the political establishment of their time. (Isaiah and Jeremiah lived here in Jerusalem, where I work.) Yet modern Israel has a poor 'track record' when it comes to anticipating, and planning for, the events in our own time that have been of vital concern to us.

Israel and Western Intelligence services did not foresee two interrelated developments in the 1950s that changed the face of the Middle East. One was the penetration of the region by the Soviet Union through backing Arab nationalism and exploiting the Israeli–Arab conflict. The other development was the domination in the Arab world of Nasser's Egypt. Through Nasser, the Soviet Union sought to bring other Arab countries into its orbit.

The years between the Sinai Campaign of 1956 and the Six Day War of 1967 saw rapid changes in the area, all unforeseen by us. In Iraq and Libya, army officers' coups followed the Egyptian example in sweeping away monarchies and installing military regimes. Egypt and Syria formed a union known as the United Arab Republic. Libya and the Sudan were incorporated into the Egyptian political–strategic system. Egypt intervened militarily and politically in Yemen in an unsuccessful bid to gain a springboard for control of the Red Sea and Arabian oil. The Palestine Liberation Organization was created under Egyptian auspices to launch a political and guerrilla struggle against Israel. In 1958, the attempt by Nasserist forces to topple the pro-Western regimes in Lebanon and Jordan led to the beginnings of civil war in Lebanon, the landing of US marines on the beaches of Beirut, and the dropping of British paratroopers into Jordan to save the Hashemite monarchy. Before the Six Day War, an eastern front against Israel had come into being which included Syria, Jordan, Iraq and Saudi Arabia, under overall Egyptian command.

In the early 1960s, when I was working in the General Staff on the long-term plans for the development of the IDF in the 1970s we did not foresee the Six Day War (1967), the War of Attrition (1968–70), the Yom Kippur War (1973) or the Lebanese War (1982) – each of which showed up shortcomings and presented us with new problems.

None of the pundits thought peace would be attained between Israel and any Arab state in our generation. When peace did come about with Egypt in 1979, it radically altered the security picture for Israel.

The geopolitical strategy initiated by Ben-Gurion in the early years of the state had been to cultivate ties with non-Arab countries on the periphery of the Arab world, and thus to alleviate Israel's isolation in the region. The most important of them was Iran, where the Shah's regime was generally regarded as a strong, pro-Western one, capable of maintaining stability in the Persian Gulf area. Even without formal diplomatic relations, we developed a network of co-operation with Iran in a number of areas (including security) and it was the main supplier of oil to Israel. Who could have foreseen that the regime would be swept away by the fundamentalist Khomeini revolution, which is rabidly anti-Western and anti-Israel, or that Iran and Iraq would become locked in the bitter Gulf War, now in its seventh year? (If Israelis are asked whom we would prefer to win that war, the answer is, 'Neither.')

Similarly, our position in the Red Sea region was abruptly changed when in Ethiopia the Emperor Haile Selassie, with whom we had extensive ties, was deposed by a left-wing military coup.

We could not know in advance how effective the Arab oil weapon would be in the West from 1973 (a weapon fortunately blunted at present by the world oil glut and the dramatic drop in oil prices).

Our region is caught up in the fluctuating global struggle between the two superpowers for positions of influence in the Third World. The Middle East is a highly strategic prize in this contest. It is a cross-roads for land, sea and air communications between three continents; and it contains our planet's greatest known oil reserves. Yet it took a long time for the United States to adopt an active Middle East policy of its own. From World War I, the region had been dominated by Britain and France. The Suez débâcle of 1956 marked the end of that era and left a power vacuum that the USSR seemed destined to fill. The 1958 American military intervention in Lebanon signalled a willingness on the part of the United States to challenge the Russian 'take-over bid'.

Each superpower has suffered reverses and gained successes in our region. It was a severe blow to the Soviet Union when President Sadat of Egypt broke off the Soviet connection his predecessor Nasser had developed, and expelled the thousands of Russian advisers and instructors Nasser had introduced. What happened in Iran was just as severe a blow to the United States, though without a corresponding gain for the Soviet Union. The Marxist coups in Ethiopia and South Yemen gave the Russians bases in the Red Sea and Indian Ocean, while Assad's Syria and Gaddafi's Libya provided them with footholds in the Mediterranean.

Meanwhile, as the only one of the two superpowers to have good relations with both sides, the US has gained a monopoly of mediation in the Israeli–Arab peace process. Consequently, the Soviet Union tries to block American peacemaking initiatives through its own protégés, such as Syria.

All these developments have had their impact on Israel's security. Yet our policy-makers could not predict them and take them into account beforehand.

Under the incredibly complex conditions of modern warfare, national defence must be planned years or even a decade ahead. On the development of armaments, one can make forecasts with some degree of assurance with the help of scientific systems analysis. But when one comes to the political–strategic sphere, the research tools have not yet been invented for making projections, and it is doubtful if they ever will be. There are too many uncertain factors, such as unstable regimes, the personal behaviour of leaders and internal upheavals.

During my years of involvement with national security planning, I maintained contact with and paid visits to major strategic institutions in the United States and Europe. With the Pentagon's experts in this field we had a permanent dialogue. On my trips abroad, I sought guidance on the problem that I found baffling – the methodology for long-term strategic projections and planning. I found that with our military successes and our simultaneous achievements in nation-building under severe handicaps, my hosts assumed that we had evolved a highly developed national security planning system, from which they could learn. I had to explain that we should have such a system, but did not.

One day I arrived from California at the National Airport in Washington, DC, and was taken to a meeting with my friend Dr Foster, Director of the Stanford Strategic Research Institute. We talked for five hours, mainly about the superpower confrontation in the Far East, the Middle East and Europe. At the end of this stimulating session, I asked him the question which was, in fact, the purpose of my visit: 'What system would you use in your Institute to form a picture of what the world might look like twenty years from now, from the political–strategic or economic aspects?'

He smiled and replied, 'My dear Abrasha, do we really have ways of finding out just how the world looks *today* in those respects?'

What, then, can serve as a basis for national long-term planning, when future events are so unpredictable? It is out of the question to make an enormous investment of national resources in order to provide for all the contingencies which may or may not arise in the next decade. Yet every Israeli government is obliged to take decisions for the future concerning military strategy, peace strategy, economic and supply systems for wars and emergencies, and the priorities in allocating our limited national resources between defence and civilian needs.

In the light of my own planning experience, I am convinced that the decision-making process must be served by high-level, centralized machinery for national security planning in the broadest sense. The country would then be in a better position to cope with the unexpected. I have been vainly advocating such a system for many years.

No staff mechanism can provide insurance against human error or miscalculation. Yet in a small, beleaguered country like ours, the decision-making process should be based on a thorough study of the relevant facts and an independent appraisal of the available options.

Appendix A

Brief Chronology

1947
29 November   UN General Assembly adopts Palestine partition plan
Arab attacks start in Palestine

1948
14 May   Israeli Proclamation of Independence
End of British Mandate
War of Independence begins

1949

Israel signs armistice agreements with Egypt, Jordan, Lebanon and Syria

1956
29 October–3 November   Sinai Campaign

1967
5–10 June   Six Day War
22 November   UN Security Council adopts Resolution 242

1973
6–24 October   Yom Kippur War
22 October   UN Security Council adopts Resolution 338

1974
16 January   Israeli–Egyptian Disengagement-of-Forces Agreement signed
31 May   Israeli–Syrian Disengagement-of-Forces Agreement signed

3 June	Rabin Government takes office in Israel

1975
1 September	Israeli–Egyptian Interim Agreement signed

1977
20 June	Begin Government takes office in Israel
19–21 November	Sadat's visit to Jerusalem
13 December	Cairo Conference opens
25–26 December	Ismailia Conference

1978
11 January	Israeli–Egyptian military committee convened in Cairo
25 March	IDF launches Operation Litani in Southern Lebanon
13 June	Israeli withdrawal from Lebanon completed after UNIFIL deployed
18–19 July	Leeds Castle Conference in UK
5–18 September	Camp David Summit Conference
12 October	Blair House Conference opens in Washington

1979
26 March	Israeli–Egyptian Peace Treaty signed in Washington

1981
6 October	Sadat assassinated
30 November	US and Israel sign Memorandum of Understanding on Strategic Co-operation

1982
6 June	Operation Peace for Galilee launched
21 August–3 September	PLO evacuated from Beirut
1 September	Reagan plan made public
14–16 September	Bashir Gemayel assassinated
	IDF enters West Beirut
	Phalange massacre in Sabra and Shatilla refugee camps

1983
17 May	Israeli–Lebanese Agreement signed

1984
March   Israeli–Lebanese Agreement abrogated by
                                         President Gemayel
14 September   National Unity Government under Peres
                                         takes office in Israel

1985
July   IDF withdrawal from Lebanon completed
                                         Security zone established in Southern
                                         Lebanon
11–12 September   Peres–Mubarak Summit Conference in
                                         Egypt
9 December   Start in Geneva of international arbitration
                                         on Taba

1987
25–27 February   Second Peres–Mubarak Summit
                                         Conference in Egypt

Appendix B

List of Israeli Ministers of Defence and Chiefs of Staff

MINISTERS OF DEFENCE

David Ben-Gurion (as Prime Minister)	1948–54
Pinchas Lavon	1954–5
David Ben-Gurion (as Prime Minister)	1955–63
Levi Eshkol (as Prime Minister)	1963–7
Moshe Dayan	1967–74
Shimon Peres	1974–7
Ezer Weizman	1977–80
Menachem Begin (as Prime Minister)	1980–81
Ariel Sharon	1981–3
Moshe Arens	1983–4
Yitzhak Rabin	1984–

CHIEFS OF STAFF (with rank of Lieutenant-General)

Yaakov Dori	1948–9
Yigael Yadin	1949–52
Mordechai Makleff	1952–3
Moshe Dayan	1953–8
Chaim Laskov	1958–61
Zvi Tsur	1961–4
Yitzhak Rabin	1964–8
Chaim Bar-Lev	1968–72
David Elazar	1972–4
Mordechai Gur	1974–8
Raphael Eitan	1978–83
Moshe Levy	1983–7
Dan Shomron	1987–

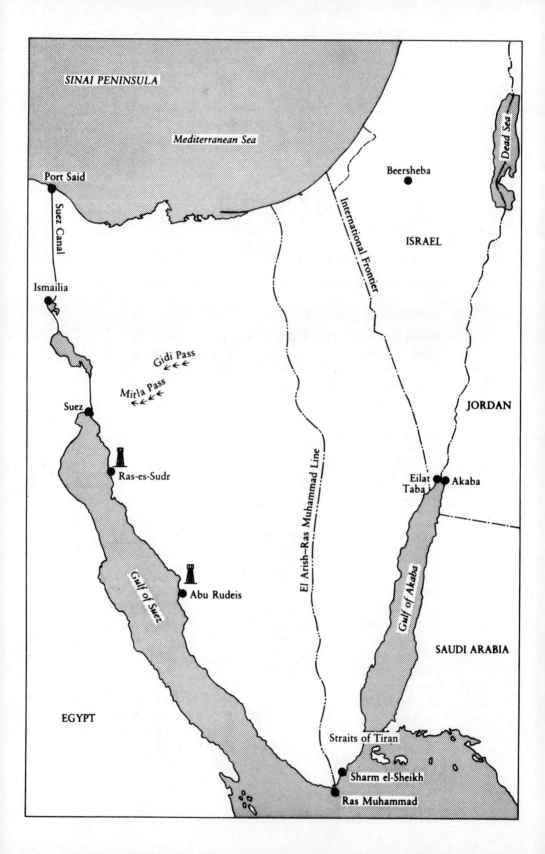

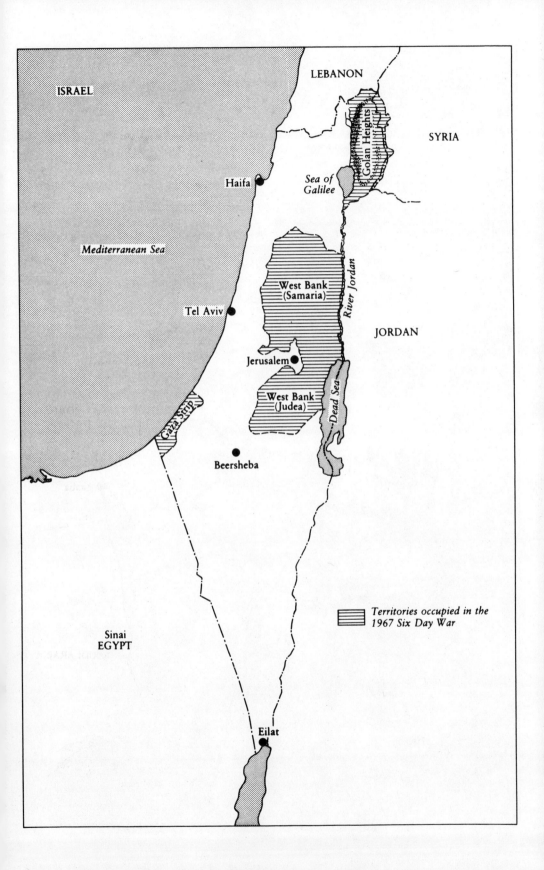

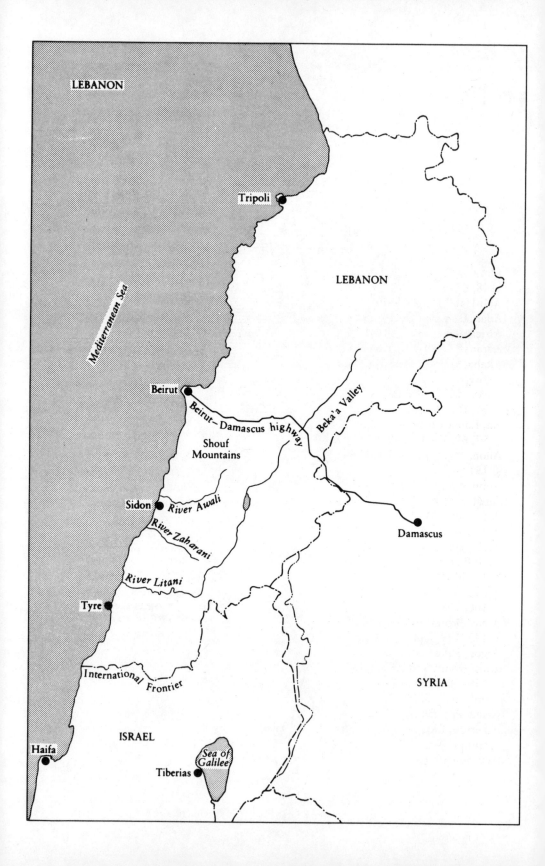

INDEX

251

Major-General Avraham Tamir was born in Tel Aviv in 1924. Most of his life has been devoted to developing Israel's national security—in the Haganah before the establishment of the State of Israel and, since 1948, within the framework of the Israel Defense Forces. He has filled many prominent positions in the General Staff and the Ministry of Defense, including Chief of the Operations Department, Chief of the Combat Doctrine Department and Chief of the Strategic Planning Branch (both of which he established), National Security Adviser in the Ministry of Defense (1980–83) and Director-General of the Prime Minister's Office (1984–86). In 1986 he was appointed Director-General of the Foreign Ministry. Throughout his distinguished career, he has been instrumental in developing the Israel Defense Forces and the infrastructure for Israel's national security; and he has also played a major role in the peace process with Israel's Arab neighbours and in developing Israel's relations with countries throughout the world.